A CONFEDERACY OF HERETICS

EDITED BY TODD GANNON AND EWAN BRANDA

SCI-ARC PRESS
IN ASSOCIATION WITH GETTY PUBLICATIONS

Published by SCI-Arc Press

Southern California Institute of Architecture
960 East 3rd Street
Los Angeles, California 90013
www.sciarc.edu

In association with
Getty Publications
1200 Getty Center Drive, Suite 500
Los Angeles, California 90049-1682
www.getty.edu/publications

Editors: Todd Gannon & Ewan Branda
Copy Editors: Justine Smith, Kevin McMahon
Graphic Designer: Kate Merritt

Printed in Canada by the Prolific Group.

Published in the United States of America.
ISBN: 978-1-60606-263-0

Cataloging-in-Publication data for this book is available from the Library of Congress.

AN INITIATIVE OF THE GETTY

The Getty

A Confederacy of Heretics: The Architecture Gallery, Venice, 1979 is part of Pacific Standard
Time Presents: Modern Architecture in L.A., celebrating Southern California's lasting
impact on modern architecture through exhibitions and programs organized by seventeen
area cultural institutions from April through July 2013.

Major support for this exhibition is provided by the Getty Foundation.

Additional support is provided by the Graham Foundation for Advanced Studies in
the Fine Arts, The Vinyl Institute, and the Pasadena Art Alliance. The publication is
underwritten in part by Furthermore: a program of the J. M. Kaplan Fund. Archival images
are provided by the *Los Angeles Times* Photographic Archive, Department of Special
Collections, Charles E. Young Research Library, UCLA.

SCI-Arc exhibitions and public programs are made possible in part by a grant from the
City of Los Angeles, Department of Cultural Affairs.

CONTENTS

WE WRITE HISTORY

ERIC OWEN MOSS

"...memory is time's truant..."
—Hart Crane

Here's the bromide query architects often field:
"What's your best project?"
And the bromide response:
"The next one."

Underneath that caricatured exchange there's
an essential meaning that belongs uniquely to
SCI-Arc's self-conception:
"What's your best project?"
"The next one."

What's current at SCI-Arc is what's next at SCI-Arc.

SCI-Arc has never conceived of itself as a repository
of architectural history.
SCI-Arc never conceived of itself as an archive.
SCI-Arc remains solely an interrogator of the future.
[Or does it?]

SCI-Arc has no pedagogy, we often insist.
SCI-Arc aspires to inspire the architects to produce
the pedagogy that SCI-Arc contests;
which provokes the next architects to formulate
the next pedagogy, which instigates the next...
If there's an enduring SCI-Arc mantra, that's it.

Pedagogy implies an allegiance, a teaching pro
forma, an agreement on what should be taught and
what should be learned.
In a prosaic, day-to-day sense, there is no school
without a dose of that structure/system/method,
SCI-Arc included.
But the SCI-Arc way is to insist that the architect-
exhibitors, lecturers, and faculty who come and go
are not voices to be revered, but rather voices to be

scrutinized, debated, and inevitably contested,
and amended, or replaced.
We demand that scrutiny.
We know that evaluative process is not easy.
We know the critical intellectual environment we
inculcate is not warranteed to produce new ways
to think or to see.
But if we continue to insist on that rigorously
discursive climate, then resurrecting, codifying,
and sustaining some a priori design allegiance will
remain antithetical to the conception of SCI-Arc.
If the present is perpetually undone to make space
for what's next, there should be no space or time left
for recollecting what we've dismantled.

And keep in mind the SCI-Arc corollary that we
remain forever open to the prospect that our
advocacy is misconceived.
So if, perhaps, SCI-Arc has a paradigm after all,
it's provisional.

What a surprise it is for the salubrious Getty to offer
SCI-Arc an opportunity to identify and reconstitute
a portion of the SCI-Arc past, to distill a portion of a
presumed pedigree, and to offer it up as a chapter in
the narrative of contemporary architecture.

Is SCI-Arc willing to acknowledge a pedigree?
Does the acknowledgement of such a pedigree
require that SCI-Arc now cede a place for its own
history?

And, by the way, isn't a war on history ipso facto a
war on oneself?

SCI-Arc agrees to collect and regurgitate a salient
portion of its past.
But understand, our memory is also provisional.
SCI-Arc reserves the future's obligation to re–
imagine our current recollection.

This Getty–sponsored exhibition is only a truce in
the long running SCI-Arc dispute with history.

And we will exploit that respite as a singular
opportunity for a new act of imagination:

SCI-Arc as temporary archive: but keep in mind that
what we are today has everything to do with our
statement of who we might have been back then.

We write our history and our history becomes the
history we write, until we write it again.

SCI-Arc offers an enormous thank you to the Getty
for this opportunity to re-imagine ourselves.

Welcome to SCI-Arc, 2013's look at SCI-Arc, 1979.

Beginning in the 1970s, a generation of Los Angeles architects launched a series of experiments that would transform architecture in Southern California and around the world. Taking on small-scale commissions and speculative projects with an energy and ambition in stark contrast to the Los Angeles architectural establishment, these architects transformed unassuming garages, galleries, alleys, and warehouses—as well as the drawings and models produced to envision them—into some of the most significant architectural achievements of the late twentieth century.

In 1979, this new architecture found a significant public forum in the Architecture Gallery, Los Angeles' first gallery dedicated exclusively to architecture, and a concurrent series of lectures hosted by the Southern California Institute of Architecture. Chronicled in weekly reviews in the *Los Angeles Times*, the events caused an immediate stir in Los Angeles architectural culture, and their impact was quickly felt around the world. In the intervening years, Architecture Gallery participants have gone on to become some of the most significant voices in contemporary architecture. They have completed important commissions worldwide, have received every available award (two among them have been awarded Pritzker prizes), and their publications and teaching in Los Angeles and around the globe have influenced several generations of architects.

Rather than attempt a faithful reconstruction of the original 1979 exhibitions, *A Confederacy of Heretics* augments selections from the original shows with additional work from the period to open new conversation and debate on the emergence, development, and enduring legacy of the so-called "L.A. School." In addition, this catalog systematically documents the original 1979 exhibitions and, in a series of essays by the curators, Architecture Gallery participants, and contemporary scholars and architects, critically assesses the work and its context, examines specific aspects of its methods and practices, and speculates on its continued relevance today.

This exhibition asks a broad set of historical questions: How and why did this new architecture emerge in Los Angeles? What was its formal and material basis? What was the relationship of this work to the emergence of architectural postmodernism as well as to corporate late-modernism? How did extra-disciplinary content and techniques reinforce disciplinary boundaries rather than dissolve them? At the same time, we are re-examining this early work to encourage a renewed and reinvigorated spirit of experimentalism and personal investment in a discipline that, today, too often exhibits signs of becoming as doctrinaire and risk-averse as the architectural culture against which the architects at the Architecture Gallery resisted some thirty-five years ago.

A Confederacy of Heretics is part of Pacific Standard Time Presents: Modern Architecture in L.A., an initiative celebrating Southern California's lasting impact on modern architecture through exhibitions and programs organized by seventeen area cultural institutions from April through July 2013. Major support for *A Confederacy of Heretics* is provided by the Getty Foundation. Additional support is provided by the Graham Foundation for Advanced Studies in the Fine Arts, The Vinyl Institute and the Pasadena Art Alliance. The publication is underwritten in part by Furthermore: a program of the J. M. Kaplan Fund. Additional support was provided by ARC Document Solutions. Archival images were provided by the *Los Angeles Times* Photographic Archive, Department of Special Collections, Charles E. Young Research Library, UCLA. SCI-Arc exhibitions and public programs are made possible in part by a grant from the City of Los Angeles, Department of Cultural Affairs.

The project would have been impossible without the participation and support of a number of people. We offer sincere thanks to Roland Coate, Eugene Kupper, Frank Dimster, Fred Fisher, Eric Moss, Frank Gehry, Peter de Bretteville, Thom Mayne, Michael Rotondi, Craig Hodgetts, Robert

Mangurian, and Coy Howard for their generous collaboration over the past two years.

Central to both exhibition and catalog were the design work and critical insights of Laura Bouwman, Dale Strong, Paul Stoelting, and Matthew Au of Zago Architecture and Rebeca Méndez, Adam Eeuwens, and Pauline Woo of Rebeca Méndez Design. Kevin McMahon of the SCI-Arc Library also played a crucial role. Kate Merritt and Justine Smith of SCI-Arc expertly designed and produced the catalog. Josh White and Tom Bonner photographed the work and the exhibition with characteristic care. We are also grateful for the insightful criticism we received from our advisory board: Jeffrey Kipnis, Patricia Morton, Paulette Singley, and Joe Day. No less important was the contribution of our student research assistants: Taryn Bone, Stefano Passeri, Nikki Karpf, Benjamin Farnsworth, Sergio Ormachea, and Jungwoo Lee, all of SCI-Arc, and Amanda Ehrlich of Woodbury University.

The difficult task of resurrecting, restoring, and retrieving models, drawings, and photographs was made easier by help from Eric McNevin at Eric Owen Moss Architects, Mary-Ann Ray and Hector Solis at Studio Works, Keith Collins at Frederick Fisher Architects, Natalie Egnatchik at Hodgetts and Fung, Takako Fujimoto at Arata Isozaki & Associates, and Legier Stahl, Nicole Meyer, and Andrea Tzvetkov at Morphosis.

Jesse Alexander, Joseph Giovannini, Grant Mudford, and Ave Pildas generously allowed us to use their work in the exhibition and catalog. Additional catalog images were provided by Julius Shulman Photography Archive, Gruen Associates, John Lumsden, Art Center College of Design, Jerrold Lomax, Jon Yoder, Helmut Schulitz, Arnoldi Studio, and Julian Wasser.

Most important, perhaps, was the unflagging institutional support this project received. Foremost, we would like to thank Deborah Marrow, Joan Weinstein, Anne Helmreich, and Kathleen Johnson of the Getty Foundation, Wim de Wit of the Getty Research Institute, and Kara Kirk of Getty Publications. At SCI-Arc, Eric Owen Moss and Hsinming Fung lent consistent support to the project. We would like to thank Dawn Mori in particular for her extraordinary efforts.

Others at SCI-Arc who lent help and expertise are Hernan Diaz Alonso, John Enright, Stephanie Atlan, Christopher Banks, Jamie Bennett, Melissa Burgess, Georgiana Ceausu, Paul Holliday, Vic Jabrassian, Bill Kramer, Reza Monahan, Frances Muenzer, Sarah Sullivan, Jessica Wheeler, and Andrea Young.

Additional colleagues to whom we owe a debt of thanks are Barbara Bestor, John Bohn, Annie Chu, Peter Cook, Neil Denari, Rosamund Felsen, Rebecca Frabizio, Paul Goldberger, Charles Jencks, Ray Kappe, Shelly Kappe, Norman Millar, Alys Pitt-Leif, Kati Rubinyi, Mohamed Sharif, Nick Seierup, Yumna Siddiqi, and Ingalill Wahlroos-Ritter.

Todd Gannon, Ewan Branda, Andrew Zago
Los Angeles, 2013

A CONFEDERACY OF HERETICS

TODD GANNON

A Confederacy of Heretics examines the explosion of activity associated with the Architecture Gallery, Los Angeles' first gallery dedicated exclusively to architecture. Instigated by Thom Mayne in the fall of 1979, the Architecture Gallery staged ten exhibitions in as many weeks by both young and established Los Angeles practitioners, featuring the work of Eugene Kupper, Roland Coate, Jr., Frederick Fisher, Frank Dimster, Frank Gehry, Peter de Bretteville, Morphosis (Thom Mayne and Michael Rotondi), Studio Works (Craig Hodgetts and Robert Mangurian), and Eric Owen Moss. Another young architect, Coy Howard, opened the events with a lecture at the Southern California Institute of Architecture, which hosted talks by each exhibiting architect. In an unprecedented move by the popular press, the events were chronicled in weekly reviews by the critic John Dreyfuss in the *Los Angeles Times*.

Commonly understood today as a set of beliefs or practices in conflict with prevailing dogma, the word "heresy" derives from the Greek αἵρεσις, meaning "choice." In classical antiquity, the term also signified a period during which a young philosopher would examine various schools of thought in order to determine his future way of life.[1] These inflections neatly capture the ambitions and attitudes held by the architects at the center of this presentation. Some had grown weary with what they viewed as the stale orthodoxies of the establishment, and saw their work as a distinct challenge to the status quo. Others were less strident, and experimented with a diverse range of historical sources as potential platforms from which to develop their individual idioms. Others still struck out in bold new directions, drawing inspiration and techniques from the art world,

literature, and other sources. Such wide-ranging activities defy any attempt to portray these architects as members of a coherent group or "L.A. School."[2] More correctly, the Architecture Gallery constitutes one of many loose, temporary confederacies into which these architects entered during their formative years. Here, the heretics found strength in numbers, and the impact of their efforts was felt across Los Angeles and around the world.

Gathering an array of original drawings, models, photographs, video recordings, and commentary alongside new assessments by current scholars, *A Confederacy of Heretics* aims neither to canonize the participating architects nor to consecrate their unorthodox activities. Rather, the exhibition re-examines the early work of some of Los Angeles' most well-known architects, charts the development of their most potent design techniques, and documents a crucial turning point in Los Angeles architecture, a time when Angeleno architecture culture shifted from working local variations on imported themes to exporting highly original disciplinary innovations with global reach. Taken together, the exhibition, symposium, and catalog that comprise *A Confederacy of Heretics* offer a unique lens through which to analyze a pivotal moment in the development of late 20th century architecture.

The Architecture Gallery opened in October 1979, a time when the continued viability of orthodox Modernism was being contested in Los Angeles and around the world. Not only had architecture by then witnessed the passing of most of its Modern pioneers,[3] but the tumultuous socio-political events of the 1960s had shaken the field to its core. By the end of the '70s, architecture's most advanced practitioners had long been developing alternative modes of inquiry. Theoretical projects, as opposed to commissioned buildings, had become widespread vehicles of disciplinary innovation, and a rift had opened between those committed to viable commercial practices and those dedicated to seemingly antithetical disciplinary pursuits and personal ambitions.

Much of this latter work addressed what many understood to be a "loss of center" in the cultural milieu, the apparent result of critical attacks on the foundational tenets of Western humanism by proponents of post-structuralist theory and deconstruction.[4] Critics from inside and outside the field called the unifying dogma of Modernism in question,[5] and architects set off in pursuit of wildly divergent agendas. Simultaneously in the mid-1960s, the Archigram group attempted to recuperate Modernism's links to technology, Robert Venturi waxed poetic about his taste for complexity and contradiction, and Aldo Rossi sought refuge in symbolic forms and collective memory. Within a few years, Venturi and his partner Denise Scott Brown had made their way west to learn from Las Vegas and other Pop and vernacular phenomena. Taking a more academic approach to signs and signification, critics such as George Baird and Charles Jencks sought to establish a new ground for architectural production in language. By the late '70s, Léon Krier, Colin Rowe, and Fred Koetter had made compelling cases for the appropriation of historical forms alongside equally impassioned pleas for a renewed attentiveness to architecture's irreducible essence from the likes of Peter Eisenman, Daniel Libeskind, and Bernard Tschumi, among others.[6] Each of these varied agendas drew strong and devoted followings whose output atomized the unified approach of Modernism into an unruly constellation of competing alternatives for a postmodern world without a center.

Los Angeles architects of the period were not immune to this widespread suspicion of orthodoxy, and at the Architecture Gallery and elsewhere, they pursued radical new trajectories. But where their counterparts on the East Coast and in Europe tended to characterize the loss of center as a burden or tragedy, the predominant reaction among Southern California architects was a sense of liberation. Such a response might have been expected in Los Angeles, which for generations had made a virtue of its peripheral status with respect to more established (and establishment) centers to the north and east.[7] Since at least the 1880s, Los Angeles architects had exploited the city's distance from established centers to develop idiosyncratic variations on imported styles, as evidenced by the Newsom brothers with Queen Anne, the Greene brothers with Arts and Crafts, and Schindler, Neutra, and the Case Study group with orthodox Modernism. In the late 1970s, the city that had perfected the periphery was the ideal place to speculate on how to organize a world suddenly bereft of the notion of center.

Concentrating primarily on younger practices operating outside the commercial mainstream, the Architecture Gallery showcased fringe members of an already peripheral disciplinary culture. But where like-minded apostates to orthodoxy in other parts of the world tended to band together in groups such as *La Tendenza* in Italy or the Institute for Architecture and Urban Studies in New York, architects in Los Angeles eschewed such collective endeavors in favor of the individual pursuit of personal and idiosyncratic agendas. In his lecture for the Architecture Gallery series, Eric Owen Moss articulated his view of the situation:

> The problem that we face in doing architecture and in defining ourselves for ourselves is, finally, a personal and individual one. There have been many, over eons of time, who have attempted to deal with that kind of fundamental irrationality in a collective sense, to try to develop an order, an underneath, a platform which seems to make the finitude of the individual a little bit more palatable and coherent and intelligible, to define a context which is broader than the individual and which will support and in fact ameliorate the problem.[8]

Though he observed that the Pythagorians and, later, the Russian Constructivists had managed to find a sense of order collectively, Moss saw no such option available to his own generation: "It will finally be my opinion that any sort of effort, on a collective level, is, at least for us, at this point in time, impossible. These kinds of searches have to be carried out on an individual level."⁹

The wide array of approaches on display at the Architecture Gallery attested to each architect's commitment to his own personal ambitions, and underscores the inability of any collective label to adequately account for their activities. Nonetheless, certain shared tendencies can be discerned. Most do not encompass the entire group, but rather loosely organize the participants into overlapping clusters of interest. A majority of these architects, for example, shared a distinctly pragmatic frame of mind and a willingness to take on commissions, such as garage renovations and small residential additions, which more established practitioners might have considered economically unfeasible or intellectually irrelevant. Several, including Eugene Kupper, Frank Dimster, and Roland Coate, grounded their endeavors in disciplinary fundamentals such as archetypal forms, functional performance, and attentiveness to the exigencies of the building site [**Figs. 1-3**]. Many, including Frank Gehry, Frederick Fisher, as well as Thom Mayne and Michael Rotondi of Morphosis, experimented with vernacular elements and materials, particularly in their residential projects. A critical reassessment of disciplinary conventions also colors much of the work on display. With the 2-4-6-8 House, for example, Mayne and Rotondi took a small project as an opportunity to perpetrate a wholesale reinvention of the conventions of construction documentation. In now iconic drawings, they outlined the building's tectonic elements and construction sequence in excruciating detail, carefully delineating even the simplest connections in an almost comically thorough sequence of axonometrics [**Figs. 4, 5**]. In this, the architects slid from reimagining fundamentals to another common tendency—the expenditure of unreasonable, even unnecessary, effort. Craig Hodgetts and Robert Mangurian's voluminous production of drawings and models for the South Side Settlement are another case in point [**Fig. 6**], as are many of the artifacts in the present exhibition. As Ray Kappe remarked,

Fig. 1: Eugene Kupper, Nilsson House, Bel Air, 1979.

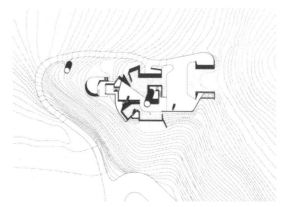

Fig. 2: Frank Dimster, Kelton Avenue Condominiums, Los Angeles, 1980.

Fig. 3: Roland Coate, Jr., Alexander House, Montecito, 1974.

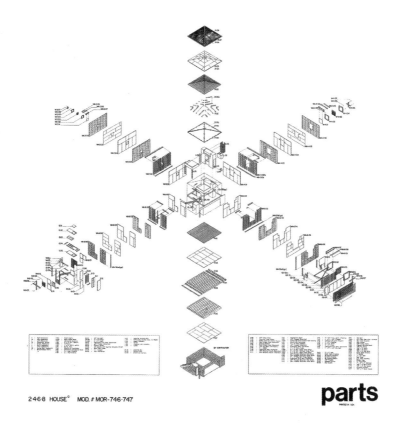

parts

2·4·6·8 HOUSE© MOD. # MOR·746·747

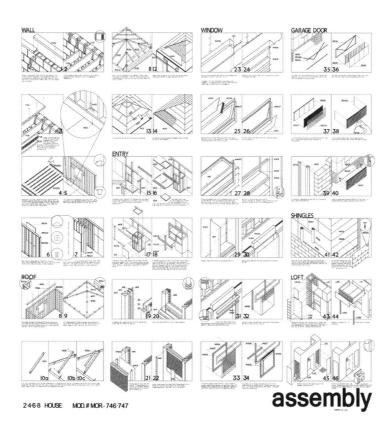

assembly

2·4·6·8 HOUSE MOD.# MOR·746·747

Figs. 4 & 5: Morphosis, 2-4-6-8 House, 1978. Parts and Assembly axonometrics.

Fig. 6: Studio Works, South Side Settlement, Columbus, Ohio, 1976-80. Posters.

TODD GANNON

"the drawing...almost became a thing in itself for a lot of these guys. ...Robert and Craig were just drawing the hell out of projects. Obviously, [this was] not necessary for construction; obviously not necessary, even, to understand the building."[10] Kappe's observation is valid, but fails to recognize the more radical proposition, widely espoused by younger architects of the period, that buildings were not always necessary to understand the architecture.

Such rhetoric, though part and parcel to East Coast architecture discourse, was rare in Los Angeles, where production typically trumped polemic. Hodgetts, Howard, and Rotondi later recounted that much of the motivation for their elaborate drawings and models had to do with the sheer pleasure of making them.[11] Love of the game notwithstanding, these labor-intensive artifacts had an additional benefit: they made for arresting publications. A widely shared ambition among these architects was a dogged pursuit of local and national design awards. Particularly prized was recognition by the *P/A* Awards, the annual competition held by *Progressive Architecture* magazine. Each of the architects in the exhibition devoted significant effort to

P/A Award submissions, and their projects were consistently found among the winners from the mid-1970s onward. Coy Howard later elaborated on his method:

> The way you won *P/A* Awards is you would draw like you were a maniac. ...All these young people were obsessive, and they're just going to draw this thing and draw this thing and draw this thing. They're so totally passionate about architecture that [the jury] just *has* to give you an award.[12]

As with the theoretical significance of their work, most of the architects downplayed the promotional aspects of their activities. Howard's recollections are typical: "...everybody probably saw it differently. I didn't do [drawings] for the *P/A* Awards. I mean, I did them and then used them in the *P/A* Awards, but I didn't do them *for* the *P/A* Awards."[13] For Howard as for all of the participating architects, architecture was much more than a career. It was a way of life.[14]

It is important to recognize that the Architecture Gallery did not occur in isolation. More symptom than cause, the events took place at a time when the

Fig. 7: SCI-Arc student presentations, c. 1974.

brought with him close ties to East Coast architectural personalities and debates. By the early '70s, he had recruited Kupper, Hodgetts, and Howard, a recent graduate of UCLA's planning program, as faculty members. Charles Jencks, at the time a rising star on the international scene, began making regular visits to the school in 1974.

In 1968, Ray Kappe was invited to lead an architecture program within the newly created School of Environmental Design at Cal Poly Pomona. A victim of his own success (the program grew from 25 to 200 students in just three years), Kappe soon came into conflict with the dean over the size of the program.[15] In 1972, Kappe left Cal Poly with six of its faculty members and roughly fifty of its students. Twenty-five additional students joined the group and in September, "The New School," officially the Southern California Institute of Architecture (SCI-Arc), was opened in a Santa Monica warehouse **[Fig. 7]**. In addition to founding faculty members Ray and Shelly Kappe, Ahde Lahti, Thom Mayne, Bill Simonian, Glen Small, and Jim Stafford, Architecture Gallery participants Eric Owen Moss, Roland Coate, and Frank Gehry were soon teaching at this unorthodox "school without a curriculum." Michael Rotondi, who would later assume the directorship of the school, was a member of the first graduating class in 1973 and joined the faculty the following year.[16]

These new institutions quickly amplified the volume of architectural discourse in Los Angeles. In 1973, SCI-Arc launched its Wednesday-night Design Forum lecture series, which drew local as well as national and international personalities from the outset.[17] The following year, UCLA convened an important conference designed specifically to insinuate a West Coast presence into ongoing East Coast debates. "Four Days in May," also known as "White and Gray Meet Silver," was conceived by Vreeland in collaboration with Hodgetts, Kupper, Anthony Lumsden, and Cesar Pelli. The group invited representatives of the well-known 'White vs. Gray' debates, with the five Los Angeles architects acting as counterparts to the five core representatives of the opposed East Coast factions.[18] The Los

city's architectural community had been working diligently to raise the level of public discourse and to make its activities known to broader national and global audiences. Through the 1970s, architectural exhibitions, lectures, and conferences occurred in Los Angeles with increasing frequency. And while many of these early efforts would not broach significant influence beyond the city limits, their increasing volume and sophistication brought important attention to highly original new work, and would prove a crucial catalyst for the Architectural Gallery.

Events often were sponsored by one of the three new schools of architecture that recently had been launched as alternatives to established programs at the University of Southern California and Cal Poly San Luis Obispo. The UCLA department of Architecture and Urban Planning opened its doors in 1964 under the direction of Henry C.K. Liu, and from the start took a distinctly anti-orthodox tack. By the late '60s, Archigram members Ron Herron, Warren Chalk, and Peter Cook were teaching in the program. In 1970, the school launched a Master's program directed by Tim Vreeland. Formerly an associate with Louis Kahn in Philadelphia, Vreeland

Fig. 8: Cesar Pelli for Gruen Associates, Pacific Design Center, West Hollywood, 1975.

Angeles participants, dubbed "the Silvers,"[19] did not present any work at the conference, which focused on the ideological and stylistic differences between the neo-Modernist Whites and the post-Modernist Grays. According to Hodgetts, the event "was more about putting UCLA on the map, I think, than trying to identify a group."[20] The Silvers put their own work center stage two years later when UCLA convened a sequel with "Four Days in April." Hodgetts did not participate, but the group swelled to six members for that presentation, adding Frank Dimster and Paul Kennon in his place.

Contrasting their White and Gray counterparts, who pursued highly formalized agendas through small private commissions, the Silvers directed their efforts primarily toward large-scale commercial projects. Major achievements, such as Pelli's Pacific Design Center [**Fig. 8**], Lumsden's Manufacturers Bank building, and Dimster's Houston Center tower [**Fig. 9**], for example, each were completed under the auspices of large corporate firms (Gruen, DMJM, and Pereira, respectively) where each architect functioned as design director.[21] These and other projects were characterized by slick glass envelopes reminiscent of recent proj-

ects by Japanese architect Kisho Kurakawa as well as Norman Foster's groundbreaking corporate facilities for Willis Faber and Dumas and IBM. A vaguely English attitude was further signaled by Vreeland's invocation of the group's use of a pragmatic "style for the job," a catchphrase previously associated with the work of James Stirling in the 1960s.[22]

The Silvers' unapologetic commitment to the mainstream brought pointed criticism from invited respondents at the 1976 conference. Charles Jencks noted the ironies of what he labeled "silver-plated capitalism." Esther McCoy, Charles Moore, and David Gebhard each questioned the lack of regional specificity to the work, and John Hejduk worried that in the presented projects, "high technology is generally wrapped up in high romanticism, with the danger that it could lead to totalitarianism." Stirling, for his part, saw the work as little more than "chic packaging," to which Pelli demurred, "All of our projects are way below the level of people such as Stirling."[23]

Such criticism, as well as Pelli's feeble response, demonstrates the continued hegemony of orthodox values over architectural culture in the mid-1970s. Carefully tailored compositions of ele-

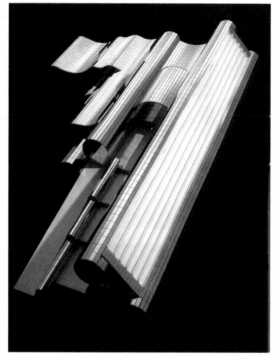

Fig. 9: Frank Dimster for William Pereira and Associates, Houston Center Tower, Houston, Texas, 1975.

Fig. 10: Anthony Lumsden for DMJM, Lugano Convention Center, Lugano, Switzerland, 1972-75.

ments, sensitively knitted to their sites and inflected by Modernism's hallmark suspicion of capitalism, remained the norm, and the radicalism of projects such as Pelli's Pacific Design Center, Lumsden's scheme for the Lugano Convention Center [**Fig. 10**], or Kupper's UCLA Extension Building [**Fig. 11**] went unacknowledged. Yet in their abandonment of traditional part-to-whole coherence for ambiguously scaled figures and open-ended systems, these projects signaled far more aggressive moves away from orthodoxy than concurrent work by Stirling, the Grays, or even—Eisenman's and Hejduk's polemics notwithstanding—the Whites. Unfortunately, the Silvers would not continue to meet after the 1976 conference, their later corporate works failed to live up to the promise of early achievements, and the episode was soon largely forgotten. Nonetheless, the Silvers made a lasting impact on architectural discourse in Los Angeles by generating significant architectural debate—and whetting an appetite for further conversation—in a city that previously simply hadn't had any.[24]

The following month, another group of Los Angeles architects debuted in an exhibition at the Pacific Design Center. *Twelve Los Angeles*

Architects was initiated by Bernard Zimmerman and organized by students at Cal Poly Pomona. The exhibition featured the work of established local practitioners Roland Coate Jr., Daniel Dworsky, Craig Ellwood, Frank Gehry, Ray Kappe, John Lautner, Jerrold Lomax, Tony Lumsden, Leroy Miller, Cesar Pelli, James Pulliam, and Zimmerman himself. Like the Silvers, the L.A. Twelve had been assembled as a local response to out-of-town groups (specifically the New York Five and the Chicago Seven), and its organizers saw in the Twelve a similar commitment to mainstream, as opposed to vanguard, practice.[25] With projects ranging from elegant Miesian assemblages by Ellwood [**Fig. 12**] to stripped down commercial facilities by Zimmerman and Lomax [**Fig. 13**] to exuberant residential projects by Kappe and Lautner [**Figs. 14, 15**], there was little formal or stylistic commonality across the group.[26] A series of twelve monthly lectures was staged at the Pacific Design Center in 1978, but the group had ceased to meet regularly the previous year.[27] Ultimately, like the Silvers before them, the L.A. Twelve never developed beyond a parochial phenomenon.[28] While many of the participating architects continued to produce significant projects (the bulk of them in an

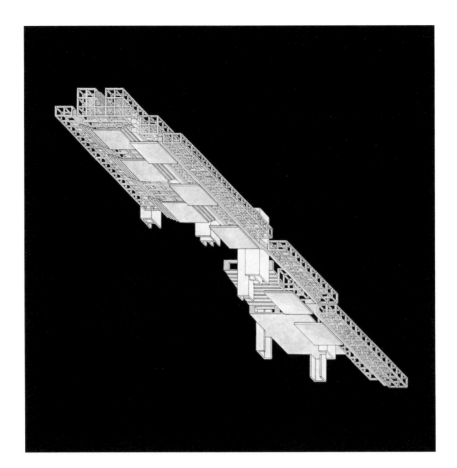

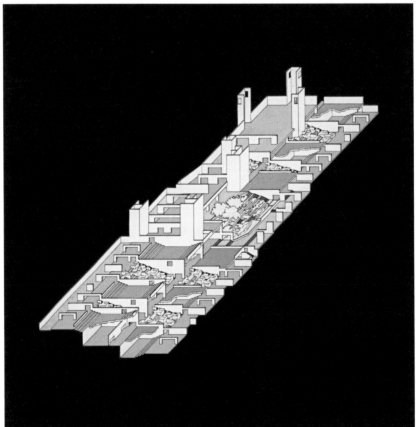

Fig. 11: Eugene Kupper, UCLA Extension Building, Los Angeles, 1976. Earth and Sky axonometrics.

Fig. 12: Craig Ellwood, Art Center College of Design, Pasadena, 1976.

Fig. 13: Jerrold Lomax, ACDC Electronics Building, Oceanside, California, 1973.

Fig. 14: Ray Kappe, Kappe Residence, Pacific Palisades, 1967.

Fig. 15: John Lautner, Silvertop, Los Angeles, 1963.

unapologetically orthodox idiom), their collective activities generated little of lasting influence.

Two additional exhibitions warrant specific mention. In January 1978, Otis College of Art and Design hosted *America Now: Drawing towards a More Modern Architecture*, a condensed representation of exhibitions held at the Cooper-Hewitt Museum and the Drawing Center in New York the previous year.[29] In a polemical catalog essay, curator Robert A.M. Stern argued that Modernism had favored "polytechnicians" over poets and had dissipated the power and importance of drawing by, among other reasons, favoring conceptual axonometric projections over perceptual perspectival renderings. For Stern, the recent renewed interest in architectural drawing coincided with a waning adherence to the tenets of Modernism and signaled a shift away from "the poverty of orthodox modern architecture" to a far richer postmodern poetry.[30]

Though Stern's critique was baldly tilted toward his own stylistic predilections, his belief that architects sought to advance beyond the stric-

tures of orthodox Modernism through drawing was widely shared. That same January, Coy Howard assembled a collection of drawings by local architects at the Los Angeles Institute of Contemporary Art. *Architectural Views: Physical Fact, Psychic Effect* featured works by Richard Aldriedge, Frederick Fisher, Eugene Kupper, Studio Works, and Howard himself that went well beyond the representation of buildings to mine the medium of drawing for untapped potential. Howard remembered his own motivations as follows:

> It basically grew out of [a feeling that] "I don't know if what I'm doing here is of any value, but let me test and see if I can come to understand what I'm trying to do architecturally in terms of the drawing." So the drawings became this incredible vehicle...I would study them and study them and study them, and try to invent different techniques to try to discover the sensibility that I wanted in the buildings which I wasn't sure was there. So, doing those drawings was absolutely pivotal for me in developing my aesthetic.[31]

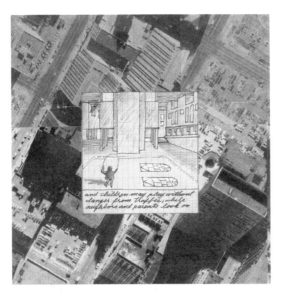

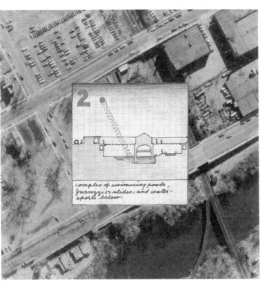
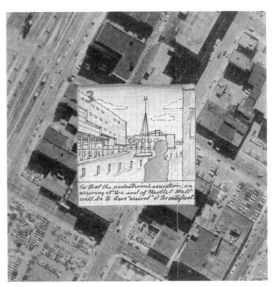

Fig. 16: Studio Works, The River and the City, Minneapolis, 1976. Sketches.

An array of techniques was on view at the exhibition. Studio Works hung a neat row of tiny, carefully mounted pen-and-ink sketches that clearly enumerated the functional and organizational elements of their scheme for Nicollet Island in Minneapolis [**Fig. 16**]. Across the room, a series of evocative collages of their South Side Settlement, assembled in part from Mangurian's meticulous construction documents, offered little in the way of technical clarity but an abundance of emotional impact [**pp. 119-121**]. Howard's work displayed a similar breadth of investigation. Two carefully inked images of his exhibition design for the 1976 Scythian Gold exhibition at LACMA [**Fig. 17**] contrasted an enormous and highly expressive perspec-

tive drawing of his Rinaldi house mounted directly to the wall with long, dynamically arrayed strips of masking tape [**Fig. 18**].[32] Kupper hung a series of six axonometrics of his UCLA Extension project [**p. 40**] as well as ink and colored-pencil studies of his house for Harry Nilsson. Fisher's large-scale rendered site plan of his scheme for Machu Picchu [**Fig. 52**] also was fixed directly to the wall with tape, while Aldriedge's careful perspective drawings in ink and watercolor were fastidiously mounted. In each case, the work on the wall went far beyond the mere representation and planning of a future building to stand as self-sufficient works of architecture in their own right. Far more emphatically than previous presentations, the LAICA exhibition demonstrated

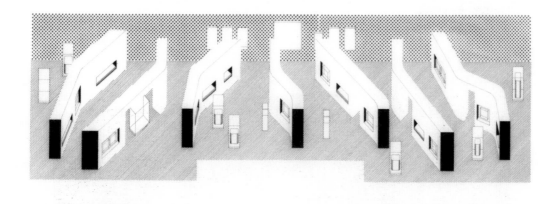

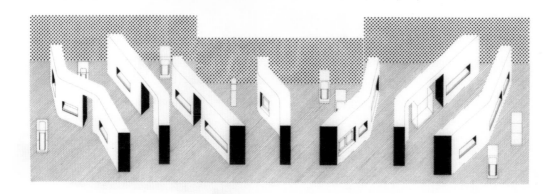

Fig. 17: Coy Howard, Scythian Gold, Los Angeles County Museum of Art, 1976.

the radical potential of alternative techniques being developed in Los Angeles.

By the late 1970s, such wide-ranging activity had begun to draw attention from local, national, and international audiences, with increasing interest going to younger practitioners. In addition to coverage in the *P/A* Awards, projects by Architecture Gallery participants such as Coate's Alexander house, Morphosis's Villas Florestas, and Moss's Morganstern warehouse received extended reviews.[33] Peter de Bretteville, Hodgetts, Mangurian, and Howard were included among the "Forty under Forty" list of significant young architects Robert A.M. Stern compiled for the Japanese journal *A+U* in

1977.[34] In 1978, *A+U* dedicated the bulk of its April issue to a survey of young Los Angeles architects assembled by Michael Franklin Ross.[35] As with previous group presentations, this collection was stylistically and programmatically diverse, held together by little more than a common desire to move beyond the International Style toward what Ross tentatively referred to as a "possibly-post-modern" interest in "indulgent complexity."[36] Unbuilt projects predominated, though recently completed buildings such as Helmut Schulitz' high-tech residence in Coldwater Canyon [**Fig. 19**], Moss's Playa del Rey triplex [**Fig. 20**], and Morphosis' small Delmer addition in Venice [**Fig. 21**] demonstrated the viability of alternative approaches. For Ross, the work represented

Fig. 18: Coy Howard, Rinaldi Residence, Los Angeles, 1978.

"a restless desire to do something more, something special, something that isn't just another repetition of what has gone before, but in some small way expands the realm of possibilities for architecture and for the people who experience it."[37] This widely read presentation drew significant attention to the younger generation from outside Southern California, and, despite Ross's attempts to disprove any collective ambitions, established the notion of a coherent group of young Los Angeles architects in the minds of many observers in the city and beyond.

By the end of the decade new local journals such as *L.A. Architect*, the monthly newsletter of the AIA's Southern California Chapter, and *Archetype*, an independent effort launched by San Francisco based architect Mark Mack, brought additional coverage and provided important platforms from which to broadcast activities and ideas. But it was the writing of *Los Angeles Times* architecture critic John Dreyfuss (1934-2004) that would prove particularly significant to the Architecture Gallery. Dreyfuss, the son of noted industrial engineer Henry Dreyfuss, joined the *Times* in 1966 and became its architecture and design critic ten years later. Often critical of the city's Downtown architectural establishment, he devoted significant attention to new projects by unorthodox Westsiders in the late 1970s.[38] Eric Moss remembers a "genuinely interested, genuinely

supportive guy. ...he was open and he was sympathetic, and he didn't come with an ideological perspective. As far as I could tell, he was just looking for ideas, looking for new stuff, looking for interesting characters."[39]

Dreyfuss took particular interest in the house Frank Gehry built for himself in Santa Monica in the summer of 1978, and in a long article in the *Times* carefully outlined the architect's unorthodox intentions and design process, the house's basic organization strategy, and described salient effects such as the perspectival illusions created by varied wall heights along the building's south façade.[40] Setting up his readers for a positive response, Dreyfuss also described a number of skeptical neighbors, including Santa Monica's mayor, who had been won over after visiting the house and learning of the architect's intentions firsthand. Dreyfuss's article was the first sustained treatment of Gehry's house in either the popular or professional press, but it was far from the last. The house was soon featured across the architectural literature and national newspapers, and even found its way into *People* magazine and a cover story on American architects in *Time*.[41]

Drawing inspiration from the work of local artists Charles Arnoldi [**Figs. 22**] and Ed Moses, among others, Gehry wrapped his unassuming Santa Monica house in a complex assemblage of glass, galvanized metal, unfinished plywood, and chain link. Inside, he stripped away finishes to reveal the bare studs and lath beneath. Formerly exterior surfaces were recast as unlikely interior elements, and typical interior spaces such as kitchen and dining were placed outside the original house, with an asphalt floor amplifying the ambiguities of the new enclosure [pp. 162-169]. The house represented a bold departure from both modern and postmodern orthodoxies and marked a significant breakthrough in Gehry's development. With it, the architect established a line of exploration he would develop over the next decade.

Gehry also used the house to take aim at prevailing tendencies on the East Coast. In his lecture for the Architecture Gallery series, he joked that a model of the house made for a 1979 exhibition in New York was assembled with a deliberate lack of traditional craft with the express purpose of "upsetting the people in New York, who are very precise about architecture" [Fig. 23]. He went on to articulate a more serious statement of his personal interests:

> There is a certain fascination with something not looking designed. I feel that a lot of buildings, a lot of architecture, a lot of work, has that 'designed' look—that everything is in place. I am really trying to get away from that, to look more like it was less contrived. Now maybe, in fact, it ends up being more contrived, but I hope not.[42]

Gehry's taste for 'carefully careless,' fragmentary compositions executed in straightforward vernacular materials would become a hallmark of Los Angeles architecture through the 1980s and '90s, leading many critics to see the architect as a trailblazer and father figure for the younger generation. In truth, the relationship was much more of a two-way street, and Gehry clearly drew off the energy of his younger colleagues.[43] But few would disagree that the house marked a spectacular achievement for Los Angeles architecture. With it, Gehry was launched into the international spotlight, and a parade of onlookers soon descended on Los Angeles' West Side for a closer look.

Fig. 19: Helmut Schulitz, Schulitz Residence, Los Angeles, 1976.

Fig. 20: Eric Owen Moss, Triplex Apartments, Playa del Rey, 1976.

Fig. 21: Morphosis, Delmer Residence, Venice, 1977.

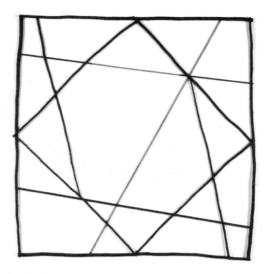

Fig. 22: Charles Arnoldi, *Untitled*, 1971.

Fig. 23: Frank Gehry, Gehry Residence, Santa Monica, 1977-78.

Fig. 24: Morphosis, 2-4-6-8 House, Venice, 1978. View from alley.

In the summer of 1978, a 34-year-old Thom Mayne returned to Los Angeles after a year at Harvard. On the East Coast, Mayne had collected a graduate degree and "realigned" himself after several years of deep involvement at SCI-Arc.[44] Michael Rotondi picked him up at LAX and drove straight to Frank Gehry's not-yet-completed house in Santa Monica. For Mayne, "It was just a startle, I'll never forget it. I had been in Boston and [it was] just dead. I was this L.A. kid...it was an enjoyable year, but there was just no way I could possibly live in Boston. ...I really had a new appreciation for L.A. and the kind of freedom I had here."[45]

Rotondi and Mayne quickly set to work on two new projects, a garage renovation in Venice and a small single-family house in Tijuana. In contrast to the more stringent functionalism of earlier Morphosis projects such as the Sequoyah School (which had begun as Rotondi's thesis at SCI-Arc) and the Stirlingesque Reidel Medical Building, the 2-4-6-8 and Mexico II houses were composed of centralized, symmetrical volumes capped by pyramidal roofs [**Fig. 24**]. 2-4-6-8's iconic progression of foursquare windows was articulated in bright yellow, blue, and red, with bands of pink concrete block running through the base. According to Rotondi, SCI-Arc director Ray Kappe was not pleased with their swerve away from more orthodox methodologies: "Kappe was really pissed off at us when we did that one because it had bright colors. He thought we were selling out to Aldo Rossi. ...Everybody was just trying things out. And Ray was Ray. He was a Modernist, with an open mind—but closed when he thought we were giving in to Postmodernism."[46]

Kappe's paradoxical stance—open to change, but committed to orthodox values—was a key catalyst for the Architecture Gallery. As younger faculty like Mayne, Rotondi, and Moss developed their positions, their architecture veered further from the status quo of Kappe's generation. By the late '70s, a distinctly adversarial relationship had taken shape. As Mayne recalled:

> At that time...Bernard Zimmerman, Ray Kappe, and a group of could-have-been,

wanna-be Case Study guys...they owned the city. And we were going, "No, we don't buy it." We were going somewhere. It was very much part of the SCI-Arc dialogue. We used to have some fantastic, really robust conversations and disagreements about where we were going, about just what we stood for.[47]

For Mayne, the Modernist project was exhausted. "The people I studied under, Pierre Koenig, et cetera, that was the end, that was the last group. ...[ours] was a group that was starting to redefine things."[48] Soon after Mayne's return to Los Angeles, an opportunity to publicly stake out alternative positions presented itself.

Ray and Shelly Kappe took a sabbatical during the 1978-79 school year, and remained away through the summer. By the time they returned, Mayne had organized the fall's Design Forum lecture series. His recollection of exactly how the events came together is vague: "I can't remember. It was my turn or they asked me to do the lecture series—we took turns doing that."[49] Kappe recalled something more calculated:

> I was on sabbatical when they put that thing together. ...I came back to kind of a surprise. ...I get back and Thom Mayne says to me, "We put together a program with guys who are doing architecture." He names the people and I said, "I do architecture, why aren't I on the list?" So it was a set-up. It was a time when both Eric [Moss] and Thom were just starting to move to a new place."[50]

That new place had little room for members of Kappe's generation. For the lectures, Mayne chose younger practitioners with the exception of Gehry, whose radical new projects aligned him more with Mayne's generation than his own, and Coate, with whom Mayne had collaborated in the early 1970s. Most were teaching at either SCI-Arc or UCLA, with Dimster and De Bretteville representing USC. Mayne drew participants from both the Silvers (Kupper, Dimster) and the L.A. Twelve (Gehry, Coate), choosing the most idiosyncratic characters from each previous group. The series' title, "Current L.A.: 10 Viewpoints," foregrounded the individualistic nature of each practice over any notions of

shared methodology. An exhibition to accompany each of the nine lectures was soon added to the agenda, with Mayne's sparsely furnished home and studio in Venice serving as the venue. Coy Howard, who would not exhibit his work, was slated to give two lectures bookending the series. Each of the SCI-Arc lectures was videotaped, and was screened on a small black-and-white monitor in the gallery.[51]

By any metric, it was a heterogeneous assemblage, and, despite its lack of approval from SCI-Arc's director, it seemed to align with the school's experimental mandate. Moss later characterized it as a natural development of SCI-Arc's unorthodox pedagogy—and the failure of its founders to fully deliver on its initial promise:

> If you set something up as a departure and then try to teach something that was no departure at all...the opportunity for departure manifests itself. I would say, in retrospect, that these shows would be a manifestation—the train had left the station, you know? First you made the station, and then you made the train, and then, finally, it took off.[52]

Howard delivered his opening talk—equal parts criticism of the establishment and poetic meditation of the nature of beauty—on October 3rd. Kupper's exhibition opened the following Tuesday. The next morning, two articles by John Dreyfuss appeared in the *Los Angeles Times*. The first outlined the series of exhibitions as a whole; the second offered a specific treatment of Kupper's installation.[53]

How Dreyfuss came to write about the shows is unclear. Mayne recalls the journalist contacting him with a request to see Kupper's exhibition, and then insisting, against Mayne's initial disagreement, that he produce weekly reviews of remaining shows.[54] Rotondi, who worked closely with Mayne to organize the events, remembers a discussion "to see if we could get Dreyfuss to write about [the shows], which he did."[55] Regardless of the motivating circumstances, Dreyfuss's contribution was crucial. With illustrations by *Times* photographer Mary Frampton and others, the reviews certainly were responsible for the steadily increasing—and largely non-professional—traffic in the gallery as the weeks progressed.[56] The articles also changed the tenor of disciplinary conversation in Los Angeles. For the participating architects, they afforded a heightened sense of significance to their ongoing experiments. For the city's architectural establishment—many of whom had close ties with the paper's owners—the attention, which meant a corresponding lack of coverage for their own output, was cause for concern. Dreyfuss soon found himself in conflict with the paper's editors, and after 1983, architectural reviews in the paper would be taken over by Sam Hall Kaplan, a critic who did not share Dreyfuss's sympathy for the younger generation.

Nonetheless, the buzz generated by the exhibitions would continue unabated into the 1980s. As Dreyfuss put it, they "catalyzed a significant segment of the Los Angeles architectural community, precipitating a steamy brew of respect, anger, pride, jealousy, excitement, and interest."[57] Dreyfuss's concluding article, which appears to respond directly to criticism he received from establishment architects, outlined an accurate prediction of developments in Los Angeles architecture through the 1980s. As architects in the exhibition—particularly Gehry, Moss, and Morphosis—rose in significance, many established practitioners indeed were "left by the wayside in terms of being movers and shakers in their profession."[58] With the Architecture Gallery, the youngsters emphatically put the city's greying establishment on notice, and their "obscure, theatrical, and trendy" output would soon become synonymous with cutting-edge architecture in Los Angeles.[59]

A Confederacy of Heretics offers the first sustained look at this crucial moment in Los Angeles architecture. Our aim is not to reconstruct the original exhibitions, but rather to unsettle prevailing understandings of this work in order to catalyze new interpretations and debate. Through the 1980s and '90s, the "L.A. School" became synonymous with a visual style of fragmented forms, intuitive compositions, expressive details, vernacular references, and varied materials.[60] As the materials gathered here attest, such a narrow description fails to account

for the array of individual—and collaborative—approaches pursued by these architects in the late '70s and early '80s. To further broaden the conversation, we pay particular attention to lesser known designs and include several notable projects and artifacts not exhibited in the original 1979 exhibitions. We privilege drawings and models over photographic documentation of built projects not because many of the exhibited projects remain unbuilt, but rather because these artifacts demonstrate most dramatically the radicalism at the heart of the Architecture Gallery. Many of the artifacts collected here have not been seen since the 1979 exhibitions and are published for the first time in this catalog.

The Architecture Gallery exhibitions were small and, in many cases, hastily assembled affairs. Many of the exhibited projects were underrepresented, and explanatory texts were often absent. Few photographs were taken and even fewer records were kept to document the events. In many cases, a reliable accounting of exhibited works is impossible, and a number of original artifacts have been lost or irreparably damaged. A Confederacy of Heretics cuts across this incomplete archive in several ways. In Part One of this volume, original drawings, models, and other items exhibited in the Architecture Gallery are presented alongside each of John Dreyfuss's Los Angeles Times reviews and new statements from the participating architects. We also include a 1979 review of the exhibitions by Joseph Giovannini, then architecture critic for the Los Angeles Herald Examiner. A selection of images by Times photographers Larry Bessel, Judd Gunderson, and Mary Frampton offers a rare glimpse at the original installations.[61]

The materials installed in the SCI-Arc Gallery and Library Gallery and illustrated in Part Two of this catalog are assembled with awareness of subsequent developments and present-day reassessments. As outlined in co-curator Andrew Zago's introduction to Part Two, we include a number of artifacts not included in the original exhibitions which demonstrate the unfolding of nascent themes at the Architecture Gallery into more mature instantiations in the ensuing decades. Rather than categorize works according to individual architects or projects, we organize the installation according to specific formal criteria which register the range of projective geometries through which the architecture of the period was disciplined. Our method re-contextualizes individual artifacts as it echoes the mobilization of counter-intuitive tactics and productive overelaboration in much of the exhibited work. Though our gambit may obscure some aspects of the exhibited work (including the architects' intentions), we wager that any losses will be offset by productive adjacencies more conventional interpretive schema would be unlikely to produce.

Part Three presents new critical essays which situate the work in current architectural discourse. Co-curator Ewan Branda introduces the section with themes by which the 1979 work might be understood from today's perspective, particularly in terms of technology. Joe Day maps the social and professional networks of which Frank Gehry was a part, while Kevin McMahon places the video documentation of the lectures within a wider history of video technology in Southern California. Patricia Morton positions the work in the broader context of postmodernism, paying particular attention to the Architecture Gallery's relationship to the 1980 Architecture Biennale in Venice, Italy, and Paulette Singley looks at Venice, California as a new locus of creativity.

All told, *A Confederacy of Heretics* gathers an array of artifacts across a wide spectrum of media. Collected here, these objects demonstrate the breadth of tactics with which progressive young architects experimented in the late 1970s and comprise a unique repository of nascent design ideas which continue to sponsor innovative architecture in Los Angeles. Not only does this collection showcase some of the earliest instances of the formal, material, and technical innovations that would develop into the hallmarks of Los Angeles architecture in the 1980s and '90s, it also maps still-potent lines of investigation to be developed—or contested— by contemporary designers wishing to exploit the promise of the periphery to imagine new possibilities for a 21st-century world without a center.

ENDNOTES

1. The theologian Heinrich Schlier outlines "the *hairesis* of the philosopher, which in antiquity always includes the choice of a distinct *bios* [way of life]" in Gerhard Kittels, ed., *Theological Dictionary of the New Testament*, vol. 1 (London: Eerdmans, 1964): 180-82. For more developed discussions of heresy's relationship to the construction of the self, see Eduard Iricinschi and Holger M. Zellentin, eds., *Heresy and Identity in Late Antiquity* (Tübingen: Mohr Siebeck, 2008). On the concept's relationship to modernity, see Peter Gay, *Modernism: The Lure of Heresy from Beckett to Baudelaire and Beyond* (New York: W.W. Norton, 2008).

2. There were several attempts to bring together these and other Los Angeles architects under a single banner in the late 1970s and early '80s. Charles Jencks claims the label "L.A. School" was invented by a group of architects that convened a series of meetings at the Biltmore Hotel in 1981. See his "LA Style / LA School," *AA Files* 5 (1983): 90. In *Heteropolis: Los Angeles, the Riots, and the Strange Beauty of Hetero-architecture* (London: Academy Editions, 1993): 132, n. 9, he lists the group's instigators as George Rand, Gene Summers, and himself, and participating architects as Roland Coate, Peter de Bretteville, Frank Gehry, Craig Hodgetts, Coy Howard, Eugene Kupper, Tony Lumsden, Thom Mayne, Robert Mangurian, Charles Moore, Cesar Pelli, Stefanos Polyzoides, Michael Rotondi, Tim Vreeland, and Buzz Yudell.

3. The twenty years preceding the Architecture Gallery saw the deaths of Frank Lloyd Wright (1959), Le Corbusier (1965), Mies van der Rohe (1969), Walter Gropius (1969), Louis Kahn (1974), and Alvar Aalto (1976). Los Angeles also lost a large share of notable personalities, including A.C. Martin (1960), Welton Becket (1969), Richard Neutra (1970), Lloyd Wright (1978), Charles Eames (1978), and A. Quincy Jones (1979).

4. Among the most influential of these attacks is Jacques Derrida's essay, "Structure, Sign, and Play in the Discourse of the Human Sciences," delivered as a lecture at Johns Hopkins University in 1966 and translated into English in Derrida, *Writing and Difference* (Chicago: University of Chicago Press, 1978): 278-293.

5. Damaging critiques include Jane Jacobs' *The Death and Life of American Cities* (New York: Random House, 1961) and Manfredo Tafuri's "Toward a Critique of Architectural Ideology" [1969], in K. Michael Hays, *Architecture Theory since 1968* (Cambridge: MIT Press, 1998): 6-35.

6. See Peter Cook, ed., *Archigram* (London: The Architectural Press, 1973) which collects much of the material published in the group's eponymous pamphlet from 1961-70; Aldo Rossi, *The Architecture of the City* [1966](New York: MIT Press, 1982); Venturi, *Complexity and Contradiction in Architecture* (New York: Museum of Modern Art, 1966); Venturi, Scott Brown, and Steven Izenour, *Learning from Las Vegas* (Cambridge: MIT Press, 1977); Baird, "'La Dimension Amoureuse' in Architecture," in Baird and Jencks, eds., *Meaning in Architecture* (New York: George Braziller, 1969); Jencks, *The Language of Post-Modern Architecture* (New York: Rizzoli, 1977); Maurice Culot and Krier, "The Only Path for Architecture," *Oppositions* 14 (Fall 1978); Rowe and Koetter, *Collage City* (Cambridge: MIT Press, 1978); Eisenman, "Aspects of Modernism: Maison Dom-ino and the Self-Referential Sign," *Oppositions* 15/16 (Winter/Spring 1979); Libeskind, ""*Deus ex Machina*"/ "*Machina ex Deo*": Aldo Rossi's Theater of the World," *Oppositions* 21 (Summer 1980), and Tschumi, "The Architectural Paradox," *Studio International* (Sept-Oct 1975).

7. Carey McWilliams' classic study, *Southern California: An Island on the Land* [1946] (Salt Lake City: Gibbs Smith, 2010), provides an excellent account of such activities throughout the city's history. I offer my own musings about the peripheral nature of Los Angeles architecture in "Downtown" [2007], *Issues-Newsletters*, Los Angeles Forum for Architecture and Urban Design. http://laforum.org/content/issues-newsletters/downtown-by-todd-gannon.

8. Eric Owen Moss. December 05, 1979. "Eric Owen Moss: Armageddon or Polynesian Contextualism" (lecture). In SCI-Arc Media Archive. Southern California Institute of Architecture. <http://sma.sciarc.edu/video/1883_moss_eric_owen_1-00-00-00/>. (October 09, 2012).

9. Ibid.

10. Ray Kappe, interview with the author. Los Angeles, 29 June 2012.

11. Personal interviews with the author, Summer 2012.

12. Coy Howard, interview with the author and Ewan Branda. Los Angeles, 16 May 2012.

13. Ibid.

14. Importantly, that way of life was widely understood to be specifically architectural. Though Howard and Frank Gehry both maintained close ties with and drew significant inspiration from the Los Angeles art scene, these and other participating architects ultimately maintained clear disciplinary boundaries between art and architecture. Eugene Kupper and Roland Coate, for example, were and remain avid painters, but they operated for the most part independently of the Los Angeles arts community. While both attempted early on to use the medium as a way to inform their architectural ambitions, each ultimately saw painting as a distinct alternative to architectural practice. Coate, in the end, chose painting, and closed his architectural practice in 1983 to devote himself to painting full-time. Kupper chose architecture, and largely suspended painting through the 1970s and early '80s.

15. Kappe had wished to cap enrollment at 250, but the dean, while Kappe was away, decided to increase to 350 students. Ray Kappe, "SCI-Arc History," unpublished manuscript, collection of the author.

16. Architecture Gallery participants Robert Mangurian, Coy Howard, Craig Hodgetts, and Frederick Fisher also had joined the faculty at SCI-Arc by the early 1980s.

17. In addition, Shelly Kappe hosted regular panel discussions at the school through the 1970s on topics ranging from "women in architecture" to "the role of the large office" to the "construction industry gap." More speculative topics, such as "Alternative Architectural Practices" and "Which Way to the Future?" also were featured. SCI-Arc videotaped the lectures from an early date and the collection recently has been digitized and made available online. See the SCI-Arc Media Archive, http://sma.sciarc.edu.

18. The White position was held by the "New York Five" (Peter Eisenman, Michael Graves, Charles Gwathmey, John Hejduk, and Richard Meier) and was galvanized in the influential catalog to their 1969 MoMA exhibition, *Five Architects* (New York: Oxford University Press, 1972). A collection of critical responses to this work from five "Grays," Allan Greenberg, Romaldo Giurgola, Charles Moore, Jacquelin Robertson, and Robert Stern, appeared in "Five on Five," *Architectural Forum* (May 1973): 46-57. Participants at UCLA included Werner Seligmann, Michael Graves, Peter Eisenman, Charles Moore, Richard Meier, Robert A.M. Stern, Giovanni Pasanella, T. Merrill Prentice, Charles Gwathmey, Richard Weinstein, and Jaquelin Robertson, with Colin Rowe (White) and Vincent Scully (Gray) each giving lectures. The event was reviewed in "White, Gray, Silver, Crimson," *Progressive Architecture* (July 1974): 28, 30, 32. A year later, the Japanese magazine *A+U* devoted an entire issue to the White vs. Gray phenomenon. See "White and Gray: Eleven Modern Architects," *Architecture + Urbanism* (April 1975). Coy Howard was commissioned to make a film of the event, but at the time of this writing, a copy has not been located.

19. Most accounts claim the name had to do with the slick, glass-and-steel aesthetic espoused by most of the group. According to Charles Jencks, the moniker also had to do with the fact that each of the architects drove a silver BMW. (Charles Jencks, telephone interview with the author, Los Angeles and London, 30 May 2012.) Hodgetts contested this assertion in a later interview with the author.

20. Craig Hodgetts, interview with the author. Los Angeles, 5 Mar 2012.

21. Eugene Kupper, who ran a small private practice, stands as a significant exception to the corporate character of the Silvers. Frank Dimster left Pereira to set up his own small practice in 1975.

22. See Reyner Banham, "The Style for the Job," *New Statesman* (14 Feb 1964): 261.

23. These quotations, and Vreeland's above, are from Peter Papademetriou, "Images from a Silver Screen," *Progressive Architecture* (Oct 1976): 70-77. Stirling had given a keynote lecture to kick off the April events at UCLA.

24. Cf. Jencks "The Los Angeles Silvers: Tim Vreeland, Anthony Lumsden, Frank Dimster, Eugene Kupper, Cesar Pelli, Paul Kennon," *Architecture + Urbanism* 70 (Oct 1976): 14. Hodgetts offered a similar assessment in a 2012 interview with the author.

25. "They might be said to exemplify the highest ideals of the architectural mainstream. Their crusade...is to illustrate their conviction that the profession of architecture can without overthrowing its traditional values successfully serve the interests of the marketplace." Nicholas Pyle, "Foreword," in N. Charles Slert and James Harter, eds., *Twelve Los Angeles Architects* (Pomona: Cal Poly Pomona, 1978): vi.

26. The catalog accounted for this by dividing the architects into four categories: The Expressionalists (Coate, Lumsden, and Pelli), the Constructionalists (Ellwood and Kappe), the Rationalists (Dworsky, Lomax, Miller, Pulliam, and Zim-

merman), and the Experimentalists (Gehry and Lautner). See Slert and Harter, *Twelve Los Angeles Architects*.

27. This inaction drew harsh criticism from *Los Angeles Times* critic John Dreyfuss. See his "Comment," in Slert and Harter, *Twelve Los Angeles Architects*, iii-iv.

28. "And Then There Were Twelve...The Los Angeles 12," *Architectural Record* (Aug 1976), appears to be the lone national publication on the group.

29. The exhibitions, curated by Robert A.M. Stern (at the Drawing Center) and Richard Oliver (at the Cooper-Hewitt) showcased a diversity of work by Charles Moore, Stanley Tigerman, Michael Graves, Robert Venturi, John Hejduk, Peter Eisenman, Coy Howard, and Franklin Israel, among others.

30. See Robert A.M. Stern, ed., "America Now: Drawing towards a More Modern Architecture," *A.D. Profiles* 6 (June 1977): 383. Local critics held similar views. The following year, Anne Luise Buerger remarked, "When the Modern Movement appeared as corporate architecture in the United States, architectural drawing suffered the consequences of a corporate specialization that too often combined division of labor with division of spirit." See "Art and Architecture: Drawing them Together," *L.A. Architect* (Feb 1978): np.

31. Coy Howard, interview with the author and Ewan Branda. Los Angeles, 16 May 2012. In a small publication on the show, other participants offered their own observations on drawing. Fisher: "Drawing serves the two aspects of design: analysis and synthesis. It facilitates dissection of a building in abstract or real terms, and replicates the selective focus of thoughtful perception." Kupper: "Architectural drawings can serve the direct purpose of technical communication, but they can also be an expression of architectural theory. Architecture is a potential of the creative spirit, not another name for real estate or construction." Aldriedge: "With my drawings I am trying to catch a glance of the moods, emotions, and ancient memories that may exist behind the architecture." Hodgetts and Mangurian, with tongues firmly planted in cheeks, flatly stated, "Drawings are a minor part of our process." See "Architectural Views: Physical Fact, Psychic Effect," *L.A. Architect* (Feb 1978): np.

32. Curved polycarbonate panels that lay strewn on the floor beneath the image were in fact a framework which could be assembled into a cylinder. The drawing—a 360-degree view of the interior of the house—could be mounted inside the cylinder to afford a viewer willing to climb inside an immersive, kinesthetic preview of the proposed space.

33. See Thomas Hines, "Coate," *Progressive Architecture* (Aug 1976): 58-61; Esther McCoy, "Everyman's Casa," *Progressive Architecture* (July 1978): 76-79; and David Morton, "Look Again: Morganstern Warehouse," *Progressive Architecture* (Jun 1979): 66-69.

34. See Stern, "40 under 40," *Architecture + Urbanism* 73 (Jan 1977): 17-142. The issue also included a synopsis of recent architectural activities in Los Angeles. See Panos Koulermos, "Los Angeles," ibid., pp. 11-12.

35. See Michael Franklin Ross, "Young, Los Angeles and Possibly-Post-Modern, Architects," *Architecture + Urbanism* 90 (April 1978): 83-154. The represented practices were Chris Dawson & David Brindle, Ronald Filson, Arthur Golding, Coy Howard, Charles Lagreco, Douglas Meyer, Morphosis, Eric Owen Moss & James Stafford, James Porter, Michael Franklin Ross, and Helmut Schulitz.

36. Ibid., 84.

37. Ibid., 85.

38. Cf. "Job Center Does its Job—and Architecture Excels," *Los Angeles Times* (23 Jan 1977), on Gehry's UCLA Placement and Career Planning Center; "Pavilion: Crater with a Stage at Bottom," *Los Angeles Times* (15 May 1977), on Gehry's Concord Pavilion; and "An Unlikely Dash of Exuberance," *Los Angeles Time* (22 Oct 1978), on Moss's Morganstern Warehouse. Dreyfuss' reviewed both Stern's Otis exhibition and Howard's LAICA exhibition in "Architects: Insights into the Sketches," *Los Angeles Times* (30 Jan 1978): E1, E5.

39. Eric Owen Moss, interview with the author, Ewan Branda, and Andrew Zago. Culver City, CA, 7 Jun 2012.

40. Dreyfuss, "Gehry's Artful House Offends, Baffles, Angers his Neighbors," *Los Angeles Times* (23 July 1978).

41. See Sally Koris, "Renegade Frank Gehry Has Torn Up His House—and the Book of Architecture," *People* (5 Mar 1979) and Robert Hughes, "Doing Their Own Thing," *Time* (8 Jan 1979).

42. Frank O. Gehry, November 07, 1979. "Frank O Gehry Part One" (lecture). In SCI-Arc Media Archive. Southern California Institute of Architecture. <http://sma.sciarc. edu/video/frank-gehry-part-one/>. (October 16, 2012).

43. Coy Howard saw in Gehry's occasional invitations to younger architects to meet for discussions at his studio deliberate attempts by the older architect to insinuate himself into ongoing conversations among the younger generation. Howard's reaction to the oft-uttered label, "the Gehry kids," was unequivocal: "It's the other way around. Gehry's our kid, in actual fact." Coy Howard, interview with the author and Ewan Branda. Los Angeles, 16 May 2012.

44. As Mayne had been involved in running the graduate program at SCI-Arc but did not hold a master's degree himself, the school granted him a sabbatical to attend the program at Harvard.

45. Thom Mayne, interview with the author. Culver City, CA, 14 July 2012.

46. Michael Rotondi, interview with the author and Ewan Branda. Los Angeles, 13 Jun 2012.

47. Thom Mayne, interview with the author and Ewan Branda. Culver City, CA, 5 Mar 2012.

48. Ibid.

49. Thom Mayne, interview with the author and Ewan Branda. Culver City, CA, 14 July 2012.

50. Ray Kappe, interview with the author. Los Angeles, 29 June 2012. Shelly Kappe was incensed by Mayne's move, and in a 2012 conversation with the author insisted that the exhibitions were a renegade action that should not be considered official SCI-Arc events.

51. Nearly all the lectures are now available online at the SCI-Arc Media Archive. At the time of writing, only Coate's lecture and Howard's concluding talk have not yet been located.

52. Eric Owen Moss, interview with the author, Ewan Branda, and Andrew Zago. Culver City, CA, 7 June 2012.

53. See "One-Week Shows by 11 Architects" and "Kupper Employs Dual Process," *Los Angeles Times* (11 Oct 1979): C25, 26, 28, reprinted in this volume on p. 35.

54. Thom Mayne, interview with the author. Culver City, CA, 5 Mar 2012.

55. Michael Rotondi, interview with the author and Ewan Branda. Los Angeles, 13 June 2012.

56. According to Mayne, the comedian and art patron Steve Martin dutifully checked out the new offerings every Saturday. Martin would later purchase Coate's Alexander House in Montecito. Thom Mayne, interview with the author and Ewan Branda. Culver City, 14 July 2012.

57. Dreyfuss, "Gallery Stirs Up Architects," *Los Angeles Times* (12 Dec 1979): E26. Reprinted in this volume, pp. 94-95.

58. Ibid.

59. Howard offered this description to Dreyfuss in a 1979 interview.

60. The best treatments of this period to date are Charles Jencks, *Heteropolis*, op. cit., and John Morris Dixon's "The Santa Monica School: What's its Lasting Contribution?" *Progressive Architecture* (May 1995): 63-71, 112, 114.

61. Complementing this catalog and the installation at SCI-Arc, Kevin McMahon has assembled an online exhibition of related materials at the SCI-Arc Media Archive, including the original 1979 SCI-Arc lectures, commentary from the exhibition curators, a film by Rebeca Méndez Design commissioned for the exhibition, and other items. See http://sma.sciarc.edu/.

PART ONE

L.A. IN THE 1970s,
12 VIEWPOINTS

ORIGINALLY PUBLISHED IN THE *LOS ANGELES TIMES*, 11 OCT 1979

One-Week Shows by 11 Architects

JOHN DREYFUSS

Behind a messy little stand of trees, past a gate concocted of chicken wire and sticks covered with sheets of black plastic, through a red door in a nondescript building with white paint peeling from red bricks—lies a marvelous space.

It is The Architecture Gallery, at 209 San Juan Ave, in Venice: a brave new idea created to exhibit the work of eleven Los Angeles architects whose common denominator is dedication to architecture as an art form.

This 20x27-foot, white walled room is Los Angeles' first gallery totally devoted to showing the works of architects. It is less than a week old, and its assured lifespan is exactly nine weeks. After that, it may continue, it may move, or it may die, depending on its popularity, on blind luck and on the will of its founder, architect and teacher Thom Mayne.

Mayne started this gallery (which is part of his home) in connection with a lecture series he organized, and because, as he said, "It's important for people to experience the artistic types of activities that lead to fine architecture."

He believes—and correctly so—that some architectural drawings and models are more than indicators of structures-to-be. They are art objects too.

The Architecture Gallery, which will be open from noon to 6 p.m. Tuesdays through Saturdays, is guaranteed at least nine weeks of life because it has booked nine week-long shows.

Each show will display work by an architect or pair of architects who will talk about their efforts on a Wednesday at 8 p.m. during the week of their exhibition.

The talks, which will be videotaped and shown at the exhibitions, are scheduled at the Southern California Institute of Architecture (SCI-Arc), 1800 Berkeley St. in Santa Monica. SCI-Arc and Mayne are co-sponsoring the gallery in Venice.

For this program, Mayne selected eleven of the Los Angeles area's particularly interesting architects. Most of them are also teachers. Many of them have not built much, at least partly because they have been unwilling to compromise their artistic principles.

While that attitude is laudable, it has created hungry times for some of those involved, in terms of both architectural commissions and groceries.

But there are advantages to being selective. "By doing fewer buildings, I have been able to make each one truly part of myself," said Roland Coate, one of the participating architects. Coate is also a painter.

"Like any artist," he said, "I feel that to do the most meaningful work means being totally committed. To develop that total commitment requires rare circumstances, and perhaps a little magic. You need the right site, the right budget, and, most of all, the right client, to name just a few of the factors."

The eleven men (there are no women in the group) have made notable contributions to California's landscape. Coate designed the exquisite Alexander House, a partially earth-covered concrete structure overlooking the ocean in Montecito. Eugene Kupper, whose work is currently at the Architecture Gallery, designed the new, highly acclaimed Harry Nilsson House in Bel Air. Peter de Bretteville built his own interesting, industrial-appearing home in Laurel Canyon.

Frank Gehry, the most successful of the eleven architects in terms of putting up structures, has designed buildings ranging from the open-air Concord Pavilion near San Francisco to his own radical home in Santa Monica.

The exhibitors are widely recognized in architectural circles, and have received their share of honors, including at least eleven prestigious Progressive Architecture national awards for buildable-project designs.

The architects, and the opening dates of their exhibitions at The Architecture Gallery (which precedes by a day the lecture at SCI-Arc) are Eugene Kupper, exhibition in progress; Roland Coate, Tuesday; Frederick Fisher, Oct. 23; Frank Dimster, Oct. 30; Frank Gehry, Nov. 6; Peter de Bretteville, Nov. 13; Thom Mayne and Michael Rotondi, Nov. 20; Craig Hodgetts and Robert Mangurian, Nov. 27; Eric Moss, Dec 4.

Coy Howard, an architect whose interest in art and ability as an artist rank him high among the lecturers, will present a concluding summary talk on Dec. 11, although there will be no exhibition of his work. ✳

ORIGINALLY PUBLISHED IN THE *LOS ANGELES TIMES*, 11 OCT 1979

Kupper Employs Dual Process

JOHN DREYFUSS

An exhibition currently at the Architecture Gallery in Venice can lead viewers on an enlightening tour through the artistically oriented design process architect Eugene Kupper employs in his work.

The show demonstrates how Kupper uses drawings to "discover architecture and explore ideas, rather than just find solutions."

Titled "Architectural Studies," the exhibit of eleven drawings and five models indicates the artistic and theoretical concepts involved in three projects.

If they can grasp the concepts, the viewers will achieve the rare, enlightening and satisfying pleasure of developing from an architectural exhibition a feeling for and understanding of both physical architecture and its emotional impact.

But architect Kupper's concepts are not easy to grasp, and, unfortunately, the exhibit does not offer much help to the layman looking for a handle.

That problem could have been avoided by means of explanatory labeling, but Kupper chose to omit labels because "the pieces in the exhibition form their own context, and labeling would tend to isolate each piece."

Notwithstanding his reasoning, the architect is depriving his viewers and selling himself short. Viewers will find themselves provided with the elements of architectural poetry, but perhaps without the considerable expertise needed to create poetry from those elements. Kupper has a lot to offer, but a lot of people won't get it.

Among his offerings are five photo prints of color-ink drawings comprising floor and superstructure studies for a proposed UCLA Extension building. The structure is designed to be an architectural metaphor reflecting the unchanging earth and the ephemeral sky.

Two floor studies indicate terraces levels that reflect the terraced site. There is a sense of permanence, of solidity about the studies, much as there is a permanence and solidity about the earth. Like the earth, the floors are not receptive to change.

Three super-structure studies, on the other hand, give a sense of three-dimensional freedom. They depict a grid-like framework that Kupper calls a "machine that can be reprogrammed" by moving panels and light fixtures. Like a cloud-filled sky, the overhead superstructure is receptive to change.

Chances are that the building will remain on the drawing boards. Kupper was asked to prepare a planning study for the structure, and he added the conceptual drawings out of personal interest.

By far the most complicated—and enlightening—segment of the exhibition is the set of five drawings and a cardboard model, all representing the recently completed house in Bel Air that Kupper designed for singer-songwriter Harry Nilsson and his wife, Una.

Two sketches in ink and colored pencil indicate the dual nature of the building: sensual and intellectual.

One drawing illustrates the principal intellectual element of the house, which is an 8-foot-wide, 22-foot-high, 130-foot-long colonnade that furnishes a processional axis through the structure. Its irregularly spaced, large-scale frames contribute what Kupper calls "a monumental neutrality" that organizes the house without reflecting its use.

The other drawing has heart. It delineates rooms, gives them color, form and warmth. "It is meant," Kupper said, "to convey the emotional quality of each room: the living room is relaxed, the bedroom is protected, the music room is lively, and so forth."

Those two drawings combine with the model and three more drawings to provide a visual essay about the Nilsson house rather than a description of it. The model adds a descriptive element.

One of the other drawings is a particularly interesting pen-and-ink work in which walls of the house are superimposed on its plan, combining three dimensions in a single plane in the manner of a cubist painter.

The third project at the gallery is a set of four models that is full of surprises.

Each model shows a wall. Each wall is thick—from three to seven feet thick, depending on the wall.

And inside the walls are all sorts of amazements: a waterfall, a sauna, a bathroom with a spa, a stairway, a rock garden, and even a bit of mundane storage space.

Kupper designed the walls into a house to be built in the Berkeley hills by Jack and Trudy Washburn. He planned the walls parallel to each other, to bracket rooms and frame what Kupper calls "magnificent views" of San Francisco and Berkeley in one direction, and woodlands in the other.

When seen from the rooms they divide, the walls are a sculptural art form, planes into which are carved doors, windows and fireplaces.

"These walls talk about architecture," Kupper said. "They contain arches, hollows, alcoves and portals reminiscent of the changing nature of walls throughout history." "They suggest a sense of the permanence of architecture."

Kupper's work will remain on display through Sunday. The Architecture Gallery, 209 San Juan Ave., Venice, is open from noon until 6 p.m. ✤

EUGENE KUPPER

Eugene Kupper was born in 1939 in Oakland, California. By the mid-1950s, he was winning high-school design competitions with convincing riffs on the work of Frank Lloyd Wright. Educated at UC Berkeley and Yale, Kupper later held fellowships at the Center for Advanced Study at the University of Illinois and the American Academy in Rome. He was a member of the faculty of the Department of Architecture and Urban Design at UCLA from 1969 until his retirement in 1994 and later taught at the University of Virginia and Arizona State University.

From 1971-73, Kupper collaborated with Craig Hodgetts and Peter de Bretteville in Works West on projects such as the award-winning Mobile Theater of 1971. In 1973, he joined the office of Frank Gehry, serving as project designer for the Concord Pavilion and the UCLA Placement and Career Planning Center, among other projects. In 1975, he entered private practice in Los Angeles.

At the Architecture Gallery, Kupper exhibited an unbuilt scheme for the UCLA Extension Building, a house he completed for singer-songwriter Harry Nilsson in Bel Air, and the Washburn House, an unrealized design for a hillside site near Berkeley. Each of the three schemes was conceived as a series of stepped habitable landscapes subdivided by parallel walls. At UCLA, ground surfaces and overhead planes were developed into complexly layered systems of interlocking spaces in a pair of arresting axonometric drawings on which a young Frederick Fisher assisted. In the residential schemes, highly varied interior volumes are gathered together under gabled roofs. Along with prominent chimneys, porticoes, and other vernacular elements, the roof forms temper the projects' otherwise abstract organizational language and resolve the schemes into stable objects in the landscape. In 1980, Kupper refashioned the materials he exhibited at the Architecture Gallery for inclusion in the Venice Biennale. Unfortunately, none were available for the present exhibition.

Kupper lives and works in Scottsdale, Arizona, where he continues to practice architecture, paints, and operates the Vitruvius Program, an art and design curriculum for students from preschool to eighth grade he founded with his wife Kathleen in 1988.

EUGENE KUPPER

Art, Architecture, Education: The alternation and fusion of these motives creates my work, stimulates my interests and forms my life. Architecture is an Art having principles that teach us. California is my site of origin: the San Francisco Bay Area is a culture that initially shaped my worldview; L.A., a place that provokes always-changing responses. Along the way, other worlds have had their say. Painting and Architecture work simultaneously and apart as practices through which my values, ideas, and philosophies have been formed and informed. Education comes from the urge to share these ideas.

Architecture is a potential that exists everywhere, manifesting a certain somewhere: a Place, a site, a location on the earth where human values reside, revealed by the project. This potential must be interpreted "on site," developed by means of the "non-sites" of design: paper, models, thought—to return to the site as architecture. A place where we live becomes a site where we build.

I am not an "L.A. Architect," but one who tries to do the best he can for any given place in the world. I have designed projects for Los Angeles, but it has never been necessary to think of industrial waste or pop commercial icons as motives for architecture. For a project in El Monte, a dismal industrial/commercial environment, a protective wall was created—a garden for the inhabitants; a solution well suited to Los Angeles, but also well known throughout the world.

The Extension project for the UCLA campus is a systematic urban building on a constrained site, yet a nearly identical program is located at Lake Arrowhead in a pine forest. The organizational complexity is similar, but the architectural character of one project is nearly the opposite of the other. The Nilsson House is a type—Villa, heir to several traditions; the Washburn House an homage to Berkeley. There is no architect's "signature style" imposed on any of these sites. To do so would be a critical and theoretical weakness for our discipline.

1979: I had been at UCLA for ten years. Thom Mayne, just graduated from Harvard, invited me to show projects in his Venice studio. Now we are celebrating an urban legend—The Architecture Gallery. Thom selected a group of people that seemed to all know each other, but had varied backgrounds and interests. I collaborated with Hodgetts and De Bretteville as Works West, and with then-students Rotondi, Fisher, and Howard. With Tim Vreeland I had joined with Dimster as a "Silver." I worked in Gehry's office at a moment of great changes in his practice. Mangurian was a colleague at UCLA and SCI-Arc. Eric Moss was always there, coaxing outrageous ideas. Roland Coate was in transition to painting. I had also been a professional artist in the 1960s Bay Area, however I had not actively painted since coming to L.A. in 1969, but would resume in Rome in 1983.

Concord Pavilion, construction of earthwork, Concord, 1975.

UCLA Extension Building, Los Angeles, 1976.

Nilsson Residence, Bel Air, 1975-79.

1979 summarized a moment, a fluctuating event for us all. For me, an invitation to participate in an international dialogue: the Venice Biennale. Assembling my work gave me the opportunity to reflect, and then to project forward. My SCI-Arc lecture was a tumultuous synthesis. Constructing word and slide montages, some themes emerged, in no particular order:

> *Architecture is an Ideal—Deriving Theory from Practice and Practice from Theory— Site measures and Site vectors—Lines on Paper, Lines on the Ground—Inhabitation through Projective Empathy—Seen and Unseen Relations of Time and Space— Marking with Drawing and Building Tools—Provisional Ambiguity checked by Retrospection—Open approach with Possible Paths of Closure—Explicit and Implicit modes of interpretation—Reciprocity of possible moves, not Step-by-Step—Vulnerability, Vagueness and Certainty—Practical, Real and Comfortable, but Exaggerated— Condensation in Models and Drawings— Energy invested in drawing / model / building / inhabitation—Whimsy and Idiosyncrasy / Decorum and Seriousness—Play: Childlike wonder, Free manipulation through reverie— Doodling and Free Association, confirmed by Critique—Collective and Urban / Individual and Private—Precision gained from gestures, smears, tearing, fragments—Seeking a Problem through a Solution—Notation and Scores rather than "Designs."*

By 1979 my career was changing, with new interests emerging: Linee Occulte, Drawing as Theory, An Architecture of Geographic Transformation, and the Vitruvius Program. An enhanced critical approach enriched my teaching and projects. The Rome Prize allowed me to resume my work in painting, continuing to the present. My thinking has deepened and my philosophy broadened to create a nationally recognized studio curriculum for Architecture in Elementary Schools, the Vitruvius Program, founded at SCI-Arc in 1988 with Kathleen Kupper. My recent architectural work is in the Central Valley of California.

At the SCI-Arc lecture, Thom Mayne introduced me as someone who began architectural practice at age thirteen. Sixty years later I am still enjoying new wonders.

Washburn Residence, Berkeley, 1978.

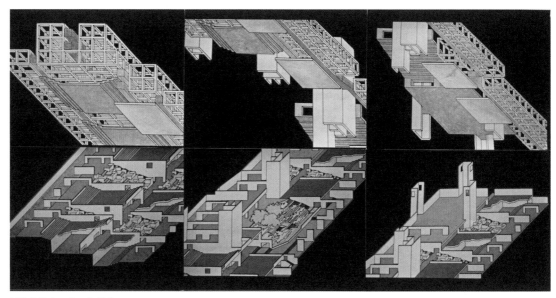

UCLA Extension Building
Los Angeles, 1976

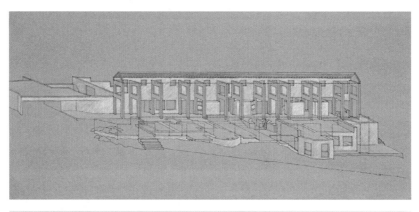

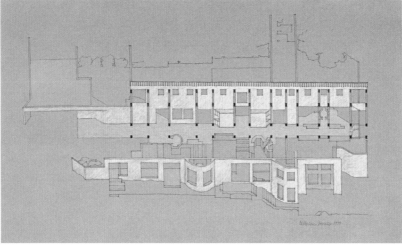

Nilsson House
Bel Air, 1975-79

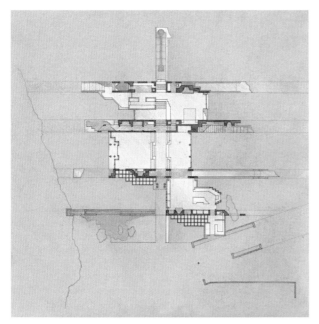

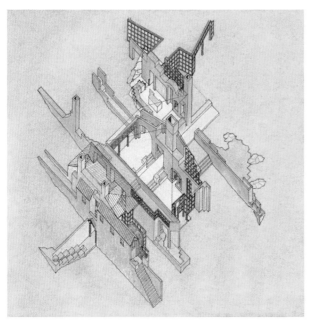

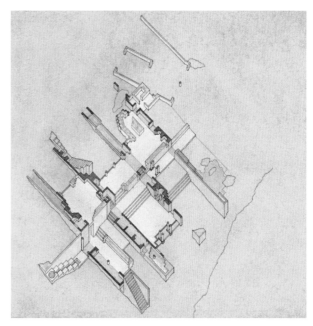

Washburn House
Berkeley, 1978

ORIGINALLY PUBLISHED IN THE *LOS ANGELES TIMES*, 17 OCT 1979

Mystery in Roland Coate's Work

JOHN DREYFUSS

There is an intriguing sense of mystery about the austere and sculptural architecture of Roland Coate Jr., on exhibition through Sunday at the Architecture Gallery, 209 E. San Juan Ave., Venice.

Drawings, photographs and models of three projects tempt viewers to explore, contemplate and seek meaning from Coate's highly structured work.

Four big paintings offer further temptation. The oils, all executed this year by Coate, relate directly to his architecture. It is fascinating and exceptional architecture.

Coate's buildings are at once harsh and inviting functional and whimsical. They are buildings that leave viewers a little disconcerted, a little surprised. And they are beautiful.

Three photographs inadequately depict the one completed project in

the exhibit. It is the richly sculptural Alexander House, overlooking the Pacific in Montecito.

The raw concrete structure stands somewhat at odds with its lush, lawn-covered setting. Its unexpected cylindrical tower (which is a sort of crow's nest from which to enjoy the view), and the apparently inexplicable angles of its walls (which provide visual channels toward framed views) would aesthetically rip the house apart from its environment, were it not for Coate's masterful job of par-

tially burying the building under its own lawn, thereby integrating the house and its site.

"The house is, in the Jungian sense, in the ground," the 49-year-old architect said. "It has an emotional connection with Mother Earth. It's a trip through the underworld in the sense Dante wrote about the underworld."

While the photos portray the beauty of the Alexander House, they fail to reveal its utility. They do not show how the house is used, how large it is or if it's practical. These deficiencies could have been rectified by exhibiting a few plans and elevations.

Unlike the Alexander House, the Leland House is fully documented with drawings and a model.

This striking work of architecture, which is under construction in the Hollywood Hills, is basically a three story box set on a 36-foot-square base. Into the southeast face of the box—the side that gets the most sun—Coate cut a huge, triangular window, two stories high. On top of the house he has set a dome 24-feet in diameter. The southeast half of the dome is glass panes. They have an insulated metal cover conforming to the dome shape. The cover can swivel around so it is over the solid, northwest portion of the dome, leaving the windows open to the sun like a greenhouse.

Coate, who calls the house a "sun temple of individual man," notes that "it has a symbolic relationship to the Griffith Observatory, visible three and one-half miles to the east."

The architect, who is interested in metaphysics, also observed that the structure's plan consists of 36 modules, each six feet square, "and the 36 squares relate in astrology to the sun."

The exhibition's third architectural project is an unbuilt development of

a dozen small houses that Coate calls "the key to the architecture of the whole tip of Baja California."

Coate's design is as intriguing as his proclamation is ambiguous.

Because the development is shaped remotely like an arrowhead, Coate sees it as "symbolizing the tip of Baja," and—since the tip is part of the whole—as representing an architectural goal for all Baja California.

It would provide, Coate said, "a nonpolluting lifestyle in houses that would not intrude on other lives."

He said the houses would furnish all their own energy through solar collectors and recirculation of waste material. Achieving that goal in a salable house is so unlikely as to verge on the impossible.

Plans for eight of the houses are simple, rectilinear and practical. The other four structures are cylindrical, and probably would provide awkward space in which to live.

Architectural relationships among the buildings, and their interaction with the site, are rigorously geometrical and highly pleasing.

Of the four architecture-related paintings Coate chose to exhibit, one blends a self-portrait with an adaptation of the Leland House. It is clearly Coate's way of saying that his architecture is both an inseparable part of him and a reflection of his thinking.

The other three paintings are also integrated with the Leland House and through it with the geometry of all Coate's architecture.

They progress from a geometric, grid-based romanticization of the house through a related landscape-seascape to a big (6x10-foot) representational painting of the house both in daylight and at night.

Coate's exhibition is the second in a series of nine weekly shows at the Architecture Gallery. The gallery is open Tuesdays through Saturdays from noon until 6 p.m.

The architect will discuss his work at a lecture scheduled for 8 tonight at the Southern California Institute of Architecture, 1800 Berkeley St., Santa Monica. ⁂

ROLAND COATE, JR.

42

ROLAND COATE, JR.

Roland Coate, Jr. was born in Los Angeles in 1930, the son of a prominent Southern California architect. Educated at Occidental College and Cornell (B. Arch, 1955), he worked in the offices of I.M. Pei and Marcel Breuer in New York before returning to Los Angeles in 1962. After two short-lived partnerships (Coate and Alexander, 1962, and Coate and McLane, 1963-65), he launched a solo practice in 1966. Coate was a member of the faculty at SCI-Arc from 1975-81 and 1986-88, and was included in the exhibition *Twelve Los Angeles Architects* at the Pacific Design Center in 1976.

Coate's interest in simple geometric forms reached a high point in 1974 with the completion of the Alexander House, his most acclaimed project. Embedded in a high promontory above Montecito and executed entirely in reinforced concrete, the house's rough materiality and bunker-like massing is contrasted by a sensitively organized courtyard plan which loosens and fans out radially to frame mountain and ocean views to the west. Later works, such as the Leland House and a group of twelve houses in Baja California, trade Alexander's subterranean lyricism for spare geometric figures that, while no less sensitive to the specificities of their sites, occupy them with a mute, tragic poetry reminiscent of ancient ruins.

Always an avid painter, Coate exhibited four large canvasses on architectural themes at the Architecture Gallery. Soon after the exhibition, he closed his architectural office to dedicate himself solely to painting. He lives and works in Venice, California.

ROLAND COATE, JR.

When I look back at my architectural work it immediately reveals to me what I used to be. The simple design elements...geometric but not rigid, correct yet subject to a certain strong emotional aesthetic... tell their personal story.

The paintings of the 1970s are architecturally based, but they do not relate directly to the architecture. The paintings stand on their own and are very much of the '70s. The 1979 exhibition was the end of an era for me. I entered the '80s with a lot of regret and left it all behind.

Environment and clean energy were important design elements. The 'solar' Leland House, the 'earth-sheltered' Alexander House, and Cabo Bello with its windmills and solar collectors were the main examples. But it was not until the turn of the century that environment and clean energy became important social issues. When we entered the '80s we entered a long period where environment and clean energy were not important socially or architecturally. Painting became a way for me to explore deep personal issues and to deal with being out of step with society.

I would like to thank Ewan Branda, Todd Gannon, structural engineer Andrew Nasser, photographer Josh White, and Thom Mayne as well for making this exhibition happen.

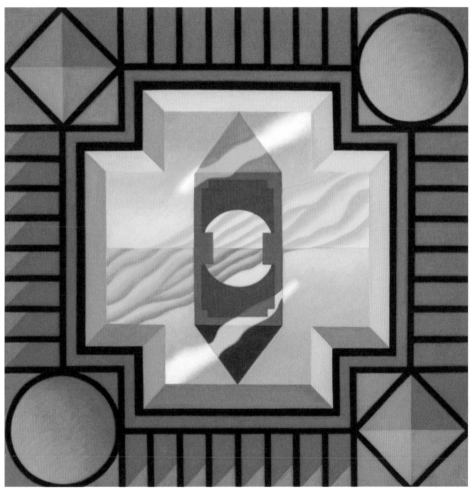

Untitled, Oil on canvas, 1979.

Alexander Residence
Montecito, 1974

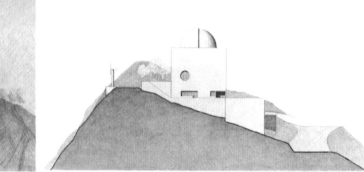

Leland Residence
Los Angeles, 1979-80

Twelve Houses at Cabo Bello
Baja California, Mexico, 1976

House for Bacchus and Philamon
Oil on canvas, 1979

Showing How to Mix Metaphors

JOHN DREYFUSS

Frederick Fisher's architecture, on exhibition at The Architecture Gallery in Venice, grows from metaphors. Those metaphors are difficult to discover in the show that runs from noon to 6 p.m. through Saturday at 209 E. San Juan Ave., but the discovery is worth the difficulty.

The reward is understanding—at least in part—what makes Fisher's work simultaneously romantic and rational, why it is at once universal and specific.

And one can learn a lot about what makes Frederick Fisher tick as an architect. "To me," Fisher said, "architecture is a cosmological art that establishes the relations between man and the rest of nature."

Those high-sounding words are basic to the creation of a building the 30 year-old architect began designing while working in the office of Santa Monica architect Frank Gehry, and completed after opening his own office this year in partnership with Thane Roberts. The structure is a residence for Laury and Loren Caplin. It is at 230 E San Juan Ave., just a few doors east of The Architecture Gallery.

In part, it is also present in the gallery: a gently arched, full-sized rafter hangs in the exhibition, duplicating a fragment of the Caplin house. It brings to the show, as no drawing or model could, a sense of the texture, shape, size, and scale of the nearby house.

The rafter also indicates Fisher's use of metaphor. It simulates a wave, relating the residence to the ocean that is less than half a mile away. It also associates the building with water in general. Fisher accentuated that association by painting the roof of the house blue.

SEEING METAPHORS' MEANING

It would be nice if everyone recognized the metaphor, and nicer still if everyone thought it was meaningful. But that is not the case. The Caplins, for example, couldn't care much less about it.

But the metaphor is extremely meaningful as a working tool for Fisher. It gave him a philosophical basis for part of his design—a design

that might otherwise arbitrarily have included a pitched shake roof, a flat tarpaper roof, or one of Spanish tile instead of an ocean-blue, curved, polyurethane-covered plywood roof conforming to wave-shaped rafters.

Another architectural metaphor that is highly significant to the architect but makes absolutely no difference to the Caplins is the precise north-south alignment of tiles in the atrium.

KNOWING ITS PLACE

To Fisher, that alignment gives the house an extremely important "sense of place in the universe."

Establishing a sense of place in the universe for a 2,500 square-foot residence in Venice, California, may seem unnecessary, silly and ostentatious. But to the architect, doing so serves to pinpoint the architectural heart of the house in a generally amorphous, unfocused world. Therefore, to Fisher, it makes the house unique.

Because Fisher sees the house as unique, it becomes very dear to him, and working on it becomes an intensely personal experience that he treats with attention approaching fervor. Fisher's metaphors are not all philosophical. Nor or they all working tools. He pays a lot of attention to his clients as well as to his theories. For example, a pen-and-ink drawing in the exhibit shows that the Caplins' curved rafters and the two-by-fours that connect them are reminiscent of the inside of a boat hull.

That metaphor brings particular pleasure to Laury Caplin, who spent fourteen years of her youth living in a boat on the Seine River.

DRAWINGS AND DETAIL

In the exhibition, Fisher uses drawings and a model to delineate the Caplin house. Seven especially handsome drawings have been transferred to a white-on-black format by a photographic and printing process.

Design changes were made in the house while it was under construction, so viewers do not get a true picture of the building. But they can gain a sense of its design, which is centered on a two-story, skylit atrium that has the

intimate quality of an outdoor courtyard surrounded by small houses.

The most beautiful drawing in the show is of a hypothetical solar crematorium. The concept won a prestigious, national *Progressive Architecture* award for unbuilt projects.

It is a metaphorical structure that architecturally represents the universe, with a rotunda (the heavens) on a rectilinear building (earth) floored with tiles arranged in wave patterns (water).

The graphite and colored-pencil drawing shows the building in a combination of plan, elevation and section beneath a dramatic, ominously black sky. An accompanying collage (yellow tape and mylar attached to a photostatic print on acetate) illustrates how the sun-powered crematorium would work.

A single pen-and-ink drawing portrays a condominium complex designed by Fisher and his partner Roberts. In an effort to break away from typical condominiums, they designed individual wooden bungalows perched on top of traditional, two-story stucco condos that surround a communal courtyard.

The wooden bungalows were intended to provide an individual architectural identity for each owner while conforming to the architecture of Ocean Park, where there are numerous wooden, bungalow type houses.

"But the client felt the concept was too unsafe and unorthodox, so he hired another architect," Fisher said.

Fisher uses a model, an ink drawing and eight photocopies of photo-

FREDERICK FISHER

graphs that he has colored with pastel crayons to illustrate a small house being built in the Hollywood Hills for movie-theater owner Kim Jorgensen.

The 1,000-square-foot structure will contain only a living room, study, bathroom and bedroom. An existing house on the same lot overlooking Sunset Blvd. will be used for cooking, eating and entertaining.

Fisher set the little house on the same north-south axis as the Caplin residence. Then, as shown in the ink drawing, he designed its patio aligned with the existing house higher on the hill, thereby associating the two structures. The new house has a combination of concrete and wooden walls. The concrete sections are made of colored blocks, arranged in horizontal lines of various earthtone hues.

"There is a latent image of an architectural ruin," Fisher said. "It acknowledges that architecture is very temporal in relation to nature."

Fisher also exhibits a large, sepia-toned print that he colored with chalk and pencil. It depicts a hypothetical hotel at the Peruvian ruin of Machu Picchu. The project was his 1975 master's thesis at UCLA. In other drawings, the architect shows his concept of a subterranean observatory, drawn for an invitational show on urban open space at the Cooper-Hewitt Museum in New York. The museum is an arm of the Smithsonian Institution. From Fisher's observatory, one would see only a point in space near the North Star.

"The significance of the observatory is that it is focused on that place in space above the North Pole that never moves in relation to earth," Fisher said. "The observer would get a view of the absolute, an Indication of a permanent phenomenon."

Fisher will discuss his work and philosophy at a lecture scheduled for 8 tonight at the Southern California Institute of Architecture, 1800 Berkeley St., Santa Monica. ✻

Frederick Fisher was born in Cleveland, Ohio in 1949. His father was an architect and his mother a schoolteacher. Fisher studied architecture at Miami University before transferring to Oberlin College to take a degree in art and art history. He earned a Master's degree from the Department of Architecture and Urban Design at UCLA in 1975.

After graduation, Fisher found work in the offices of A.C. Martin and William Pereira, and assisted Eugene Kupper with the drawings for the UCLA Extension Building. He also worked with Leonard Koren on several issues of *Wet* Magazine. In 1977, Fisher joined Frank Gehry's office to work on the Mid-Atlantic Toyota facility, Santa Monica Place, the Cabrillo Marine Museum, and other projects. After a short partnership with Thane Roberts, he launched his own practice in 1981.

At the Architecture Gallery, Fisher exhibited drawings and a model of his recently completed Caplin House, located just a few doors down from the exhibition. The presentation also featured a full-scale mock-up of the house's curved roof beams suspended from the gallery ceiling. With exposed framing, chain link railings, and a careful juxtaposition of off-the-shelf materials, the house owes much to Fisher's mentor Frank Gehry, though it is handled in a far more painterly manner than the older architect would sanction. The Jorgensen House in the Hollywood Hills delved deeply into the Picturesque, starkly contrasting ruin-like masonry elements with ephemeral wood and stucco construction. Picturesque themes also color the village-like collection of gabled units which comprise the Ocean Park Townhouses. Rounding out the presentation, Fisher included highly expressive drawings for an Observatory, a proposal for a hotel at Machu Picchu, and plans for a Solar Crematory, a project completed in response to the death of his father.

Fisher taught at SCI-Arc from 1980 to 1985 and was head of the Environmental Design Department at Otis College of Art and Design from 1986 to 1992. He has also taught at UCLA, the University of Pennsylvania, the University of North Carolina, and Harvard's Graduate School of Design. He is a Fellow of the American Academy in Rome.

FREDERICK FISHER

Prior to entering the architecture program at UCLA, I studied art and art history at Oberlin College. My interests in art history included English Romanticism, with its reflections on temporality. Surrealism, and collage in particular, was another area of interest, both historically and in my art practice. While at Oberlin I read the relatively new and controversial essay by Robert Venturi, *Complexity and Contradiction in Architecture*. This book brought together architecture, art, and history into a synthetic narrative that inspired me to pursue architecture. The threads of my background in art and art history formed the early direction in my work: imagining a building

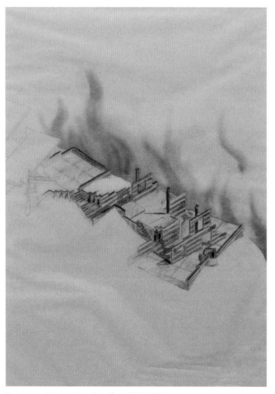

Jorgensen House, Los Angeles, 1978-1980.

as a collage of real materials, rather than a formal abstraction, and drawing on cultural ideas such as Romanticism and metaphor. Coming from studio practice as well as art history led me to focus on the character and craft of the drawings that I produced,

beyond the conventions of architectural documentation. The 1979 show was one of many exhibits and publications during this time that focused on the "art" of architects' drawings and models.

The Crematory and Observatory projects were explorations on metaphors for mankind's relationship to the larger universe as explored by ancient cultures. The Jorgensen house continued this exploration of time and the forces of nature, expressed by superimposition of inconsistent forms and materials, collage as an index for time. The form of the Caplin house was based on a metaphor for a personal narrative of the client. Collage was a compositional strategy to reflect to complexity of the lives within the house.

The Solar Crematory project was developed when I was a graduate student at UCLA's architecture program. It was a response to the passing of my father, who was an architect. The basic ideas were to connect the cycle of life and death to the cycle of the sun and to accomplish cremation in a more sustainable and symbolically meaningful manner. The process drew on the nascent large scale solar furnace technology which applied a large array of heliotropic mirrors to focus sunlight on a parabolic reflector, which in turn concentrated the energy into a crematory furnace. The site plan of the crematory complex derived from Leonardo's famous diagram of the human figure inscribed in a circle and a square. This geometry also related to Chinese symbolism of the circle of the heavens and the square defined by the four cardinal points of the earth. A chapel at the center of the complex repeated the circle in the square plan.

My interest in archeo-astronomy led to another theoretical project based on natural cycles, the Observatory. I studied the astronomical structures at Jaipur, India; European Neolithic structures such as Stonehenge; and structures from Pre-Columbian Americas. The Observatory was designed as a reflection on stability and change in nature. The viewing shaft, parallel to the ecliptic, focuses on the North Star, the one point in the heavens that does not appear to move through the sky. All other stars and planets appear to revolve around that point in the sky. It is believed that if one looks through a long enough shaft, the refracted light of daylight breaks down and one can theoretically see stars in day time. The Observatory was imagined as a place where one could go—day or night, at any time of the year—to

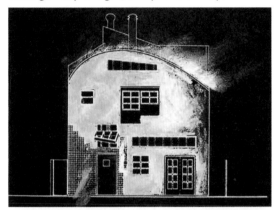

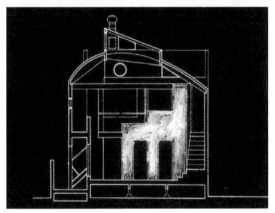

Caplin House, Venice, 1978. Elevation and section.

see the North Star as a fixed point through the shaft. One would descend a deep stairwell to a viewing chamber and look through the shaft to the Pole star.

Loren and Laurie Caplin were part of the Venice cultural scene in the late 1970's. In particular, Loren was the publisher of *Wet* Magazine, a publication started by Leonard Koren, who was one of my classmates at UCLA. *Wet* became a focal point in the flourishing cultural mix of art, design, graphics, architecture, food, music, and "gourmet bathing." I took on the project of designing a live/work space for them as I was leaving Frank Gehry's

office. The project was done in the spirit of creativity and speculation. Both Loren and Laurie are artists, Loren a musician and writer and Laurie a sculptor. Each had a studio in the house. The master bedroom suite was complemented by a separate guest suite. At the center of the house is an atrium living space. My interest in collage is manifest in the front elevation, a purposely intuitive mix of different sized doors, windows, bay, canopy, and tile. The roof of the house was conceived as an upside-down boat hull, a memory device for Laurie's childhood life on a barge in France.

My second house continued the themes of metaphor, narrative, and collage. It was designed for a movie producer and theater owner, Kim Jorgensen. It is a small retreat house on a promontory in the Hollywood Hills with panoramic city views. The area had recently been burned by the Hollywood fire and there were scores of burned out ruins of houses in the neighborhood. I imagined the house as if it was built on the ruins of some unknown structure. The project is a rumination on the ephemeral nature of our works, a theme explored in art, landscape design, and literature of the 19th century Romantic tradition as well as in Asian art. As there were no ruins on the site, we built a set of ruins. The simple, pavilion-like house was blended into the "ruins." The resulting collage of structures expressed temporality and the forces of nature.

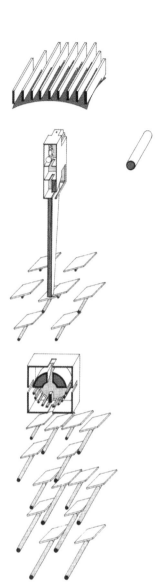

Solar Crematory
1976

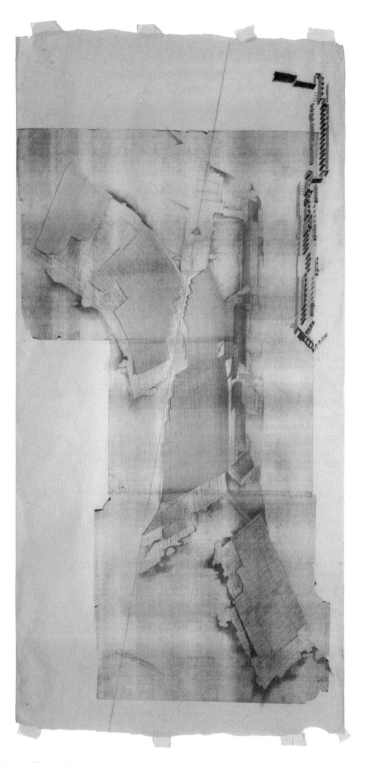

Machu Picchu Hotel
1978

Jorgensen House
Los Angeles, 1978-80

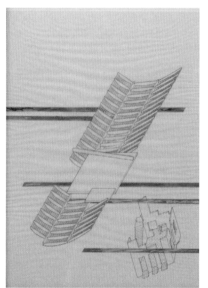

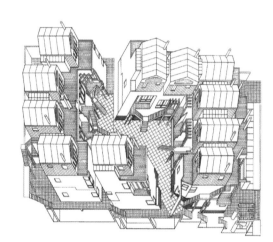

Ocean Park Townhouses
Los Angeles, 1979

Caplin House
Venice, 1978

ORIGINALLY PUBLISHED IN THE *LOS ANGELES TIMES*, 31 OCT 1979

Designs in Social Relationships

JOHN DREYFUSS

To Frank Dimster, architectural work is social work. In designing a house, he worries first about how people relate to people and then about how people relate to aesthetics.

"There's a lot of room to improve family relationships with architecture," said the 41-year-old Los Angeles architect whose drawings, models and photographs will be exhibited from noon to 6 p.m. through Saturday at the Architecture Gallery, 209 E. San Juan Ave., Venice.

While Dimster is particularly interested in architecture's effect on families, his concern for the social impact of buildings extends far beyond family circles. For example, he cares about how people relate to cities, and he views the potential relationship with extraordinary optimism.

PLACE OF OPPORTUNITY

"The city," he said, "is a place of opportunity, a place of choice, a place of excitement. I do not see the city as a place of corruption."

Dimster's exhibition is the fourth in a series of nine at the Architecture

Gallery, and it is thoroughly different from the first three.

Earlier exhibitors (architects Eugene Kupper, Roland Coate Jr., and Frederick Fisher) emphasized artistic and metaphorical aspects of their work. In general, they presented exhibitions noteworthy for aesthetic content and architectural imagination.

"My colleagues like to emphasize the unusual," Dimster said. "I like to contribute to the commonplace.

"I like to be noticed because I'm doing something that contributes to how people live, decreasing friction in a family, serving old people, having a living unit flexible enough so an older couple can have a young student living with them without loss of identity, either for the student or couple.

WANTS TO CREATE CHOICES

"I want to create choices. I want to be noticed for doing things like that, not to be noticed because my work is 'different.'"

Dimster is no idle talker. His architecture reflects his attitude.

It is a great shame that his exhibit does not adequately reflect his architectural philosophy. The viewer is the loser.

Part of the problem is with what is in the show: drawings illustrating different objects are jammed up against one another, elevations drawn from eye-level perspective are hung at knee level, one photograph is printed askew, another seems underexposed, and a third is actually printed backwards.

But the major problem is with what is not in the show. Written explanations are totally lacking, so it is impossible to grasp the architectural-sociological message of the exhibition.

"I didn't document it," Dimster said. "I didn't think that documentation was particularly interesting." He was particularly wrong.

COMPETENTLY EXECUTED

Lack of written explanation detracted from the three previous shows at the Architecture Gallery. But the exhibitors got away with the deficiency because their work was artistic in itself, creating an aesthetic reason for being beyond its architectural and philosophical meanings.

Dimster exhibits competently executed architectural drawings and adequate models. However, they are not exceptional in and of themselves. What is exceptional is their sociological import.

An example of the architect's attention to sociology stems from his recognition that it is becoming increasingly difficult for young adults to afford to move out of their parents' houses. Besides which, he said, "I think the family is a basic unit."

He also thinks that family members need privacy, and if two or three generations are to live successfully under one roof, they must be able to stay apart as well as get together.

So Dimster often provides private, outside entrances to bedrooms, going so far as to install stairways to make upstairs bedrooms accessible without passage through a house or condominium.

Also, he frequently relates bedrooms to other parts of the house so they can virtually be separate apartments. Condominiums Dimster designed in Westwood and Santa Monica have entire floors that can be used either as apartments or as integral parts of larger dwelling units.

In both those condominiums, the architect showed sensitivity to the street environment by skillfully designing entries that simultaneously protect privacy by partially obscuring the front door from the street and promote a relationship with the street scene by providing a version of the old-fashioned front porch where one can sit or stand.

Dimster's exhibited work has other interesting aspects. He frequently uses sawtooth-shaped skylights for the triple benefit of letting in north light, providing a slanted south-facing surface on which to mount solar collectors, and increasing the volume of a room.

In an era when many architects all

FRANK DIMSTER

but ignore the design of surrounding buildings, Dimster takes care to fit his structures into their neighborhoods.

The architect frequently provides sliding glass doors that effectively increase the size of a room by making it part or the outdoors.

Those and other architectural and sociological characteristics are important factors in Dimster's architecture. It is unfortunate that his exhibition fails to reveal them clearly.

Dimster will discuss his work at a lecture scheduled for 8 tonight at the Southern California Institute of Architecture, 1800 Berkeley St., Santa Monica. ⁑

Born in Romania in 1938, Frank Dimster earned a B.S. in Architectural Sciences at Washington University in St. Louis in 1959. He went on to receive a Diploma from the Academy of Creative Arts in Vienna before returning to Washington University for graduate studies in architecture and urban design. After graduating in 1964, he relocated to Los Angeles to join the newly formed faculty of Architecture and Urban Design at UCLA. After stints at the offices of DMJM and William Pereira, he launched his own practice in 1975. Dimster was one of five Los Angeles Silvers, UCLA's answer to the East Coast's White-Gray cliques, and participated in both of the group's conferences in 1974 and '76. He joined the faculty at USC's School of Architecture in 1977.

At the Architecture Gallery, Dimster exhibited a collection of single- and multi-family residential projects including recently completed condominiums in West LA and Santa Monica. These projects cleave to an established modernist idiom of white planar surfaces and Platonic massing, though complex façade compositions and forceful massing in projects like the Yancy Residence and the Kelton Condominiums impart a Mannerist air reminiscent of Charles Gwathmey's early houses on Long Island. Dimster's Euro-Caribbean House, like his later project for his own Los Angeles house, demonstrates his tendency to articulate a cubic volume with peripheral geometrical intensity, and showcases the architect's sensitivity to domestic planning. Ample terraces and multiple entries transform bedrooms into semi-autonomous apartments to offer occupants both community and independence in equal measure.

Dimster was elevated to the AIA's College of Fellows in 1997, and remained at USC until his retirement in 2000. Since that time, he has been principal of Dimster Architecture in Venice, California.

FRANK DIMSTER

Los Angeles in the mid-century was a very interesting major city in many respects—social diversity, physical context, a promise of change, all uninhibited by a dominant history. An additional set of influence came from the aggressive development in the space program to put a man on the moon. We came to Los Angeles, in my case from Washington University in St. Louis, in hope of professional opportunity, but with well formulated values and goals. These value systems were basically rooted in the Bauhaus point of view. One could call it a functionally based problem-solving approach, with a strong appreciation for craft and materials.

As a result of a diverse and rapidly growing population, Los Angeles provided great opportunities for young professionals to experiment in the area of individual and multiple housing projects. The universities started to develop Urban Design programs. There was UCLA, where I started. Professor Ray Kappe started a new school called the Southern California Institute of Architecture. There was also USC, the oldest architectural school of the three, which at that time also changed direction towards a philosophy sympathetic to the Bauhaus way of thought. Professor Konrad Wachsmann was a former Bauhaus member teaching at USC for many years. In all of these places in different parts of Los Angeles, technologies were influencing the planning and formal directions of the faculty, and consequently the students' work. One can imagine from this very brief description the architectural networks which were reinforced, influenced, and validated by frequent visits from the East Coast as well as European practitioners and teaching professors. There was the London-based group Archigram, as well as others such as Herman Hertzberger, Hans Hollein, Fumihiko Maki, and Arata Isozaki. The most regular and articulate spokesperson was Professor Reyner Banham who helped to create the

intellectual foundation for both practical and theoretical work, particularly with his book about Los Angeles. Meaningful work was going on here in Los Angeles, and it was pursued at different scales in an interdisciplinary fashion.

My work was always influenced by the need to build and the instructive value that building has on the teaching of architecture. After I left UCLA, I led large-scale projects at the office of William Pereira. Later, I went out on my own to do smaller projects. These small-scale experiments, sometimes additions to existing buildings, dealt with current issues of changes in the social life style. A pivotal idea for many of these projects revolved around the combination of public and private spaces within the single-family dynamic. The idea was one of adaptability, allowing for changes to the family over time. The groups of houses in Switzerland are the clearest built example of this idea that I displayed in the 1979 exhibition. There was a flexible plan contained within a larger envelope that allowed separation between generations within one unit. Private areas were separate and distinct, connected through common areas used by all. Each unit was in a way a combination of separate units unified through common areas.

In the eight Santa Monica townhouses a similar idea was developed, in this case within a vertical sequence of spaces. The entry level was eating and cooking, with one adjacent bedroom. The second floor contained a two-story living room and mezzanine, further emphasizing the verticality of the space. The mezzanine afforded all occupants access to a private rooftop garden. Adjacent to the living room was the master bedroom and its adjoining private spaces.

The five townhouses in Westwood on Missouri and Kelton Avenues are in a three-story building, adding an additional floor to this vertical

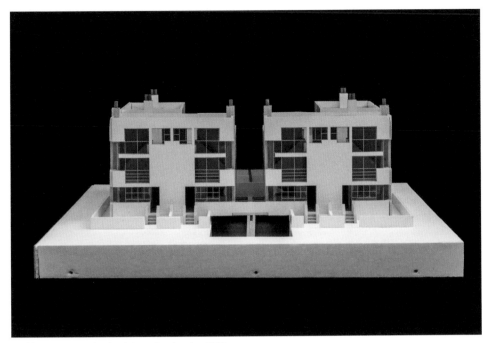

Washington Avenue Condominiums, Los Angeles, 1980.

organization concept. In this project we used an open central stair as both the visual and physical connecting element between the more public and private spaces. There is a gradual transition through the floors from more public spaces on the lower levels to the most private spaces on the top level, with its own separate means of egress.

This idea of open-ended planning was well known and promoted by many architects. This was a reaction to traditional plans, which were usually a combination of static and separate spaces, relying on a 'one size fits all' approach. Adaptability became paramount in the new plans. This was a response to the mobility of the users and the rapid development of new technologies in communication and building systems. This central idea of evolving use continues to be an important response to the ever-changing living situations most people find themselves in throughout their lifetimes. It extends the usefulness of buildings, as new conditions redefine living programs. I also found it interesting to explore the aesthetic implications this idea can have on the appearance of the work, usually pronounced through the use of color, materials, and fenestration patterns. I take great satisfaction is seeing the longevity of these concepts as they continue to respond to social developments.

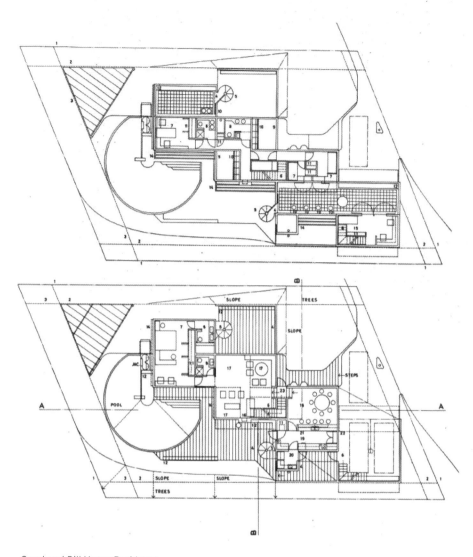

Carol and Bill Yancy Residence
Los Angeles, 1979

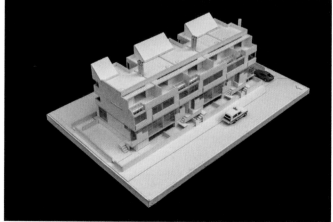

Kelton Avenue Condominiums
Los Angeles, 1980

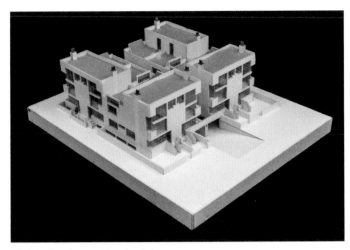

Washington Avenue Condominiums
Santa Monica, 1980

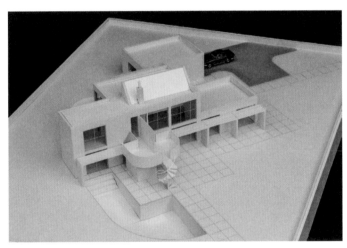

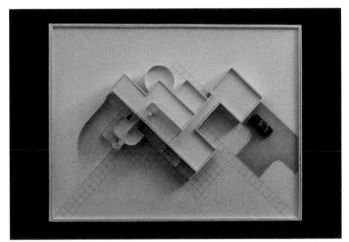

Euro-Caribbean Residence
Freeport, Bahamas, 1979

ORIGINALLY PUBLISHED IN THE *LOS ANGELES TIMES*, 7 NOV 1979

Courage of his Conceptions *Gehry: The Architect as Artist*

JOHN DREYFUSS

In terms of age and success, Frank Gehry is a leader among the artistically oriented architects putting on exhibitions at the Architecture Gallery, 209 E. San Juan Ave.

That Gehry is also a leader in terms of imagination and professional courage is the loud and clear message delivered by his work being shown at the gallery from noon to 6 p.m. through Saturday.

A lot of architects don't like having their work called "sculptural." They correctly consider the word a cliché for buildings comprised of anything approaching bold forms.

But Gehry is unabashedly a sculptor. His use of architectural form and line is so sculpturally oriented that elements of his buildings often escape the limits of that broad zone where architecture and art blend. When that happens, those elements become pure art.

Gehry's architecture-art is aesthetically strong and beautiful. But it is also highly unconventional, and therefore not for everyone. A house using visual tricks that make it appear to be sliding down a hill doesn't engender a sense of security. A carport with a roof that looks like a fluffy cloud seems thoroughly goofy to some viewers. Others will be put off by the galvanized, corrugated metal of Gehry's own radically designed home in Santa Monica. And many people find his sculptural use of chain-link fence more prison-like than sculpture-like.

What Gehry has done in his mind—and subsequently in his architecture—is transcend the traditional uses of building materials.

He sees galvanized, corrugated metal not only as something from which to make a barn roof, but also as an aesthetically pleasing, beautifully textured surface. To Gehry, chain-link fence is the stuff of which geometric sculpture is made, not just a barrier to keep people out of places where they want to be (or in places where they don't want to be). House framing covered with glass instead of walls suggest to some observers that Gehry forgot to complete a building, but to others it creates abstract

artworks that also act as "picture frames" to isolate interesting views.

It is important to see all of Gehry's work from a perspective of blissful ignorance, to observe his structures from the childlike viewpoint of one who has no preconceptions about what architecture must be.

Given that approach, the viewer has the best chance of understanding, judging—and appreciating—the work of Frank Gehry.

The easiest part of the exhibition to appreciate consists of a series of superb photographs of Gehry's house. Photographer Grant Mudford proves his own artistic ability with a camera while illustrating artistic details of the house.

Basically, it is a two-story house that might have been lifted off a Kansas prairie.

But Gehry added a corrugated metal wall around three sides of the structure. Between that wall and the outside of the old house is a roofed space in which the architect put his kitchen and dining areas. Other parts of the house are within the vastly remodeled original residence.

Studying the Mudford photos, eight photocopies of sketches by Gehry and three large photographs of the house (inconveniently mounted across the gallery from the other pictures) gives viewers a fairly clear idea of the Gehry residence. For those desiring more, a trip to 22nd St. and Washington Ave. in Santa Monica will provide a view of the real thing.

The two newest projects in the exhibit are both just out of the design stage: three studios to be built on Indiana Ave. in Venice and a house for Calabasas Heights.

The adjacent studios, represented by three models, are among the most intriguing and excellent works of art and architecture in the exhibition.

One building is finished in pale blue stucco, another in unpainted plywood, and the third is covered with green asphalt shingles.

Essentially, the buildings are three boxes, each accentuated by one or more sculptural elements cut into the box. Those elements—such as an angled chimney on one building, steplike shapes climbing the upper parts of another, a marvelous bay window dropped into the corner of the third—create illusions of perspective that visually disconnect the accents from the main structures.

The viewer is left fascinated, mystified, intrigued, baffled, confused—or all of the above.

A model of the Calabasas Heights residence for Mr. and Mrs. Robert Benson plays two simple, crisp architectural boxes against one another and against radical art, thereby creating a home that will leave some people elated and others shocked.

A low building contains eating and living rooms. A separate, higher building serves as a sleeping house.

An abstract sculpture of raw lumber covers the entire roof of the taller structure. Like so much of Gehry's work, it appears to be a contractor's catastrophe unless one makes the mental effort to disconnect the design from the traditional use of the material from which it is built. Only after that separation is made does it become possible to evaluate the sculpture for what it is.

Behind the sleeping house is a carport with a roof that looks like nothing more or less than a cloud

FRANK GEHRY

floating on four vertical sticks.

Gehry—not to mention the Bensons—is taking a huge gamble with the house. It could turn out to be an architectural pratfall—or a work of art. The jury must remain out until the house goes up...

Other work in the show includes the extraordinarily complicated and inadequately exhibited Toyota distributorship building in Maryland: plans, sketches, and photos of the model of the never-to-be-built Gary and Liz Familian residence in Santa Monica (The plans are labeled "A. C. Egg Residence," which Gehry said refers to "a shell company owned by Familian.") and a model, plans, and sketches for the residence of George and Sue Wagner that appears to be sliding down a Malibu hillside.

Also exhibited are a graceful (and quite comfortable) cardboard chair, and a rather lonely photograph of the ticket booth for the Concord Pavilion in Northern California. That booth, designed about four years ago, was Gehry's first big chain-link architectural sculpture.

Without exception, the exhibited projects reveal Gehry's unflagging effort to remain in the vanguard of excellent architects who are artistically oriented. It is a successful effort.

Gehry will discuss his work tonight at 8 at the Southern California Institute of Architecture, 1800 Berkeley St., Santa Monica. ⁂

Frank Gehry was born in Toronto in 1929, and moved to Los Angeles in 1947. He studied at Los Angeles City College and the University of Southern California, where he earned a Bachelor of Architecture in 1954. After a time in the office of Victor Gruen, he served in the Special Services Division of the U.S. Army. He entered the Harvard Graduate School of Design's Urban Planning program in 1956, but returned to Los Angeles after one semester. Gehry went on to work in the offices of Hideo Sasaki, Pereira & Luckman, Gruen Associates, and André Redemont in Paris before entering into partnership with Gregory Walsh in 1962. The two were joined briefly by David O'Malley in 1966 and Frank O. Gehry and Associates was launched in 1967. Architecture Gallery exhibitors Eugene Kupper and Frederick Fisher worked in the office in the mid-1970s.

By the time of the Architecture Gallery exhibitions, Gehry had already achieved wide acclaim in local and international architectural circles. His exhibition featured a suite of photographs of his own house in Santa Monica by Grant Mudford. In addition to earlier commercial projects and an example of his recent Experimental Edges furniture, Gehry including four recent residential designs. Two from 1978 which would remain unbuilt, the Wagner and Familian Houses, develop fragmentary yet carefully controlled compositions of planar elements constructed of wood studs. In two later schemes—the Indiana Avenue artists' studios in Venice and the Benson House in Calabasas (both later realized) Gehry shifts to a more volumetric and figural exterior expression, while maintaining the inexpensive material palette of the earlier houses.

Gehry's projects were regularly among state and local AIA award winners from the mid-1970s, and he was included among the *Twelve Los Angeles Architects* exhibitions and lectures in 1976. He held teaching appointments at USC, SCI-Arc, and UCLA through the 1970s, as well as visiting positions at Rice, the Cooper Union, the University of Texas at Houston, and Yale, where he held the William Bishop Chair in 1979. He was elected to the AIA College of Fellows in 1974, to that of the American Academy of Arts and Letters in 1987, and won the Pritzker Prize in Architecture in 1989. The current iteration of Gehry's office, Gehry Partners, LLC, was established in 2001. Gehry Technologies, a project management and software enterprise, was launched in 2002.

FRANK GEHRY

Citing insufficiently detailed memories to offer anything substantive about the Architecture Gallery events, Frank Gehry declined our invitation to provide a statement for this catalog.

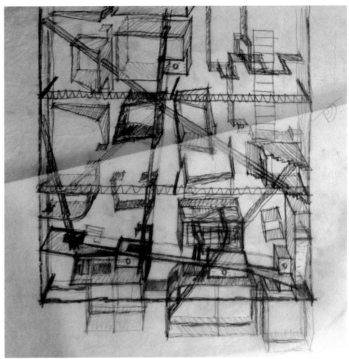

Mid-Atlantic Toyota
Glen Burnie, Maryland, 1976-78

Gehry House
Santa Monica, CA, 1977-78

Familian House
Santa Monica, 1978

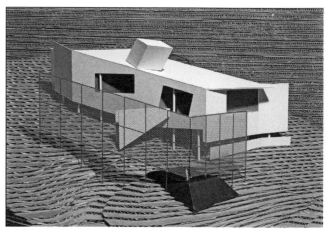

Wagner House
Malibu, 1978

Indiana Avenue Studios
Venice, 1979-81

Benson House
Calabasas, 1979-84

Experimental Edges Chair
1979

De Bretteville in Exhibition

JOHN DREYFUSS

Four of Peter de Bretteville's projects in an exhibition of his work at the Architecture Gallery in Venice illustrate the path of his professional growth and emerging independence.

Many architects don't grow. They may react to current fads or new design trends by imitating them. That is changing, not growing.

But De Bretteville's work, on display from noon to 6 p.m. through Saturday at 209 E. San Juan Ave., reveals increasing sensitivity and a progression from architecture that perfects an existing design approach to architecture that is more original.

There are at least two reasons that the trend is hard to see. For one thing, it is not fully delineated in the exhibit. Also, De Bretteville's early work appears deceptively original although it actually represents an existing style. What the Los Angeles architect did with notable skill was to refine that style to nearly its ultimate degree.

De Bretteville, who is 38, became an independent architect in 1971, so his "early" work is not very old.

His first completed project was his own house on Willow Glen St. in Laurel Canyon.

Designed in 1975, the building has a stringent, industrial appearance that relies on severe building materials (mostly metal) and expansive, warehouse-like spaces for its strong architectural impact.

A breaking up of big spaces and an aesthetic softening, largely due to use of wood and plaster instead of metal, is evident in a house in the West Hollywood hills that De Bretteville designed in 1977.

The third stage in the architect's continuing growth is represented by a 1978 plan for a house in Bel Air. Emphasis in that house is on curving walls that all but embrace people in rooms, and on distinctly cellular spaces as opposed to the linearity and the big volumes in his earlier work.

Where De Bretteville will go from here is a mystery, even to him. "I have no idea of what's next," he said. What is clear—and what is good— is that he is going somewhere. He has abandoned a highly distinctive but basically unoriginal style and

is developing his own architectural direction.

A PLETHORA OF PLANS

De Bretteville's show at the Architecture Gallery is a very simple, rather stiff exhibit that suffers from a plethora of plans and a shortage of photographs and models. There is not enough information about the interiors of his buildings. The exhibit fails to evoke a sense of what it would be like to live in one of them.

For example, there is only one interior shot among five excellent photos by architectural photographer Marvin Rand of De Bretteville's own house. It is left to a picture of a model and several drawings to provide an idea of what is inside the house, and the idea doesn't come across very well.

De Bretteville's house is actually two houses separated by a small court. The architect occupies one dwelling with his wife, designer Sheila de Bretteville, and their son. The other house belongs to writers Dyanne and Roger Simon and their two children.

Both houses are corrugated metal with exposed steel frames. Wood and metal trusses support the roofs. The houses' industrial appearance is emphasized by perforated, galvanized metal "catwalk" interior balconies and steel, factory-type stairways. In the West Hollywood hills house, the stern linearity and uninterrupted volumes of De Bretteville's home give

way to interior spaces more broken up by walls and to an exterior that reflects many of the rooms inside by articulating them on the outside.

BURSTING THROUGH WALLS

"All the interior spaces of the building burst right through the walls," De Bretteville said. Elements of industrial architecture remain, including metal balconies and stairways similar to those in De Bretteville's house. The balconies, however, are on the outside of the West Hollywood hills home.

The Bel-Air house is a remodeling project that De Bretteville, with his tongue in his cheek, has dubbed Villa Belaria [later renamed Villa Calzino, - ed.]. It is represented in the exhibit by two plans.

One plan has double lines with shading between them to depict the existing house, and double lines separated by white space to show De Bretteville's additions. The second plan uses shading throughout to give a sense of the finished unit.

The plans indicate that De Bretteville is something of an architectural Pygmalion. He took an ordinary house full of uninviting, undistinguished rectilinear spaces, and transformed it into a warm, embracing, distinctive home.

Since the project has been canceled, there is no way to be sure exactly what the plans would look like in three dimensions. It is certain, however, that the nucleus of some very good architecture is in those plans.

CUBES BECOME A BUILDING

Other projects in the exhibit include two cubes with 8-foot-long sides. The cubes combine to become an imaginative little prefabricated building, complete with furniture.

The building was designed (but never manufactured) as a car-rental office to be put up in a day on an empty lot. A greenhouse like enclosure would fold out of one box, almost doubling its floor space and volume. The other box, containing lighting,

PETER DE BRETTEVILLE

heating and air-conditioning equipment, would be set atop the first cube and—presto—an office. Some furniture would be built into the structure, the rest would be bolted to the floor for shipment and detached later.

Photos and drawings of a remodeled World Savings Bank in Northridge, elevations and plans for a school in Studio City, and plans for two unbuilt houses complete the exhibition.

De Bretteville will discuss his work at 8 p.m. tonight at the. Southern California Institute of Architecture, 1800 Berkeley St., Santa Monica. ⁂

Peter de Bretteville (b. 1941) grew up in Woodside, California in a house designed by his godfather, noted Bay Area architect Gardner Dailey. He earned undergraduate and graduate degrees at Yale, completing his master's in architecture in 1968. After working with Giancarlo di Carlo in Milan, De Bretteville relocated to Los Angeles in 1970 to team up with Craig Hodgetts, Keith Godard, and later, Eugene Kupper at Works West.

At Works West, De Bretteville and Godard were assisted by a young Michael Rotondi on the design of the 1973 Ajax Car Rental project. The scheme is a clever experiment in prefabricated fiberglass construction, and included a colorful re-imagination of the company's logo, stationary, and even a key chain. In 1974, De Bretteville launched his own practice. In projects such as the Willow Glen Houses in Laurel Canyon, the Country School in Studio City, and the Sunset House in the Hollywood Hills, he combined lightweight steel-and-glass assemblies with pragmatic wood construction to produce elegantly scaled buildings in a distinctly modernist idiom. By 1979, De Bretteville had begun to shift to a somewhat Rationalist, postmodern language of axial colonnades and figural spaces in projects such as the cheekily named "Villas" Calzino (for an importer of socks) and Cambiamento (a large renovation in Malibu). This manner continued through his later collaborations with Stefanos Polyzoides in the 1980s.

De Bretteville taught at California College of the Arts from 1970-73, at UCLA from 1973-76, and at USC from 1976-90. Since 1990, he has been a member of the faculty at the Yale School of Architecture and principal of Peter de Bretteville Architect. He lives and works near New Haven in a house of his own design.

PETER DE BRETTEVILLE
—*Wherefore 1979?*

Soon after the two houses on Willow Glen were completed, an architect visiting from England remarked that they represented an extraordinary display of optimism. Because my focus was so embedded in the work of the moment, I was not at all certain what he meant by that and supposed that the rigorous highly rationalized order somehow must have seemed idealistic. The intention behind that order was to create a liberating strategy which the differences of the two houses manifest. While employing the same material and construction elements, I had strived to make them quite different based on both the aesthetic predilections and the program of my clients. To that extent I saw the work as dynamic, adaptable, and variable, even changeable. It was an exploration of user interaction, if not in real time, at least in the conceptual work. My interest was in establishing an interactive relationship between the buildings and the user or the site such that the design would act on or manifest the variability of site and program or whatever forces might make demands on the design and use. So the Willow Glen houses are opposites, almost a figure ground reversal, not as a formal exercise but because of the differing requirements for the arrangement of rooms and for natural light. In addition the entire color scheme for each house was radically different. What I intended to demonstrate was that within a single method of construction, I could achieve a

high degree of differentiation, individualization, and identity.

While the material and structure of the Sunset House were quite different, the aspirations were not dissimilar. The principle elements of that building were the standard wood frame with stucco and the steel stairs, decks, handrails, etc. which were to address the exceptional, even "hardware," of the program. So some volumes push through the orthogonal envelope and another volume occupies a portion of the cantilevered balcony. Thus the regular systems and order of the building are appropriated at exceptional places to achieve specific local goals.

The discussion of layering which I introduced in my talk at SCI-Arc in 1979 and which is explored in both the interior and exterior balconies of the Willow Glen Houses—most obviously in the canvas sun shades—is examined in a wall form in the Villa Cambiamento and in the Villa Calzino. Those outer layers were employed as both sun control devices and to scale and organize the facades in a manner free of the particulars and openings governed by the interior. This is also true of the Sunset House and is even more fully explored later in the adjacent Guest House. As a building within a building, the "yellow submarine" defining the tellers and vault areas of the bank inside the green box, the World Savings project is also exploring another kind of layering.

On the other hand, the Country School and Ajax, while different, have in common an interest in the assembly of prefabricated elements and an architecture shaped by site and or circumstantial deployment issues. The Country School is an assembly of single and double prefabricated modules organized along an open spine with classrooms to the south and other support activities to the north. Besides the entry points from the main street and from the cul-de-sac, the most powerful

Ajax Car Rental, Los Angeles, 1973.

Sunset House, Los Angeles, 1977-79.

loss and strategies for advanced fabrication and building techniques. While there is currently a lot of compelling exploration of layered glass, it seems that the language could be expanded into a richer mix of wall types, including transparent and translucent glass as well as opaque walls. An additional potential that is inherent in some of these strategies is a more interactive architecture, one that responds in real time to both climate and use. So while in 1979 all of us were caught up in the moment and certainly optimistic, we were then and I believe are now equally excited by the radical changes and potential of the moment.

Willow Glen Houses, Los Angeles, 1973-75.

site influences were the giant sycamore trees which interrupted what was understood as the continuous edge of classrooms on the South. While Ajax was also based on a prefabricated steel frame, it is more choreographed on site and in real time. The closed container arrives at the site and turned up to the vertical, at which point the greenhouse room hinges down and the toilet and seating capsules are deployed. This process is also reversible meaning that the same module can be redeployed. This returns to the other aspect of the Willow Glen Houses which were strictly organized on a four-foot cube and made up of components fabricated off-site, namely the insulated and wired 4′ x 8′ wall panels, the steel frame and the trusses. My interest in prefabrication and my understanding of that notion in contemporary terms was advanced when I was told that the physical dimensions of trusses was not what was standardized but instead it was the software. It was my first experience of infinite customization as it was not the physical but rather the method that was standardized.

So there are at least two critical themes that can be extracted from this work which relate to contemporary practice, the management of a multilayered exterior envelope to control heat gain/

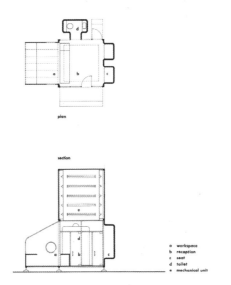

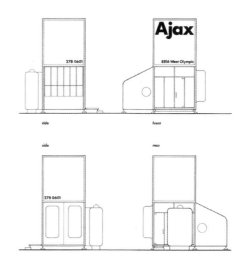

Ajax Car Rental
Los Angeles, 1973

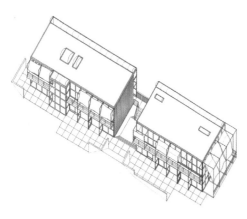

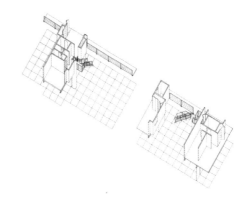

Willow Glen Houses
Los Angeles, 1973-75

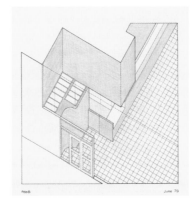

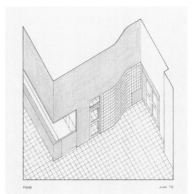

The Country School
Studio City, 1977

World Savings Bank
Northridge, 1979

PETER DE BRETTEVILLE

70

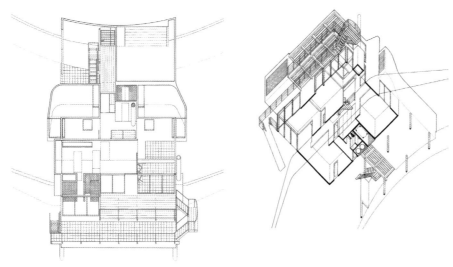

Sunset House
Los Angeles, 1977-79

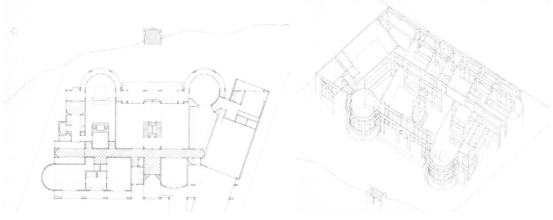

Villa Calzino
Malibu, 1979-80

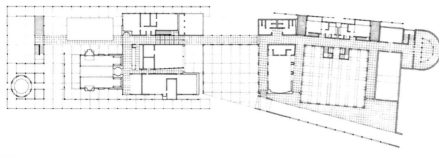

Villa Cambiamento
Malibu, CA, 1979-80

ORIGINALLY PUBLISHED IN THE *LOS ANGELES TIMES*, 28 NOV 1979

Sampler of a Duo's Whimsy

JOHN DREYFUSS

Viewers entering the Architecture Gallery in Venice to see an exhibit of work by Thom Mayne and Michael Rotondi will always find someone there ahead of them.

He is a short, rather gray complexioned fellow wearing a rakishly tilted, bright yellow hard hat labeled "Morphosis," which is the name of Rotondi's and Mayne's architectural firm.

Sunglasses hide the eyes of this apparently humorless observer, who is quite sure to haunt the gallery at 209 E. San Juan Ave. for the duration of this show: from noon to 6 p.m. through Saturday.

He wears a T-shirt on which is printed what seems to be a house with its walls folded down flat against the ground.

His legs—which number a disconcerting three—look like a camera tripod. They are metal. His face is plastic. "We call him our conscience," Mayne said. "He watches over everything we do."

Inserting their homemade Conscience in a show they take very seriously is a not-so-subtle indication of the delightful whimsy that Mayne and Rotondi build into some of their architecture.

The fanciful element dovetails with a seriousness of purpose that combines precision, pragmatism, and innovation.

The result is good design.

Another result is an excellent exhibition. This seventh in a series of nine shows by Los Angeles architects is clearly the most polished presentation so far.

The biggest problem with the exhibit is its short duration. The most obvious problem is a nasty reflection of studio lights from plastic sheets covering drawings and models.

Rotondi and Mayne present their work in a wide variety of ways: color photocopies, blueprints, a drawing from which a model grows, color photographs, pencil sketches, working drawings, models, color overlays, and photographs of ink drawings.

Consistently, the work is executed with so much care and precision that perceptive viewers will surely sense the total investment Mayne and Rotondi have in their profession.

Projects in the show range in size and diversity from a tiny garage-studio that is under construction in Venice to a large residential-state office building complex that won't ever be built anywhere (it was a competition entry).

While there are some design forms that appear in several Morphosis projects—notably pyramid-shaped roofs—the firm tends to find special solutions to special problems rather than to repeat its successes.

One project appears to have been purchased at a hobby store. Indeed, part of the exhibit is a box in which the "2-4-6-8 House" kit was packaged. Contents listed on the box cover include assembly instructions, a complete parts list, working drawings and a picture of the finished house. For good measure the kit contains a T-shirt (one is worn by Conscience) and a book that the architects happen to like.

The project is a cube, 18-feet on each side, with a pyramid roof dropped on. The ground floor is a garage, the second story a studio, with a window in each wall. The four windows progress regularly in size from 2 feet square to 8 feet square (hence the "2-4-6-8 House"), and are given emphasis by bright yellow wooden frames and cross bars that divide each opening into four equal quadrants.

For what it's worth, by standing in the middle of the room and turning to look out each window sequentially, one can create the illusion of growth or shrinking, à la Alice in Wonderland, as the windows grow or shrink. It is an eerie sensation, but it's fun.

The whole project has a childlike quality about it. On the outside, bright blue vents mimic beams above each yellow-framed window. Above the vents lie brilliant red scuppers to keep water out of the vents.

Gray concrete blocks interrupted by bands of pink blocks make up the garage walls. Exterior walls of the studio are pinkish asphalt shingles.

Mayne tells a story about the building that indicates how much he and Rotondi care about their architecture.

He says that when concrete forming for the stairs appeared shoddy, he had the contractor rip it out. Later, when the stairs were poured the work was sloppy and the contractor was told to do it over. He refused, according to Mayne. So Mayne rented a jack hammer and destroyed the stairs. They have been rebuilt to his satisfaction.

The house can be readily understood from the exhibit. Drawings show all four walls, a blueprint indicates component parts and a series of blueprinted drawings shows how to assemble them. A "pocket-sized" book of working drawings is also displayed.

If that information is not enough, the almost completed "kit" can be seen life size in Venice, half a block west of Lincoln Blvd. on Amoroso Place, which is three blocks north of Venice Blvd.

Most Morphosis work is not so frivolous as the "2-4-6-8 House." For example, a highly refined design for a vacation house in Mexico makes maximum use of a tiny (25x80-foot) lot through sophisticated handling of light, space and interior landscaping.

It is typical of Rotondi and Mayne that, when they lost their client halfway through the design phase of the house, they completed the design anyway.

"We learn from doing that," Rotondi said. "We get ideas to use later. We grow."

The architectural focal point of the house is a sunken atrium. Entry to the building is via a skylit hall that leads straight to the atrium. But, because walking directly across that central space would detract from its importance, railings were built so people would have to walk around it to reach the rest of the house. The skylight that begins above the entry hall loops over the walkway, providing an overhead "sign" to guide people. The atrium is readily accessible by side entrances.

Since the house is so small, Mayne and Rotondi wanted to expand its apparent space. So they provided for interior planting, including vines to

MORPHOSIS

grow up the atrium walls, thereby bringing the outside environment in.

The structure is depicted in the exhibit by a model and a series of drawings that progressively "builds" the house from the ground up.

Beautiful drawings depict the most recent completely designed work in the exhibit: a distinctive addition to a nondescript house in Pacific Palisades.

A vaulted metal roof covers the addition, which includes a dining room, a bedroom suite and a loft.

Its outside wall, covered with ivy, is separated by a 14-foot-wide deck from an ivy-covered trellis parallel to the wall. Balconies hang from the trellis.

The show includes a house for a Nigerian doctor that combines Western architecture with concepts of African tribal tradition through a design based on a tribal compound. The house is divided into four equal blocks separated by interior "hallways." Bay windows hang over the "hallways," creating an exterior atmosphere enhanced by rough stucco walls similar to those on the outsides of many houses. The result approximates a compound of four structures sheltered under one roof.

Other work in the show includes the big residential-state office complex designed for construction in Sacramento, a medical building under construction near Tijuana, a corrugated metal addition to a Venice house that sits on the traditional old structure like a lunar module sitting on the moon, a set of "stamps" Rotondi and Mayne produced to depict their work for another exhibit, and some sketches on tracing paper showing their most recent design, which is another studio over a Venice garage.

Mayne and Rotondi will discuss their work at 8 o'clock tonight at the Southern California Institute of Architecture, 1800 Berkeley St., Santa Monica. ⁑

Morphosis was founded as a loose, Archigram-inspired collaboration in 1972 by Thom Mayne (b. 1944, Waterbury, CT) and James Stafford. Early collaborators included SCI-Arc students Michael Brickler and Michael Rotondi (b. 1949, Los Angeles). By 1975, Stafford and Brickler had moved on, and Mayne and Rotondi had established a partnership which would remain in place until the end of 1991. Prior to joining Morphosis, Rotondi had practiced with DMJM and Works West. Mayne studied at USC (B. Arch, 1969) and taught briefly at Cal Poly Pomona before moving to SCI-Arc as a founding faculty member in 1972. He earned a Master's degree from the Harvard Graduate School of Design in 1978. Rotondi was a member of SCI-Arc's first graduating class in 1973, and joined the faculty the following year. By the time of the Architecture Gallery exhibitions, the office had been recognized with two P/A Awards, had exhibited in California and Germany, and had been featured in several local and international publications.

Morphosis's show at the Architecture Gallery demonstrated the wide range of influences from which the young architects would forge their unique style. The Reidel Medical Building in Tijuana and, to a lesser extent, the Sacramento State Office Building, owe much to the work of James Stirling, while projects like Mexico II and the Modebe House signal their interest in recognizable vernacular forms and materials. With the Delmer Addition, the 2-4-6-8 House, and the Flores addition, Morphosis hinted at the autonomy of individual architectonic elements and taste for brash juxtaposition which would characterize slightly later works such as the Sedlak House, which had just begun development at the time of the Architecture Gallery. Morphosis also displayed an array of drawing styles at the exhibition. Of particular interest are the firm's obsessive drawings for 2-4-6-8 and Flores, and their axonometric studies of Reidel and Modebe. These efforts reached a crescendo in the highly original drawings for the 6th Street House of 1986.

In the wake of the Architecture Gallery, Morphosis quickly rose to international acclaim with influential projects such as Kate Mantilini Restaurant, the Venice III House, and the Crawford House. In 1987, Rotondi succeeded Ray Kappe as the Director of SCI-Arc, holding the position until 1997. In 1992, he left Morphosis to launch Roto Architects in Los Angeles, which continues to produce award-winning projects. Mayne continues to lead Morphosis Architects as its sole principal. In 1992, he left SCI-Arc to join the faculty at UCLA, where he remains a full-time professor. In 2005, Mayne was awarded the Pritzker Prize in Architecture.

THOM MAYNE

At the time of the Morphosis exhibition and lecture in 1979, we were beginning to work out of and against a quasi-scientific notion of architecture that had grounded the educational model in the late 1960s and early 1970s. As students, we had been inculcated with an idea of architecture as a responsive system, generated from a rationalized analytic process. A clear separation had been drawn between intellectual and intuitive reasoning, with "design" redefined from its association with invention to become synonymous with "result." There was an ambivalence in locating the agency of architectural production; this would become a driving site of inquiry as we developed our approach.

Our initial methods, undertaken in early projects such as the Reidel Medical Office Building in 1976, evince the architectural climate we were growing from in their focus on infrastructure, reflected in a neutral architecture that emerged out of the prioritization of program and flexibility. Over the period of a few years, our concerns shifted substantially. Conflict and intentional disjuncture became key formal and conceptual concerns, as a way to arrive at more expressive and private sensibility. We were beginning to find critical sites of contention for generating forms and possibilities. The work embodied a generative relationship between willfulness and responsiveness, between the active and passive, between the idealized and the idiosyncratic, in order to develop a reworking of grammatical rules. The intent was to create a dialogue between the rational and the idiosyncratic to reflect a more pluralistic and complex worldview.

In attempting to come to terms with the specificity of place and use, we understood our practice as a means of both responding to and redefining an urban environment. At the most basic level, each project was designed to make general and specific observations about its immediate context. Contrasting structural and nonstructural elements and manipulating the program and materials for specific environmental conditions were two crucial techniques used to create visual and spatial dialogue between building and site. The 2-4-6-8 House and the Flores Residence are both early examples of these investigations. Even with the intimate scale of many projects, the buildings became vital interventions into existing social situations. History provided an indispensable framework for developing our organizational strategies. We sought an alignment between materiality and concept that could express the inherent physical qualities of the process of construction while maintaining conceptual integrity.

As Colin Rowe had asked, we questioned whether the architect was "a victim of circumstances" or whether the agency of the architect could be understood as an active force in the social and political fabric of society. We ultimately believed in architecture as a form of communication that was both a willful activity and one that could reflect and accommodate complexities in human experience.

MICHAEL ROTONDI

A story was being told over and over among colleagues searching for a way to describe the openness of Venice and to explain why it was the place in Los Angeles for contemporary art and architecture to emerge. It was coherent as a geographic place but incoherent as a social system. To those of us who spent most of our time there, it felt like a center of an intense beehive, an attractor with the pull of gravity.

It looked like the margins where conformity is repelled out like a toxin. The diversity of life forms seen in one place was the full-scale version of a Petri dish. A new hybrid culture was coming to life. What we saw when we took our daily walk along the four-mile boardwalk was central casting for the bar scene in Star Wars, we often said. The unusual fact was that everyone belonged and everyone looked normal here, a hybrid society was giving birth to a hybrid culture. We thought this was only possible because the umbilical cord from Europe had been severed by the Rockies, allowing us the freedom to be heretics in an orthodox world. We imagined being invisible and Venice was our cover. It was the city version of a rainforest—great diversity intertwined advancing one step beyond mere coexistence. In an inexplicable way we all needed to be there embedded in this world of difference to inspire us. This would enter our aesthetic psyche and would be sorted out through the work we did.

It was a quantum, non-recurring, non-Newtonian world in which we came of age. We were living the effects of a theory that explained how the universe worked on a small scale (Spherical Harmonics) but in the greater context. Probability and self-similarity had given way to spontaneity and strangeness. It was made to order for a generation in the midst of inventing a life and unwittingly playing a role reinventing the world that had already been cracked open in 1968. Those years of anger had given way to joy and optimism. We were young Archi-

tects after all. Merely responding and adapting was too limiting, was not in our scope. We constructed the world we imagined we wanted to be a part of. We knew this time and place was an opportunity to construct a world one project at a time. There was never an ambition to lead and definitely no expectations of followers. It was a horizontal world without need for social hierarchy. Our worldview was emerging. Context brings out our intrinsic capacities to do and be.

We traveled as a small posse (more nimble that way). How we moved and what we thought about were one and the same: while the ideas were being tested through a variety of media and scale, we invented projects and a life. We also invented ways to test and convey our ideas, which were always evolving even as we expressed them. Mistakes? We were always among friends who defined failure as trial and error, speaking in silence a lot of the time, multiple bodies and one mind.

It was such a joy feeling a sense of belonging to a tribe like this and to experience a special type of unity. One thing we seemed to have in common was that our ambitions were connected to the energy and intelligence that flowed through our hands into matter. We made things to try and answer questions about everything we were curious about. Material relationships were a metaphor for social and political ones. The things we made were a way for us to better understand the world and our place in it. On an intimate level we were curious about the worlds within worlds we envisioned in our mind's eye and at the intermediate mezzo scale we wondered if space and form were truly the trigger of our deep memory and imagination. At the macro scale we wondered if Architecture could retain its integrity and autonomy as it entered a difficult and unrelenting world.

At this time in the late '60s and '70s, Architecture was in crisis, confused about its own nature and its varied responsibilities in the world.

The modern era had yielded a new orthodoxy: although abstract it was no different than the old orthodoxies. It required us to follow the party line. It required allegiance. There was no tolerance for self-expression or rolling the dice. This did not make sense to us, at all. We had an affinity to placing ourselves at the epicenter where the idiosyncratic met the ideal. There were rules but they were invisible. This may have been confusing but to us, it was where creativity resided.

Our confusion was coincident with our curiosity and our motivation. Confidence and a willingness to take risks compelled us to test our ideas by constructing them in as many ways and formats we could think of and make happen: drawings, buildings, teaching, endless debates, and exhibitions. We often looked around for precedent but found none to our liking so we invented what we had to. We learned how to move fast in slow motion. Venice seemed like the right place to be doing this.

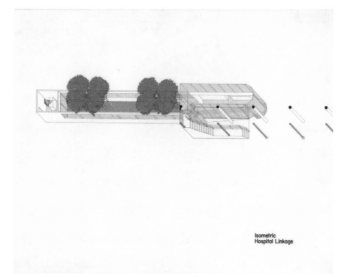

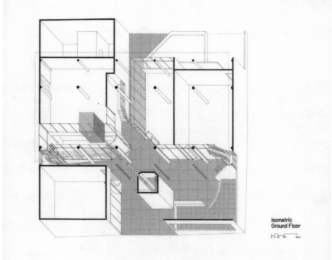

Reidel Medical Building
Tijuana, Mexico, 1976

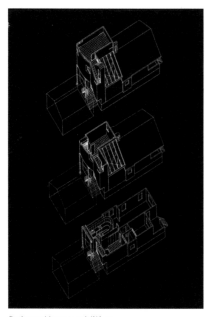

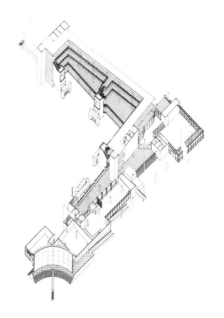

Delmer House addition
Venice, 1976

Sacramento State Office Building
Sacramento, 1977

2-4-6-8 House
Venice, 1978

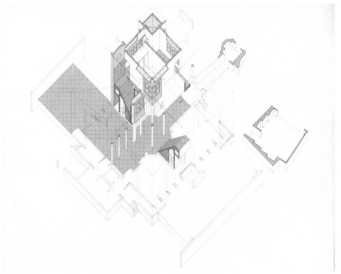
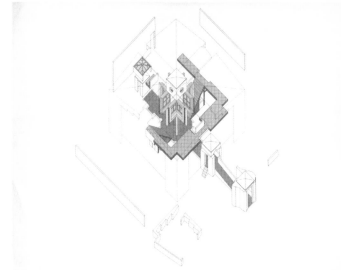

Modebe House
Onitsha, Nigeria, 1979

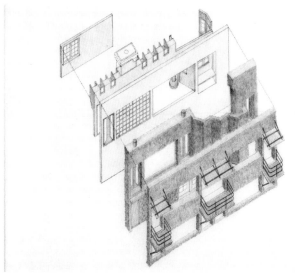
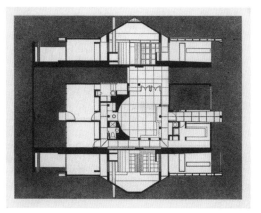

Flores House addition
Los Angeles, 1979

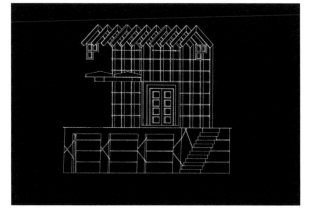

Sedlax House addition
Los Angeles, 1979-80

Mexico II House
Tijuana, Mexico, 1978

ORIGINALLY PUBLISHED IN THE *LOS ANGELES TIMES*, 28 NOV 1979

Their Aim: Social Change

JOHN DREYFUSS

If a job does not provoke social change, they don't want it, say Craig Hodgetts and Robert Mangurian, who run an architecture and design firm in Los Angeles called Studio Works.

Seven drawings and two models, plus a big table of design-related goodies that would do honor to an architectural rummage sale, represent some of their work for social change at the Architecture Gallery. 209 E. San Juan Ave., Venice.

The exhibit, open from noon to 6 p.m. through Saturday, contains important and interesting messages. But the show fails to deliver the messages.

All the drawings are skillfully executed and intentionally severe. Models are craftsmanlike. And the table holds a treasure of touchable miscellany ranging from paint chip samples to renderings of scenes from a proposed movie.

While severe drawings, craftsmanlike models and a table full of fascinating fun from the architects' attic are interesting, and perhaps meaningful to perceptive members of the architectural community, they do not warrant a public exhibition.

The show needs some transition between what is on display and what the display represents, both architecturally and socially.

That bridge could be built with drawings, written explanations or—preferably—a combination of the two.

HAULED MODEL TO OHIO

As the exhibit stands, it is a treasure hunt in search of clues. The treasure is there, directly in front of the viewers' noses, but there are not enough clues to reveal how very rich the prize is.

Most of the show is devoted to a private, nonprofit community center in Columbus, Ohio, called the South Side Settlement. To design the center, Hodgetts and Mangurian virtually integrated themselves with the community.

"It was an incredible break from the normal, relatively detached programming of a building," Mangurian said. "We got our information from being in the client's operation."

The architects met with settlement house staff, literally living with them while in Columbus.

They learned firsthand about needs for such facilities as a theater, gymnasium (also to a serve as a banquet hall, meeting room and disaster housing area), kitchen, childcare center, medical clinic, coffee house, teen center, arts and crafts workrooms, counseling offices, and administrative offices.

Then they built a model, loaded it in the trunk of a bright red, rented car, and hauled it to Ohio.

The model depicted a 40,000 square-foot, $1.3-million building that essentially was a concrete box containing five parallel "streets."

Inside, three of the rather impersonal "streets" were roofed over and filled with rooms designed in a wide variety of styles, giving the building an aesthetic warmth and human scale.

Two "streets" were left uncovered. They provided pedestrian circulation, and a number of "houses" were built on the uncovered "streets" to serve various purposes.

In keeping with the working-person nature of the community and the center's clients, numerous small contracting firms were to be hired to build the numerous components of the project.

Officials at the center thought the model was wonderful. So did judges of the annual *Progressive Architecture* competition for unbuilt structures, who gave it their top design award in 1976.

Two years later, Hodgetts got a heartbreaking phone call. Center officials had changed their minds. They said they would scrap the design and start over with local architects.

The building cost too much, the design seemed impractical, and Mangurian and Hodgetts were too far away to maintain contact with the job, the officials said.

"We'd been living and breathing this project," Hodgetts said. "That phone call felt like an incredible betrayal."

When Hodgetts got the bad news, he called Mangurian, who was in Rome as a fellow of the American Academy there.

"We did a new design on the phone," Hodgetts said. "The next day I flew to Columbus with two little sketches."

Board members at the center liked the sketches. They gave the job back to Hodgetts and Mangurian.

NEW DESIGN INFINITELY BETTER

The new building, represented by the other model in the exhibit, is half the size of the original, twice as dramatic, and infinitely better.

Instead of "streets" with architectural additions, the building is a collection of a lot of specific, special places.

Principal entrance is via a ramp that deposits visitors on the stage of an outdoor theater overlooking a stairway-sculpture by New York artist Alice Aycock.

An indoor theater, gymnasium, and a kitchen-dining area occupy separate, distinctive spaces bracketed by two wings housing the center's other facilities.

In contrast to the old plan, which was a group of personalized spaces within a decidedly impersonal box, the new design provides a group of dramatic volumes that relate to one another without a strong sense of containment by an overriding geometrical plan.

The new design will give building's users a sense of relating to individual spaces that happen to be part of a complex, whereas the original design clearly consisted of an imposing structure circumscribing (and thereby controlling) a series of personalized spaces.

While the old plan ingeniously created individual architectural volumes, those volumes were forced into a grand design that was formal and impersonal.

In contrast, the new design eliminates the controlling element (the concrete box divided into "streets") and creates an atmosphere of architecture designed to serve the personal needs of the users, leaving them in control of their environment rather than being fitted into it.

STUDIO WORKS

When the center opens next year, Hodgetts and Mangurian hope to see their work encouraging innovation and personal freedom among its users, as well as creating a feeling that the center belongs to them rather than they to it.

Drawings in the exhibit depict three other projects, none of them readily understandable from the show.

One drawing shows a 1975 plan for a proposed housing project on Roosevelt Island in New York City's East River. It provides apartments for between 5,000 and 7,000 people. The low-rise units are interspersed with green belts. Parking is limited to a big garage near the development. All movement in the area is on foot or by bicycle.

The design encourages individuality by allowing residents to design their own apartments. It promotes contact among residents by eliminating auto traffic and by laying out public spaces so people easily can be close to each other.

Another drawing indicates a plan to "tune up" two shoreline sections of the Mississippi River and the small island they bracket, all within the Minneapolis city limits.

The project was done in 1976 for an exhibition at the Walker Art Center in Minneapolis. Proposed facilities on the northwest side of the river include housing on canals, boutique shopping facilities, and a sports center. On the opposite bank, which is near the city's existing business district, Hodgetts and Mangurian show expensive riverfront housing, monumental corporate headquarters, a park and a concert hall.

On the island, the architects put a hotel, a museum, and a monumental, 2,558-foot-long scale model of the Mississippi River (one foot of model equals one mile of river).

Two other projects are shown: a hydroponic planter drawing about six times actual size, and an extraordinarily complicated plan-elevation-perspective combination of an art dealer's gallery-residence under construction in Venice. ∗

Craig Hodgetts was born in Cincinnati in 1937. He was educated at the General Motors Institute, Oberlin College (B.A., 1962), San Francisco State University, and Yale (M. Arch, 1967). Robert Mangurian was born in Baltimore in 1944. He studied at Stanford before completing a bachelor's degree in architecture at UC Berkeley in 1967. After graduating, both worked with Conklin & Rossant Architects in New York, where Hodgetts also helped establish a local office for James Stirling in 1967.

In 1968, Hodgetts and Lester Walker, another Conklin & Rossant alum, launched Works in New York. Mangurian joined the following year, not long before Hodgetts left to take a position at the California Institute of the Arts. Walker and Mangurian remained in New York as Works East, and Hodgetts teamed up with Peter de Bretteville and Keith Godard to form Works West in Los Angeles. Coy Howard, Eugene Kupper, and Michael Rotondi each collaborated with Works West in the early 1970s. The two offices pursued work independently under their geographical monikers, with bicoastal collaborations such as the South Side Settlement in Columbus, Ohio credited to "Studio Works." Mangurian joined the Los Angeles group after a fellowship at the American Academy in Rome in 1977.

The young architects quickly gained notoriety for their technologically progressive and exuberantly drawn designs. Hodgetts' MAXX Housing scheme, completed while a student at Yale, was published in *Archigram* in 1967. Works West earned a 1972 *P/A* Award for their Mobile Theater scheme, on which Kupper collaborated. In 1977, Hodgetts and Mangurian were included in *A+U* Magazine's "40 under 40."

At the Architecture Gallery, the pair exhibited urban design competition schemes for New York and Minneapolis, their recently completed Gagosian Studio in Venice, and two proposals for the South Side Settlement. The urban schemes betray both the architects' clear debt to James Stirling as well as a canny ability to push their mentor's language into new territory. The two Columbus schemes outline a trajectory pursued by many architects through the 1970s, with an early indeterminacy in plan giving way to a more controlled composition of figural spaces and overt historical references. The latter tactic also was employed in Venice for the Gagosian Studio, organized around a circular courtyard and often referred to in publication as a "palazzo." Contrasting many of their more overtly postmodern contemporaries, Hodgetts and Mangurian retained close ties to the language of technology and in particular hot rods, evidenced at the Architecture Gallery by their clever Hydroponic Planter, a "high tech herb garden" designed for Mattel. Sadly, no documentation of this project survives.

In 1983, Hodgetts left Studio Works. After forays into film-production design and an aborted novel, he joined forces with Hsinming Fung to form Hodgetts + Fung in 1984. Mangurian continues to lead Studio Works with Mary-Ann Ray, who joined as principal in 1987. Hodgetts was Associate Dean of California Institute of the Arts from 1969-72, and a member of the faculty at UCLA from 1972-82. He taught at Rice, the University of Pennsylvania, UC San Diego, and Yale before returning to UCLA in 1993, where he is currently Professor of Architecture. Mangurian taught at City College of New York in the late 1960s and early '70s and joined the faculty at SCI-Arc in 1977. He directed SCI-Arc's graduate program from 1987-97, and continues to lead studios and seminars at the school.

CRAIG HODGETTS & ROBERT MANGURIAN

Whatever brought this bunch of guys to the desolate Pacific fringe, Los Angeles, in the late seventies and early eighties is not clear—nor does it matter very much. What matters is that they were all recent graduates from architecture schools spread all across the country, and that they shared a discomfort—disdain even—for the trappings of the then dominant architectural culture. Maybe they liked being on the actual edge of the country as well. What is clear is that they felt profoundly disenfranchised. What is unclear is how they found each other.

Venice, in those days, was a haunt of mostly vagrants, itinerant trailer people, Hells Angels, and the remains of the hippie culture. The beach was littered with battle-scarred motorhomes, careering seagulls, and bordered by a few scabby coffee joints. Artists were the first to arrive— Eric Orr, Ron Cooper, Ron Davis, the Dill brothers, and others. The cheap rent, left-over storefronts, and desolate ambiance had a considerable appeal to them and, never far behind, architects.

Thane Roberts, Robert Mangurian, and Craig Hodgetts at Studio Works, Venice, 1974.

It was not a pre-ordained, structured, manifesto *à la* the New York Five. Far from it! There was no sheltering institution, no MoMA, no Philip Johnson. The players were all playing out their own hands, together in their ennui, their search for a sympathetic audience, but ultimately, acutely on their own. Consensus, such as it was, was always implicit, apparent in the work itself. The nearest approach to a codified, unified front was the "Silvers" conference initiated by Tim Vreeland at UCLA, which proposed a West Coast retort to the "Whites and Grays" on the East Coast.

There were some collaborative arrangements: Coy Howard and Hodgetts worked together briefly on designs for a then forward-thinking computer firm (1980) and Michael Rotondi helped to refine the Hodgetts-designed Punchout line of furniture before joining Thom Mayne to form Morphosis. But overall, the orbits of the Venice studios were principally tethered to two institutions: UCLA which, under the stewardship of Vreeland, looked eastward for succor, and SCI-Arc, which had gathered together most of the talented and vocal young architects under the leadership of Ray Kappe. It was Kappe who led a revolt at Cal Poly Pomona, commandeered a decaying West Los Angeles metal shop, and began the school from scratch with a group of students which included Rotondi.

Between them, the schools were able to lend a modicum of support to the growing body of younger architects—partly financial—but much more importantly by offering them a platform from which to promote a unique vision. A vision which in retrospect was intransigent, iconoclastic, and—shudder—doomed to be regional, but which was, in fact, solidly grounded in a fresh appraisal of the unexplored material potential unfettered by European antecedents.

Where there are artists, of course, there will be galleries, and in the late seventies two galleries that were to assume major roles set up shop on Main Street in Venice rather than join the flourishing, established scene on La Cienega. Ace led off with a Robert Irwin installation which removed the entire façade of the building and replaced it with a transparent fabric skin. The other, commissioned by Larry Gagosian, resulted in the first Los Angeles project by Studio Works, then a bicoastal operation with Mangurian in New York, one floor above Warhol's Factory, and Hodgetts, who had come to Los Angeles from NYC to head the design department at Cal Arts, in a studio at the foot of Rose Avenue, which he shared with artist Eric Orr.

Others in the constellation of young architects had found similar spaces pretty much within walking distance of one another. Roland Coate, Eric Moss, Howard, and Mayne occupied storefronts strung out between Speedway and Electric, and entrepreneurs like David Greenberg, who founded Environmental Communications, and artists-turned-developers Tom Sewell and Guy Webster had a presence on nearby Pacific Avenue. Soon thereafter, Tony Bill, the producer and director of *Shampoo*, L.A.'s first boutique grocery, and Leonard Koren's *Wet* Magazine fleshed out what was fast becoming an enclave of young, energetic, shoestring endeavors which were defiant misfits in the prevailing culture.

When Frank Gehry, then conducting a largely commercial practice from a spacious industrial loft, decided to join the club and relocate into a cramped, messy storefront a few yards from the beach, it was clear that what had begun as a coagulation of misfits was emerging from the shadows.

Los Angeles Times reporter John Dreyfuss and *Examiner* critic Sam Kaplan noticed. A flurry of articles documented the scrappy architecture then emerging in Venice, which contrasted vividly with the polished, corporate architecture then favored by both papers. The controversy expanded as Dreyfuss dug in, highlighting design events like Hodgetts' Venice biennale proposal and offering intelligent commentary on the scene. At times, Dreyfuss seemed to channel the DNA of the emerging architects, championing those who designed it as well as the work itself. It felt like Hollywood.

By the time Mayne captured that energy—self-sponsoring a series of exhibitions at the storefront where he practiced and lived—the 'gang' had a modicum of success. Projects, exhibitions,

installations, rhetoric, and manifestoes were multiplying rapidly, while opportunities for lectures and teaching—mostly at SCI-Arc and UCLA—were lending both visibility and credibility to what had been a far-out fringe.

Each exhibit was self-curated by the participants. Often assembled at the last minute, without a budget, and with only minimal promotion, the series played out like an off-off-Broadway production, attended by a motley crew of students, fellow teachers, and friends of friends. No one had any expectations, yet the fire had been lit. Dreyfuss contributed detailed articles on each show. The word, somehow, got out.

Our own contribution, coming as we were from completing the construction documents for our first two Los Angeles commissions, was firmly grounded in the philosophy made famous by writer-director Bertold Brecht. We had an innate distaste for self-promotion, and decided that the only honest posture was to present exactly what we were doing as exactly as possible. By positioning a couple of long tables in the center of the storefront, and covering them with an assortment of drawings, pencils, model fragments, and references to late nights, we hoped to convey an impression of process. The hard work, attention to detail, and common materials we saw as antidotes to a more pragmatic design practice.

Predictably, the shows had little or no effect on the largely disinterested local population. After all, there were no fashionistas, no sidewalk cafés, no museums of contemporary art, and no gourmet bakeries. It was another time, a time when Case Study houses were being demolished with the same fervor that Lautner's string of tiny Naylor restaurants was being replaced with strip malls. Los Angeles was still innocent, and it would be many years before Rodney King kicked off an urban revolution.

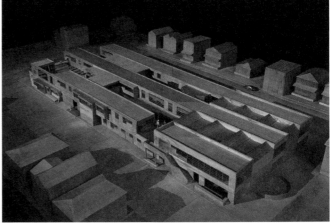

South Side Settlement, first scheme
Columbus, Ohio, 1975-78

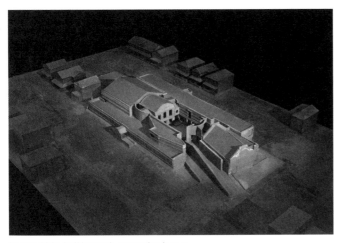

South Side Settlement, second scheme
Columbus, Ohio, 1978-80

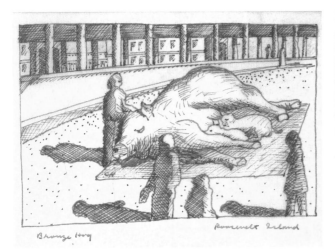

Roosevelt Island Competition
New York, 1976

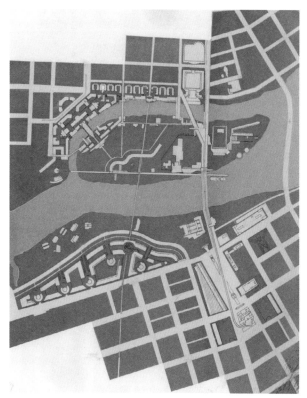

The River and the City
Minneapolis, 1976

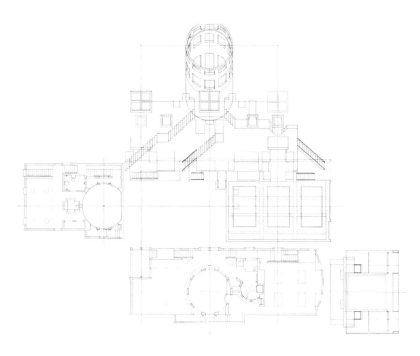

Gagosian Studio
Venice, 1979

ORIGINALLY PUBLISHED IN THE *LOS ANGELES TIMES*, 5 DEC 1979

Nine Entrées: Eric Moss' Architectural Feast

JOHN DREYFUSS

Eric Moss is serving an architectural banquet at the Architecture Gallery, from noon to 6 p.m. through Saturday at 209 E. San Juan Ave., Venice.

It is a refreshing, innovative, effective and amusing exhibition of work by the Los Angeles architect and his partner, James Stafford.

With a little help from Abbey Rents, Moss set a formal, 25-foot-long table for nine guests. Each "entrée" is a model of a different building.

Most settings include a "menu" of drawings and words describing the architectural fare.

With so many dishes to sample, the banquet never gets dull. It is a feast too good to miss.

Like traditional meals (but unlike many architectural exhibits) this one is enjoyable on a number of levels. It can be approached from the perspective of a casual visitor not deeply interested in architecture, or with the refined palate of an architectural gourmet, or it can be gobbled up with the greed of a gourmand.

ARBITRARY AND PRAGMATIC

Moss' buildings are graphic combinations of the arbitrary and the pragmatic. He works to satisfy his clients' needs, be they a savings and loan building that doubles as a steam-billowing signboard, or a beach house that goes to great lengths to frame specific views for its owner.

But the forms of his buildings often are arbitrary "statements." He places windows in a Pasadena condominium so they approximate facial features on ancient Easter Island stone sculptures. He designs mysterious concrete cylinders in front of a Los Angeles warehouse-office building that are intriguing shapes from the outside, but awkward storage areas on the inside.

Moss may be Los Angeles' most broadly intellectual and scholarly young architect. At 36, he has a bachelor's degree in English literature from UCLA and master's degrees in architecture from UC Berkeley and Harvard University.

He sprinkles conversations with references to and quotes from sources as diverse as Nietzsche, Phidias, James Joyce, Ludwig Mies van der Rohe, and the Bible.

Moss knows what he's talking about. The quotes are accurate and the references pertinent.

With his background, Moss understands and appreciates the rules of architecture. But he thinks that rules—be they mathematical, philosophical, political or architectural—are inadequate.

DOCTRINE AND DOGMA

"As soon as you demand strict consistency according to rules," he says, "you get doctrine and dogma, and you die." Moss pays enough attention to the rule books to make his buildings work, but not so much that they become predictable.

The results, as anyone can see at the exhibition, keep those buildings very much alive in that they are exciting, lively looking structures.

Some of Moss' buildings are unusual to the point of appearing supernatural. They are not the kind of architecture found on every street in town.

So if you are looking for traditional architecture, don't look for Eric Moss. If you seek innovative excellence, he may be your man.

The most striking model in the exhibit is of a pink, blue, orange, and beige house designed around five pinball machines and a Porsche.

Part of the roof on the hillside house to be built in Laurel Canyon will be a "bleachers" from which to enjoy the view of Los Angeles, the surrounding hills and the vivid house itself.

Five pods will hang from the front of the building that will look a lot like a locomotive. Each pod is to house one of the client's pinball machines. The garage is designed with a window separating it from the living room to show off his sports car.

The impenetrable-looking corrugated metal facade of the house will bend to become a vaulted roof leading to a surprise in the back yard: a roof mostly made of gray, mirrored glass supported by walls that also are largely glass.

PAINTBRUSH IN BRIGHT COLORS

Moss dipped his paintbrush in bright colors that will all but make the house jump: exposed blue ductwork and chimneys, orange sections painted on the beige roof, and pink details.

A lesser architect would have combined those highly unusual colors and design elements to create a garish, even ridiculous residence.

But Moss, in exploring new architectural territory, provides excitement, creativity and a decidedly livable house. It is extreme architecture that works.

All of Moss' work is not so extreme. His condominium to be built in Pasadena is relatively subdued, with emphasis on the word "relatively."

To blend the three-story, five-unit building with bungalow-style homes in the neighborhood, Moss designed a rectilinear facade facing the street. Then he broke up the facade with reflective glass blocks caricaturing the

ERIC OWEN MOSS

silhouettes of nearby houses.

While the relationships between the condominium and nearby homes seem abstract, Moss said residents of the neighborhood are supportive of the planned building.

The structure is unusual in that each of its four sides could easily belong to a different work of architecture. One side is fenestrated and painted so each unit suggests the face of an Easter Island stone sculpture. The opposite side has ordinary, rectangular windows set at an angle that reflects interior stairways, but that reflection is really just an excuse for a distinctive design element. From the back of the building hangs a big, hemispherical window that doesn't relate to anything else about the place.

For all their emphasis on arbitrary design, the condos, like most of Moss' architecture, are good looking. They may also be efficient living units, although one can't tell because there is no "menu" of plans to go with the model. Other models on the table include a unique Malibu beach house, a savings and loan association building, a very strange looking studio-guest house for a Malibu site, a huge annex for the Minnesota state capitol building (it was a competition entry), a warehouse-office building in the Los Angeles garment district, a remodeled facade for the building adjacent to the warehouse-office, and a home in the Hollywood Hills.

Moss will discuss his work at 8 tonight at the Southern California Institute of Architecture, 1800 Berkeley St., Santa Monica. ⁂

Eric Owen Moss was born in Los Angeles in 1943. He earned a B.A from UCLA in 1965, an M. Arch from UC Berkeley in 1968, and a second M. Arch. from the Harvard Graduate School of Design in 1972. After working with Skidmore, Owings & Merrill and Paffard Keatinge-Clay in San Francisco and Gruen Associates in Los Angeles, he entered private practice in 1973.

At the Architecture Gallery, Moss presented models of nine projects arranged as entrées on a long dining table, complete with linens, silver, and stemware. Drawings were presented as menus (now lost) to be perused by exhibition visitors. Projects included his recently completed Morganstern Warehouse, which had been widely published that fall. Like other exhibited projects, Morganstern demonstrated Moss's penchant for brash compositions of enigmatic, often awkward, forms rendered in bright contrasting colors. Quotidian elements such as address numbers and mechanical equipment were scaled and placed to give them a cartoon-like graphic quality which extended onto the roof of the building. Unlikely elements such as the concrete drainage pipes-cum-towers along the street façade hinted at Moss's more aggressive later work in Culver City and elsewhere through the 1980s.

Where many of the young Architecture Gallery participants were still working through the stylistic idioms of various mentors (cf. Stirling's influence on Morphosis and Studio Works, for example), Moss's output of the time often was set in deliberate opposition to prevailing trends. In contrast to the Euro-centric postmodernism of many peers, Moss's references, when present, were obscure and decidedly non-Western, as evidenced by the echoes of the Nazca Lines on the roof at Morganstern or of Easter Island's Moai statues on the façade of the Pasadena Condominiums. Some elements, such as the crooked column at the La Faille House, the canted trusses in the section of the Pinball House, and the supergraphic patterns and texts at the Login House, would comprise something of a personal signature for Moss in later projects. Elaborations of these elements can be found in such projects as the exuberant 708 House in Pacific Palisades, the idiosyncratic Fun House project of 1980, and his widely published later projects in the Hayden Tract in Culver City.

Moss joined the faculty at SCI-Arc in 1974, and has served as the school's Director since 2003. He has taught at major universities around the world, including Harvard, Yale, Columbia, and the University of Applied Arts in Vienna. His numerous awards include an Academy Award from the American Academy of Arts and Letters, an AIA/LA Gold Medal, the Arnold W. Brunner Memorial Prize, and the RIBA's Jencks Award. He continues to lead Eric Owen Moss Architects in Culver City.

ERIC OWEN MOSS

"Don't look back. Something may be gaining on you."
— *Satchel Paige*

I'm not confident I can reconstitute the Moss office mindset, vintage 1979. I never considered the office an object lesson, or the exemplar of a particular moment in the architecture chronology. Our focus has never been on preserving an in-process process that could, at some moment, be recreated, evaluated, taught, and learned.

The history-writing pro forma typically traces developmental lines from a presumed pivotal moment, then extends those lines forward and backward to inter-connect past, present, and future. The assumption is what was initiated at a certain point comes to fruition at another, i.e., the future is a logical consequence of a line drawn from the past through the present.

Or is it?

I insist our past remains open, not an inevitable prognosticator of our future. (If it were, I would be the most dependable of soothsayers). Time lines are discontinuous—break, divide, multiply, disappear and reappear. So our contemporary condition is a result of design options invented, options retrieved, options discarded, and in some cases options sustained.

When I was in school in Berkeley and in Cambridge, I began to think of architecture as an opportunity to contribute to the culture, and simultaneously to comment on it. Things are as they are; things could be other than they are. Both, simultaneously. Architecture is a bridge between what is and what might be, and the bridge (if it's in working order) remains in a state of tension. That tension is a demand for resolution, stretching between contradictory possibilities. Now and in 1979.

And somewhere in that tensed mindset I would include mischief and subversion as vantage points contributory to a conceptual process of the idea of building in the process of becoming a beginning. A start, not an end was what we looked for in the Pinball and the Petal and Guangzhou and the Mariinski.

I've always been interested in the production of unanticipated architecture—how to make what we don't yet know how to make. There's a conviction here that the prospect of architecture can forever be re-imagined, and it's the architect's job to discover what we don't yet recognize.

In our first Rizzoli book we explained the surprise quotient in two conceptual venues: one, the "Hole in the Sky," the other, "Penelope." The hole in the sky was a borrowed quote from an old saxophone playing pal in Oakland who claimed that his music making always exceeded its imagined limits, and punched a hole in his sky, and that he came to understand there was always a new sky above the one he once perceived as the ultimate lid. The more he played the sax, the more new skies were revealed, so that after a while he no longer recognized where the process began.

The second hypothesis came from the *Odyssey*. Penelope waits twenty years for Odysseus to return to Ithaca. Toward the end of that time the suitors insist Odysseus is dead and she must marry one of them. She agrees, saying she'll pick one as soon as she finishes knitting the shroud on her loom. During the day she knits, and at night she takes the knitting apart in order to begin again the following day.

The idea that there's always another sky above the above, always another way to feel and think and see (hole in the sky), and the sense that what we imagine can always be taken apart and reconstituted (Penelope) were germinating principles in 1979 and continue to be so today.

There are those contemporary opinion makers who insist architecture is in a period of consolidation now. The exploration's done, and now's the time to implement what we've learned going back to the 1979 period. The Parametricism debate is a reflection of this "time to consolidate" conclusion.

That implementation mandate suggests that a period of innovation must be followed by a period of rules, that, strangely, innovation would necessarily lead to a subsequent rule system to which we and others would subscribe. (Hitchcock and Johnson, *The International Style*, 1932, and Schumacher's *Autopoesis*, 2011, are for instances.) And in the history of ideas the fragile and experimental conception followed by a regulatory/consolidation process reflect an evolutionary truth. But in terms of the Moss office we've never accepted a ruled method or system derived from what we did back then, so our constant is intransigence against constants. We're not interested in consolidation as an implementation corollary. The aspiration is to keep the fragile fragile.

For us 1979 is fundamentally 2013. The project scale is different today. The site locations are different today. The clients are different today. The technical apparatus surrounding the production of buildings is different today. The surrounding social and political context is different today. The responsibilities are different today. Most important, undeniably, the sympathy for an anomalous voice, so rare then, is much greater today. (Which may bring into question whether a sustained anomaly remains an anomaly at all.)

The fact of the Getty-sponsored exhibitions confirms that current sympathy.

But I'm not concerned with, and probably incapable of offering a stabilizing rendition of architecture. Not then; not now. The 1979 aspirations endure. Which means that I can talk about today, and feel comfortable that the priorities aren't so different from what they were in '79.

It was the best of times, as Dickens said; it will be the best of times, as Dickens should have added.

And somewhere in this discussion is the "LA story," a city sometimes supportive, sometimes opposed, and often uniquely complacent in the face of the ongoing adventures of architecture here yesterday and today.

I listened to Charley Moore in Berkeley in 1967. I listened to Shad Woods, Jose Luis Sert, and Kenzo Tange at Harvard in 1971. But maybe the strongest and most enduring recollection that forecast the office tone was hanging out on the Berkeley street corners in 1968; strikes and sit-ins and marches and Hendrix and Dylan and Joplin and Bobby and Vietnam, and realizing it was impossible for me to know where and with whom to sign-up, to join, and to march lock-step. Not that I didn't want to. Just didn't know how to do it. Still don't.

Modern? Postmodern? Metabolism? Deconstruction? Digital coding?

"I had to re-arrange their faces, and give them all another name," the song said.

Life is personal, not interchangeable. Architecture, one architect at a time.

That status remains quo.

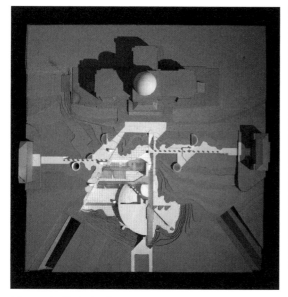

Minnesota State Capitol Annex Competition
Minneapolis, 1977

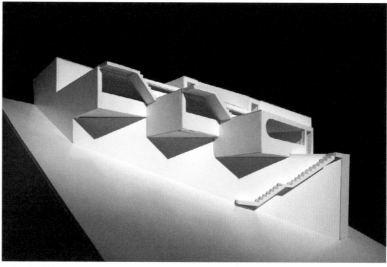

Cobb Residence
Hollywood Hills, 1977-78

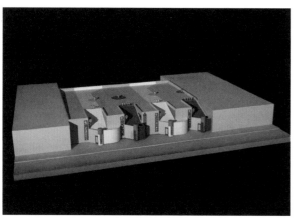

Morganstern Warehouse
Los Angeles, 1977-79

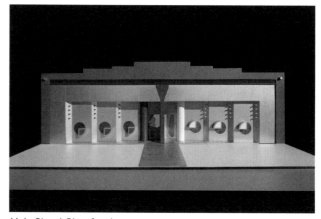

Main Street Storefront
Los Angeles, 1979

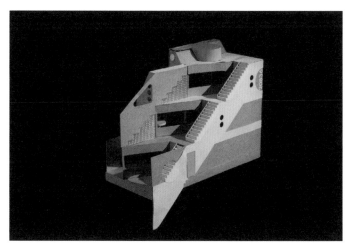

Login House
Malibu, 1979-82

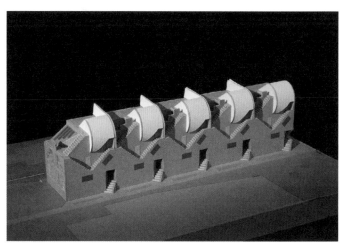

Pasadena Condominiums
Pasadena, 1979-81

Pinball House
Los Angeles, 1979-84

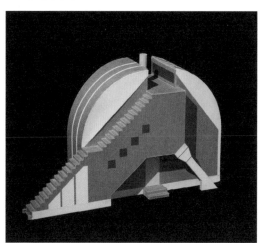

La Faille House
Malibu, 1979

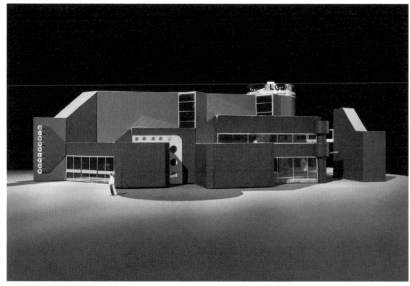

Gibraltar Savings and Loan
Los Angeles, 1979

ORIGINALLY PUBLISHED IN THE *LOS ANGELES TIMES*, 12 DEC 1979

Gallery Stirs Up Architects

JOHN DRYFUSS

Like the guest who knows when to go home and the lecturer who concludes before his audience nods off, the Architecture Gallery in Venice is about to make a well-timed exit. Saturday afternoon, at the tender age of ten weeks, it will go out of business.

In the established sense, the gallery at 209 E. San Juan Ave. hasn't been much of a business. It's never made a dime.

What it has done is more important. It has catalyzed a significant segment of the Los Angeles architectural community, precipitating a steamy brew of respect, anger, pride, jealousy, excitement, and interest. The brew seems hot enough to go on steaming for a while.

Beyond creating a healthy stir among architects, the gallery has provided a surprisingly receptive public with a chance to see work by an avant-garde group of art-oriented architects.

During each of the past nine weeks it has exhibited drawings, paintings and models by a different practitioner or small firm.

FINAL SMATTERING

The gallery's swan song offers a glimpse of work from each previous exhibition. This final show will be open from noon to 6 p.m. through Saturday.

What is there for all to see is a smattering of architecture from the drawing boards of Los Angeles men (there have been no women in the series), some of whom will almost surely emerge in the next decade or two as significant, original-thinking designers of the built environment.

One of them, Frank Gehry, already is in that exclusive circle.

The series of exhibitions illustrated that a few of his colleagues have the wherewithal to join him, and that others don't.

Architect Coy Howard, who introduced the series in a lecture at the Southern California Institute of Architecture (SCI-Arc), nicely evaluated the situation in a subsequent interview:

DEVELOPMENT PROCESS

"Things don't bloom full grown," he said. "This group is developing. Some will sell out. Some will drop out. And three or four will be significant."

Howard, who is a highly perceptive, strongly opinionated architect, pointed out that work by members of the "will-be-significant" faction tends to be obscure, theatrical, and trendy.

Critical as the adjectives sound, Howard intended no indictment. He considers those qualities part of the growing, searching process that can lead to work that is at once excellent, original and significant.

He is right. Only a few architects ever develop work that is simultaneously original, significant, and excellent. Those few are likely to experience growing pains reflected by obscure, theatrical, and trendy designs.

The tragedy and the indictment are reserved for architects whose work fails to progress beyond those reflections.

It is the obscurity, theatricality,

and trendiness of work in the series of exhibitions that has engendered much of the criticism from some established architects.

Why, they ask, is so much attention being showered on undeveloped architects? Why does the "me-too-ism" of eclectic work receive so much acclaim? Why do architects whose designs represent so few built projects rate all the publicity that comes from weekly reviews in the press?

Part of their deeply felt response seems to stem from pride and jealousy. The well-established professionals have worked long, hard years to get where they are, and they'd like a bit of the attention falling to the young Turks.

Another part of the reaction sounds suspiciously like fear. An architectural mode may be growing from the trend toward building design that pays old-fashioned attention to function but treats form with extreme, artistic innovation. Would such a mode leave some respected, successful practitioners by the architectural wayside?

DESERVING PUBLICITY

There are answers to all those questions.

Architects whose work has been exhibited in the series deserve publicity because some of them are making designs that are courageous and thoughtful and—above all—may be cobblestones on the road to new emphasis on art in architecture.

If established architects are jealous of those designs or the publicity they spark, their reaction is understandable.

It is worth noting, however, that no one seems jealous of the professional gamble the designs represent, nor of the miniscule income they produce for all the exhibitors but Gehry, who has spent many years working toward the recognition and cash flow he enjoys today.

Some architects may harbor justifiable fears of eventually being left by the wayside in terms of being movers and shakers in their profession. But they won't be left behind in terms of work. There will always be clients who

COY HOWARD

prefer their time-tested approach to excellence in architecture.

It would be gratuitous to present a pecking order in an effort to predict which developing architects are most likely to become historically significant, which ones may drop out, which may sellout.

But it would be equally unjustifiable to ignore Craig Hodgetts and Robert Mangurian, whose combined efforts show such great promise.

Their South Side Settlement community center in Columbus, Ohio (which was the mainstay of their exhibit), combines historicism, originality, and practicality to an extent demonstrated by no other architect in the exhibition series except Gehry.

If they can overcome some professional problems (not the least of which are a history of having built very few projects and of being two of the world's worst businessmen), Mangurian and Hodgetts appear most likely to achieve the significance predicted by Howard for three or four of the series' exhibitors.

Regardless of which, if any, exhibitors achieve such significance, they all have furthered their professional causes through the series of shows at the Architecture Gallery and related weekly lectures at SCI-Arc.

They have created an increased aura of legitimacy around their work. They have engendered a sense of community and excitement among artistically oriented architects, thereby increasing their professional momentum. And they have fired serious discussion among other architects about initiating exhibitions and lectures.

Credit for those results goes to architect Thom Mayne and to SCI-Arc, where he teaches. Mayne developed the series and co-sponsored it with the school.

Coy Howard will summarize the lectures and exhibits in a talk at 8 tonight at SCI-Arc, 1800 Berkeley St., Santa Monica. ⁂

Coy Howard was born in Dallas, Texas in 1943. He studied architecture at the University of Texas (B. Arch, 1966), and after a three-year teaching stint at Oklahoma State University, relocated to Los Angeles to study urban planning at UCLA. Upon graduation in 1971, Howard joined the UCLA architecture and urban design faculty, where he remained until 1977. He founded Coy Howard and Company in 1973. By 1977, he had won his first *P/A* Award (for the Boudov Residence) and had been named one of Robert A.M. Stern's "40 under 40."

Though he did not exhibit work at the Architecture Gallery, Howard's two lectures at SCI-Arc set the tone for the events and his opinions gave shape to much of John Dreyfuss's concluding review of the exhibitions in the *Los Angeles Times*. His work during the period spanned from architecture to graphic design to furniture. In each, he deployed a range of media as he attempted to move beyond the functional determinism of orthodox modernism to engage more emphatically architecture's social, psychological, and perceptual dimensions. His crisp ink-on-mylar drawings for the Rinaldi Residence and LACMA's 1976 Scythian Gold exhibition, for example, stand in stark contrast to his evocative graphite renderings for the Wolfenstein and Boudov residences. Howard maintained close ties to the Venice-based art scene through the 1970s, and his interdisciplinary ambitions at the time are perhaps best captured in his "drawls," a kind of hybrid drawing/model he invented and executed in cardboard, encaustic, wood, bronzing, and other materials. Eerie, if unintended, premonitions of the "Dead Tech" aesthetic later pursued by many Los Angeles architects in the 1980s and '90s, the drawls combine the abstract precision of architectural projections with an entropic physicality that resonates equally with Rauschenberg's combines and the anonymous grunge of Pico Boulevard, one of Howard's oft-invoked muses.

Howard taught briefly at SCI-Arc in 1979-80 and returned permanently in 1986. He directed SCI-Arc's undergraduate program from 1986 to '87 and continues to lead studios and seminars at the school. In 1991, while still teaching at SCI-Arc, he created the Environmental Arts program at Otis College of Art and Design, which he directed until 1995. In 2008, he was the Eliel Saarinen Distinguished Visiting Professor at the University of Michigan and he was the Bernoudy Architect in Residence at the American Academy in Rome in 2011-12. Howard continues to work across a range of media, recently turning significant attention to computer-generated renderings. His work has been published and exhibited widely and has been included in the permanent collections of the Museum of Modern Art and the Metropolitan Museum of Art in New York, the Museum of Fine Arts in Boston, and the Denver Art Museum.

COY HOWARD—*Roar*

Dylan started it
He sang "Ballad of a Thin Man"
Someone mumbled, "Go West Young Man"
Weeks pass
Ten
Mumbling again
Terry Allen ended it with "The Art Mob"

Somewhere between mumblings
Ten guys
Some soloists, others duets
Placed their bets
And then
No password just a look
Boarded the train
Each picking
Carefully
Which car, which seat
Avoiding others,
Or getting close enough to hear
Whispered confidences
Insecurities, bravado
Sounding the same
Squeaky
Young
Voices change
White hats, Black hats
Circus performers, cowboys
And stow-away tramps, wannabe princes
And sometime sorcerers

Traveling, "Go West Young Man"
Through Burma-Shave towns
Seeing what counts and what doesn't
What lasts and what shouldn't
From ice cream stick forts
To tuned carburetors
Hijacking history

Truth traveling
In the shadow
First one side then the other
The train snakes the terrain
Rocking like a cradle
Climbing for the high chair

Two fathers
The Ring Master and the Engineer
Stoking
Every log a longing
This engine can't break
Hex signs, voodoo symbols, biblical curses
Revival tents and secret handshakes
Everywhere

Traveling to places
With no names
Peeking through keyhole tunnels
Flickering lights Plato shadows
Looking for clues for crimes to commit

Way station dogs
Chasing their tails
Speechifying
Angel finger drawings
Dr. Caligari visions

Not footprints just bread crumbs
Desires don't explain
They just draw lines
To see who might step across
Strutting rock stars
Or just waiters
Waiting to be legends
Assaulting, seducing

Some riding the train like a horse
The Pony Express from there to here,
Changing cars
Sensitivities hidden
In their eccentricities
Habits more than visions
Those mannerisms and quirks
Sometimes with and then against
A timeless changing world
The weirdness of the ordinary
The wealth of the vernacular
More black shanty town than Parisian Palace

Whitman wails, Ginsberg howls
A "coulda-been-a-contender"
Challenge to a duel

Cards are played
Poker-faced bluffs are called
Traveling
"Go West Young Man"
Tracks fork
Trains change
Snakes lose their skins
Guardians and Gatekeepers
The demons of discarded logics
Proselytizing in the aisles

But this engine won't break
"Go West Young Man"
Every log a longing
This engine roars

Back alleys and junkyards
Celebrating a world
Unfinished
Echoing east

Through white silences of old traditions
Traveling to unmapped corners of the psyche
Seeing only
Reflections
Themselves and phantom towns
Rising fading
Mutely
Echoing
Like a racing rumor
Way out ahead
No need to dress
Echoing
Echoing
This engine roars.

October 2012

SELECTED WORKS, 1975-1980

Although Coy Howard did not exhibit work at the Architecture Gallery, this selection of roughly contemporary projects is included to offer a sense of his architectural output at the time.

Wolfenstein Residence
Los Angeles, 1975

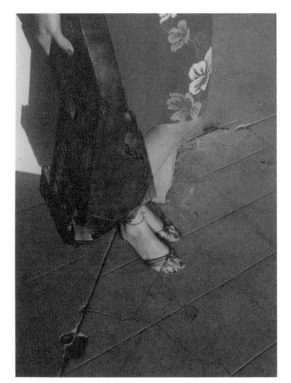

Gross Residence
Los Angeles, 1978

Daniel Studio
Los Angeles, 1980

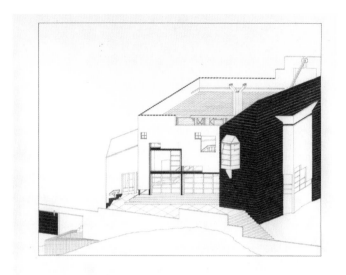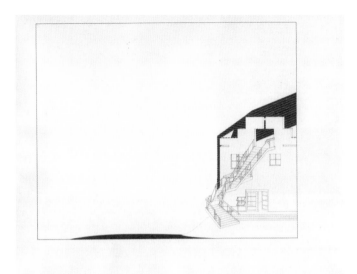

Rinaldi Residence
Los Angeles, 1976

Boudov Residence
Los Angeles, 1976

ORIGINALLY PUBLISHED IN THE *LOS ANGELES HERALD EXAMINER*, DECEMBER 19, 1979

The Importance of Being Coy

JOSEPH GIOVANNINI

The magnetism of New York's Architecture scene has long distorted architecture in Southern California—many local architects have lined up like so many filings pointed east, attentive to the latest trends.

There is indeed, much work of interest built on the East Coast, and many of the leading national architecture schools are located there. Most architecture publishing is done in the east, and the publications naturally take on an East Coast emphasis. While eastern architects have only a vague awareness of what is going on in California, architects in California are all too aware of ideas emanating out of the east.

Deserved or not, Southland architects have acquired a regional inferiority complex similar to the broader cultural sensitivities many Southland residents feel toward the east. Recent graduates of Ivy League architecture schools take on a certain cachet once they arrive in Southland. Students, and architects, from California are treated in New York like exotic creatures fresh out of the manzanita—aboriginal Californians: raw, nonverbal, blissed out on sun, one too many motorcycle rides, without a helmet. Frank Gehry is the most recent native to be shown off in a city that devours the exotic—the cosmopolitan Philip Johnson has paraded the probably befuddled, certainly rumpled, Gehry around town in his limousine, like the first Samoan to visit St. James' Court.

The draw of the east has long bothered whatever sense of cohesion Los Angeles architects might feel in their dispersed city. It has therefore been refreshing to see Los Angeles' "alternative" architecture school, the Southern California Institute of Architecture, in Santa Monica, initiate a series of lectures that has featured Southland architects exclusively—a series called "Current LA: 10 Viewpoints." The lectures rippled into the city via a temporary architecture gallery in Venice where the architects' drawings and models were shown, along with video tapes of the lectures.

The series primarily focused on work done locally; it incidentally grouped the architects into more of a community than they themselves were probably aware of. Los Angeles, as a city, disperses architects, like everyone else, and the series was an occasion for the architects to see each other's work as well as to show their own.

Although there was little debate after any of the lectures, there was some larger controversy in the larger Los Angeles architectural community about the series as a whole—about what was considered by some to be a narrowly, implicitly elitist, and finally self-isolating approach to architecture. The series did not draw widely from across Los Angeles, but it did draw deeply within the more specific West Side art-oriented architecture community.

The work presented was too diverse to represent a school of thought—possibly because Los Angeles itself is too centrifugal to bring opinions into a "school"—but it did demonstrate a common attitude. All the architects were serious about architecture nearly to the point of cult; they approached architecture as a search rather than a question they have already answered; there was an implicit freshness, tentativeness, and optimism about their explorations. Avant-gardism was the accepted mode of design—the conventional mind set was to violate expected architectural behavior, and think the always new architectural thought. In this consciously avant-garde group, the most radical architect was, by default, the most traditional and commercial—Frank Dimster—someone who was not generally accepted by the rest of the group. The architects were, generally, not interested in sedate, comfortable, familiar design, and would be more prone to look for their images in a Sears catalogue than in the inventory of modern architecture classics.

Frank Gehry was the spiritual uncle of the group—the Establishment naughty-boy who has brought chain-link fence off the parking-lot and into the museum. Avant-gardism was so accepted as a thought mode that Mr. Gehry could actually show a dismembered house scattered like a body over its hillside site, and not elicit any comment from the apparently accepting audience. Throughout the lecture, the lack of debate was conspicuous by its absence; the only real dialogue was perhaps the sequence of opinions expressed on a weekly basis by each lecturer.

Except for Gehry's and Dimster's buildings, the work presented was limited in extent, and confined primarily to single-family residences. Southern California, despite the high cost of building, is still one of the great enclaves of the detached house, and in the buoyant real estate market of the last several years, young architects eager for a showcase building have poured their ideas into residential commissions. For architects, the single-family house has traditionally been a building type that supports experimentation—possibly because the clients' ego is so firmly identified with it. Most of the work shown was so individualistic that it is no surprise the young architects have attracted few corporate or commercial clients. Architectural experimentation does not interest banks.

Given the small volume of work, it is difficult to generalize about the buildings of even a single architect, let alone about those of the whole group. Still, there was some overlap. Most of the architects went beyond the traditional boundaries of their profession for images and thoughts, and many used other arts as a tool or an analogy to shape and inform their architecture: Gehry used painting and sculpture; Frederick Fisher, collage; Roland Coate, painting; Eugene Kupper, drawing and modelmaking; Peter de Bretteville, technology as art; Craig Hodgetts and Bob Mangurian, the machine as art. Eric Moss, the most verbal of those presented, resorted to his formidable arsenal of concepts, cynically interpreted. All lavishly explored their buildings in drawings and models that would pain an efficiency expert.

Indeed, many of the projects were overdrawn and overstudied. Gehry's weren't, and they generally retained their vitality. Hodgetts and Mangurian's Settlement House in Columbus, Ohio, achieved a gravity so fundamental, and satisfying, that one doesn't care how much labor was spilled over the compulsively inked drawings.

In most cases, time and effort spent studying the buildings by nature of drawing and modelmaking, tended to turn the buildings into formalistic objects. As objects, some of the most interesting effects were simply artistic compositions of architectural elements and colors—compositions that are difficult, and sometimes embarrassing, to talk about in the usual architectural language of function ("this does that"). Eric Moss' buildings, though cloaked in ratiocination, were often striking simply because of a sculpted or painted effect. Gehry's buildings have considerable presence because they use just the right wrong images that are abrasively correct for their time and place—chain link, unpainted plywood, blacktop. There is on the West Side, a loosely "punk" aesthetic (the beauty in being nasty: *Wet* magazine, *Stuff* magazine, etc.) that has filtered through to some architects who presented their work at the SCI-Arc lectures.

Although it was refreshing that almost no one presented work imitating the New York schools of White Architecture, warmed-up Le Corbusier, or historicism, it was disappointing that so few showed any sustained interest in solar energy (except Dimster) and in the regionalism of where they were building (except Coate and Fisher). Most of the architects addressed formal issues such as the layering of architectural elements and the architectural response to a particular site, but few explored specifically California images. For people who by and large professed contextualism, the omission was surprising. No one even glancingly referred to the larger, current issues in Los Angeles—the millions of square feet of office space being built downtown, the Library issue, the pending earthquake ordinance, or the historic neighborhoods now threatened with redevelopment.

Perhaps it takes some personal isolation to develop an individual architectural vision, but protracted isolation may finally diminish the scope of the architectural vision and impoverish the images. If the avant-garde is too far in front of the society it supposedly leads, it loses its own context and becomes irrelevant.

The SCI-Arc lecture series was a valuable event for Los Angeles. One hopes that the school will not lose the momentum of this strong precedent by waiting several years for the same architects to generate more buildings. There are other interesting architects in the area, and so many more subjects to explore. ⁂

PART TWO

A CONFEDERACY
OF HERETICS

ECCENTRIC PROJECTIONS
ANDREW ZAGO

Though it is always inflected by tangential circumstances, the most significant discourse in any field involves close attention to the developmental tendencies and organizational specificities of the work itself. Such discourse—of barely audible subtleties of tone and rhythm among musicians, of arcane pathogenic trajectories among medical doctors, of obscure rhetorical constructions among lawyers— unfolds primarily as an expert conversation among colleagues. Where a historian rightly constructs links between subject matter and broader social, political, and cultural contexts, an architect attends first and foremost to the problem of form as such. This is the nature of disciplinary conversations at SCI-Arc. Though its public and scholarly profiles are expanding, SCI-Arc remains at its core an architects' school. As in other fields, its discourse ranges widely, but a recurrent and seminal theme involves the close reading of architecture's form, geometry, and underlying spatial scaffolding. Close attention to such particulars is the only way to address what is truly radical—etymologically, of or going to the root—in a work of architecture.

A Confederacy of Heretics is best understood with this condition in mind. Rather than dwelling on the usual musty tropes of what characterized the emerging Los Angeles scene in the late 1970s—inexpensive materials, seemingly unfinished construction, garish colors, and an informality of lifestyle— this exhibition calls attention to the subtle progress of spatial and geometric invention found in some of these works. It has less to do with specific historical projects or architects exhibited than with articulating an ongoing conversation among colleagues.

On first examination there was little of current relevance in the nine one-week exhibitions held in Thom Mayne's Architecture Gallery in 1979. Barring a few notable exceptions, most of the work

on the display was either by architects still finding their voice or by others who never would. This assortment of juvenilia and dead-ends seemed to offer little fodder for an architectural exhibition beyond presenting a curious historical footnote. Closer examination, however—of the works, of the concurrent lectures, and of other later works by some of these architects and of others not in the shows—revealed the nascent stirrings of genuinely new features within the discipline, features that seem to occur here first and which went on to have an outsized influence on the field. So, like paleontologists interpreting protomorphic wing bones in the fossilized remains of dinosaurs, we sought for this exhibition not just those features that were common and commonly understood in that period but also those that would prove relevant only later. Thus, A Confederacy of Heretics does not recreate the content of the original shows. Rather, it attempts to identify and extract a few potent strands of disciplinary DNA which passed through the Architecture Gallery to impact the development of architecture in the ensuing decades.

We selected and organized the materials in the exhibition according to a taxonomy of increasingly eccentric spatial projections outlined on the following pages. These projections are found at times in the buildings themselves, at times in their depiction, and at times in both.

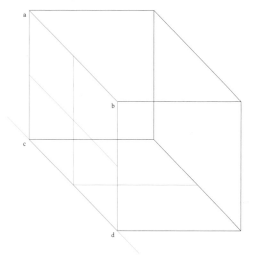

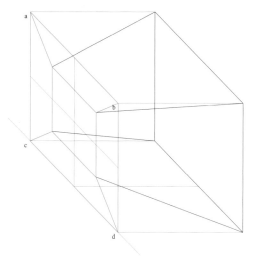

PARALLEL PROJECTION

Parallel projection, chiefly the axonometric, was a dominant spatial model for progressive architecture in the 1960s and early 1970s, as exhibited in work ranging from the intellectual abstractions of Peter Eisenman to the suggestive figurations of James Stirling. In this exhibition, projects such as Peter de Bretteville's Ajax Car Rental, Morphosis's Reidel Medical Building, and Studio Works's first scheme for the South Side Settlement operate within this dominant model. More extreme experiments conceived of the parallel projection as the extrusion of novel figures as is seen in Cesar Pelli's first Pacific Design Center building (the so-called Blue Whale) of 1975. Examples of this sort of figural extrusion here include Eric Owen Moss's Morganstern Warehouse and Gibraltar Savings and Loan Bank and, more overtly, his Pinball House and his first design for the Pasadena Condominiums.

PERSPECTIVE

A renewed interest in perspective was part of a reactionary postmodern tendency that emerged in the field in the 1970s. As a mannered re-introduction, it was accompanied by an interest in historic references, stable geometries, and evidence of authenticity (the use of Prismacolor pencils, for example, as opposed to the more mechanistic effect of Pantone adhesive sheets for coloring drawings). Perspective is here used broadly, referring to a general sensibility even when literal perspectival constructions are not employed. This sensibility is seen in many of the works exhibited in the original Architecture Gallery shows. Here, it can be seen in Studio Works's second scheme for the South Side Settlement, in Frederick Fisher's Solar Crematorium and Observatory, and in the exhibited projects by Frank Dimster and Roland Coate.

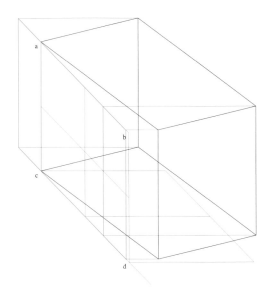

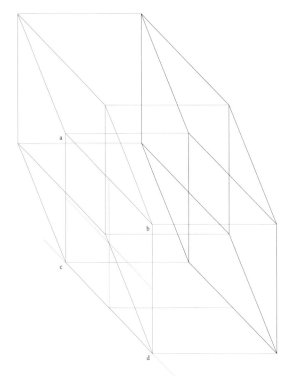

PLAN ROTATION

In the late 1970s and early 1980s, the plan rotation (sometimes referred to as a "grid shift") was a dominant feature in East Coast architecture especially among the students and protégés of Colin Rowe. With the exception of Morphosis, who used it often in early projects, it was a recessive trait among Los Angeles practices. Examples included here are Morphosis's Sedlak House and, to a limited degree, Moss's La Faille House.

FLAT PROJECTION

This period saw a new interest in drawings and models and, importantly, a willful conflation of their status with that of the building itself. This is most clearly seen in experiments with flat and near-flat projections. In building, this is seen in Frank Gehry's facade of his World Savings Bank building in Burbank, where the mullions are arranged to simulate a perspective projection of the interior volume. More ambitiously, Gehry's Wagner House negotiates between volumes with a geotropic orientation and those normal to the hillside slope, creating, in certain views, the sense that the house is an axonometric projection. In this it is reminiscent of the axonometric model of Peter Eisenman's House X, but in the Wagner House the flattened and eccentric projections are a feature the architecture itself, whereas Eisenman's projective eccentricities only occur in the models and drawings. (In his publication of the project in his 1985 monograph, Gehry shows a detail of a Chinese painting depicting persons seated at an isometric table. It is labeled, simply, "dining room.") In a fascinating pair of models, Frederick Fisher delaminates the facade of his Caplin House into two distinct, bas-relief models at wildly different scales—one of the interior and one of the exterior. A more explicit conflation is found in Coy Howard's drawls, hybrid constructions of his own invention that operate somewhere between traditional drawing and model-making. Shown here are two drawls for the Daniel Studio and one each for the Gross Residence and the Palmer Eckard Condominium.

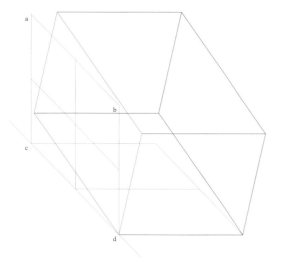

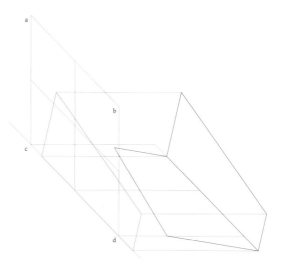

SECTIONAL ROTATION

Though it later would be widely adopted, the sectional rotation was nearly unique to Los Angeles architecture in this
period. More radical than the plan rotation—which disrupts
a building's organizational logic but leaves its tectonic logic
intact—the sectional rotation defies tectonic logic. It disrupts
the gravity-responsive orientation of construction and introduces the diagonal line liberated from the plan. A precursor to
Deconstruction, the feature is seen in several of Frank Gehry's
projects in the 1970s and achieves its iconic expression in the
kitchen window of his own house in Santa Monica. It may also
be observed in Moss's 708 House, and as a recessive feature in
Moss's Pinball House and in Morphosis's Sedlak House. Note
that in the Sedlak House it is the plan rotation, coupled with a
sloped skylight, which produces the resultant angled surface
in elevation. This device is seen first in Gehry's building for
Gemini GEL in 1976-79.

GRAPHIC WRAP

Part of the interest in the autonomous life of architectural
drawings and models was the obsessive production of graphics
derived from projects. From the working drawings of the South
Side Settlement, Studio Works produced a series of graphic
works incorporating marbled papers and color Xerox transfers
of pop imagery. An extensive series of experiments with the
then-novel technology of color Xeroxing resulted in a series of
faux postage stamps by Morphosis, which stand as important
precursors to Thom Mayne's ongoing production of autonomous and semi-autonomous drawings and assemblages. If
with his drawls Coy Howard made drawings that were like
buildings, another tendency—the graphic wrap—introduced
the flat and wrapped graphic as a building technique. This is
seen most clearly in Eric Moss's Fun House, his 708 House
and, later, in Morphosis's Sedlak House. Moss's Petal House,
to the extent that the splaying of the roof may be understood as
a graphic rather than a tectonic modification, also exhibits this
tendency.

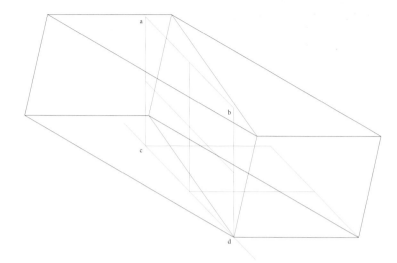

ECCENTRIC PROJECTION

In a 1979 SCI-Arc lecture Eric Moss illustrated his comments
on the progressive disintegration of the concept of the collective with a series of theaters. His final example was a small
theater in Arata Isozaki's 1974 Gunma Museum of Modern
Art, in Takasaki, Japan. Here, a cube was rotated eccentrically
within the theater volume and then projected as a graphic line
onto the inner walls of the theater. Isozaki referred to it as a
"shadow of slanted frame." This complex geometric construction (albeit built only as a series of painted lines) goes beyond
the previous categories of projection. While not unique to Los
Angeles (Daniel Libeskind's Micromegas were completed in
1978) the eccentric projection can be seen, in part, as an out-
growth of Los Angeles experiments. Also, in Los Angeles these
eccentric projections were seen early on as a building problem.
Eccentric projections open paths to the increasingly destabiliz-
ing, fragmented, and convoluted architecture of the late 1980s
and beyond. Such projections can be seen in Moss's Petal
House, Morphosis's Sixth Street House, and most completely
in the Gehry house.

The form and layout of the exhibition evokes these projections. Three shaped walls—one bisecting the library gallery and two dividing the main gallery—bracket the exhibition spaces into a series of geometric volumes that roughly parallel the sequence of projections here described. The wall in the library gallery sits sloping on the floor as a fragment of a perspective. In the main gallery, each side of each wall constructs a sectional rotation, followed by two complementary sides of a flat projection to, finally, an eccentric projection. Additionally, outside each gallery, giant enlargements of exhibited work by Morphosis and Studio Works take on and extend aspects of the graphic wrap.

Thus, *A Confederacy of Heretics* addresses a central question of space. As the scaffolding for cultural production, space has evolved through modernity from a rational, homogeneous, and extensive matrix into an increasingly complex, fragmentary, and irrational web. Just as European architects and explorers in the Renaissance sought control of and projection into deep space, these Los Angeles architects, facing the edge of the Western World and the end of Modernity, explored alternative avenues for spatial projection in the 1970s. Some of their work—not just buildings but also drawings, models, and other artifacts—confounded traditional principles of architectural organization and eventually outstripped East Coast architectural experiments. Though met with a degree of skepticism at the time, this Los Angeles work proved uncannily prescient of subsequent architectural directions.

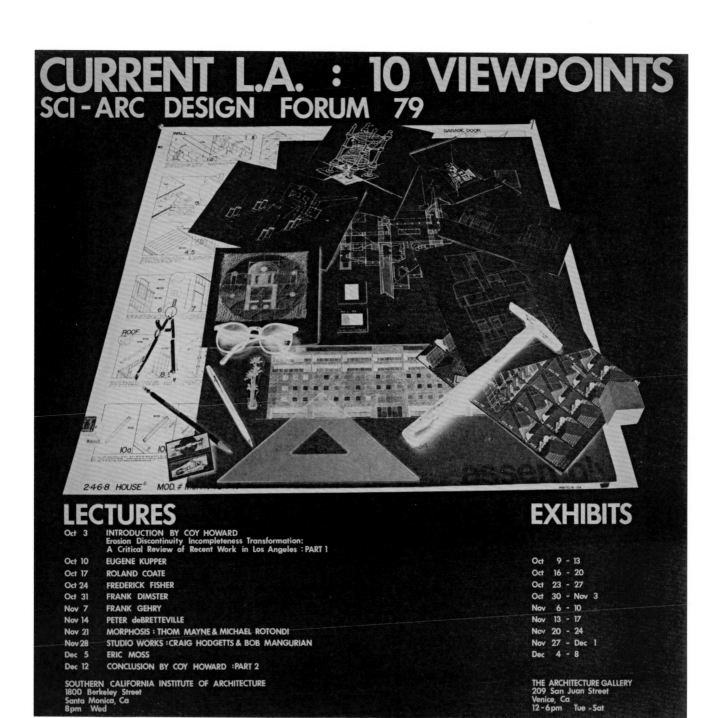

CURRENT L.A. : 10 VIEWPOINTS
SCI-ARC DESIGN FORUM 79

LECTURES

Oct 3	**INTRODUCTION BY COY HOWARD** Erosion Discontinuity Incompleteness Transformation: A Critical Review of Recent Work in Los Angeles : PART 1
Oct 10	EUGENE KUPPER
Oct 17	ROLAND COATE
Oct 24	FREDERICK FISHER
Oct 31	FRANK DIMSTER
Nov 7	FRANK GEHRY
Nov 14	PETER deBRETTEVILLE
Nov 21	MORPHOSIS : THOM MAYNE & MICHAEL ROTONDI
Nov 28	STUDIO WORKS : CRAIG HODGETTS & BOB MANGURIAN
Dec 5	ERIC MOSS
Dec 12	CONCLUSION BY COY HOWARD : PART 2

SOUTHERN CALIFORNIA INSTITUTE OF ARCHITECTURE
1800 Berkeley Street
Santa Monica, Ca
8pm Wed

EXHIBITS

Oct 9 - 13
Oct 16 - 20
Oct 23 - 27
Oct 30 - Nov 3
Nov 6 - 10
Nov 13 - 17
Nov 20 - 24
Nov 27 - Dec 1
Dec 4 - 8

THE ARCHITECTURE GALLERY
209 San Juan Street
Venice, Ca
12 - 6pm Tue - Sat

Current LA: 10 Viewpoints
1979
Morphosis (Thom Mayne and Michael Rotondi)
Diazo print. 20" x 20"

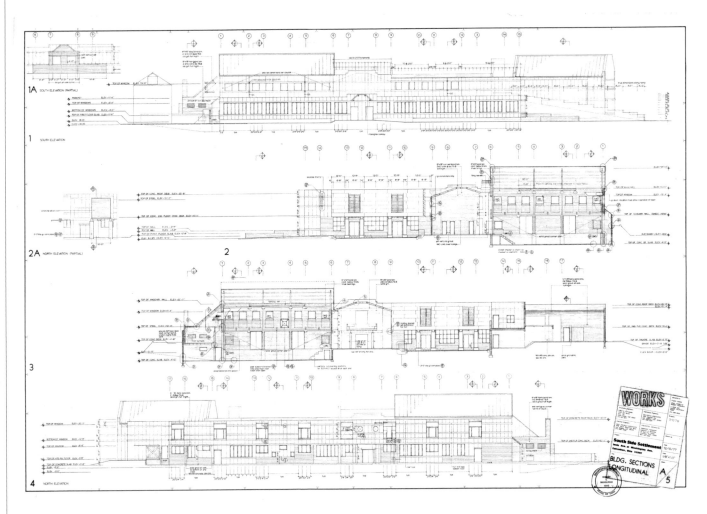

South Side Settlement
Columbus, Ohio, 1975-1980
Studio Works (Craig Hodgetts and Robert Mangurian)
Working drawings, second scheme
Graphite on linen. 45″ x 31″

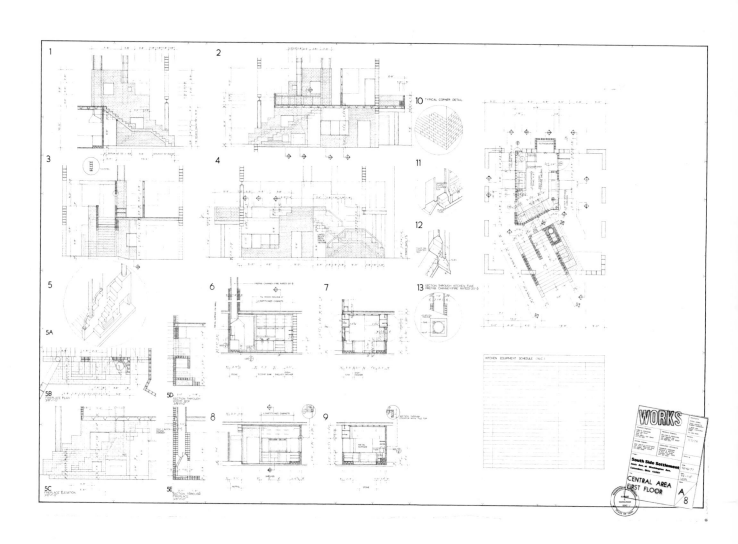

South Side Settlement

CENTRAL AREA
FIRST FLOOR

A
8

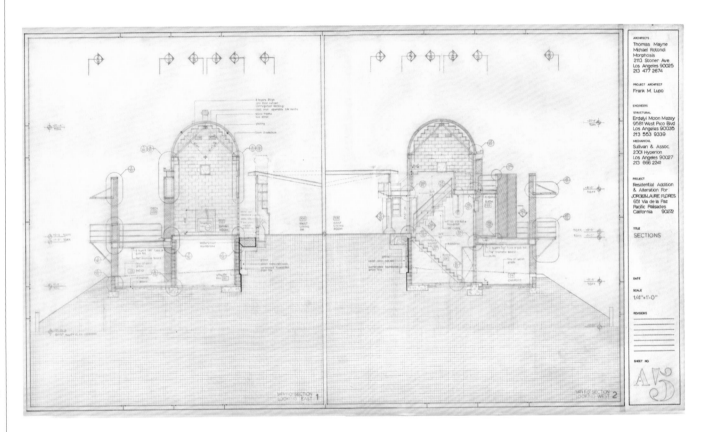

Flores Residence
Los Angeles, 1978
Morphosis (Thom Mayne and Michael Rotondi)
Working drawings
Graphite on linen. 30″ x 19″

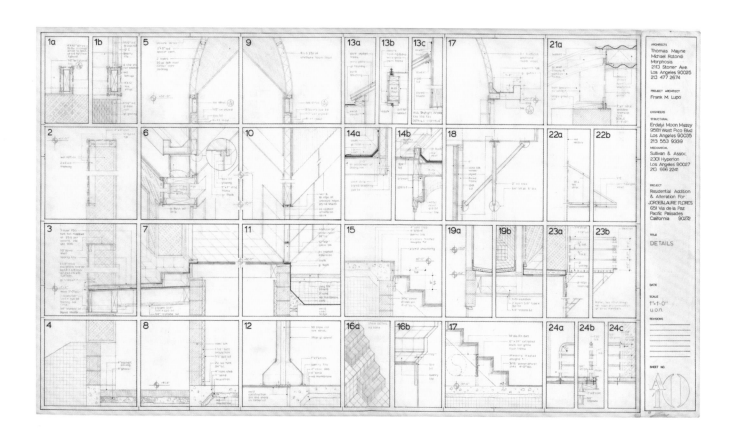

ARCHITECTS
Thomas Mayne
Michael Rotondi
Morphosis
2113 Stoner Ave.
Los Angeles 90025
213 477 2674

PROJECT ARCHITECT
Frank M. Lupo

ENGINEERS

STRUCTURAL
Erdelyi Moon Mezey
9581 West Pico Blvd
Los Angeles 90035
213 553 9339

MECHANICAL
Sullivan & Assoc.
2301 Hyperion
Los Angeles 90027
213 666 2241

PROJECT
Residential Addition
& Alteration For
JORGE&LAURE FLORES
651 Via de la Paz
Pacific Palisades
California 90272

TITLE
DETAILS

DATE

SCALE
1"=1'-0"
u.o.n.

REVISIONS

SHEET NO.

A0
10

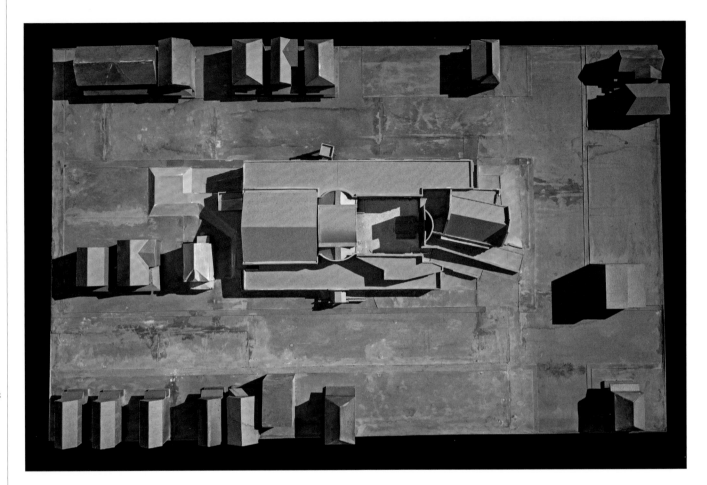

South Side Settlement
Columbus, Ohio, 1975-1980
Studio Works (Craig Hodgetts and Robert Mangurian)
Model, second scheme
Chipboard and wood. 64½″ x 39½″ x 5″

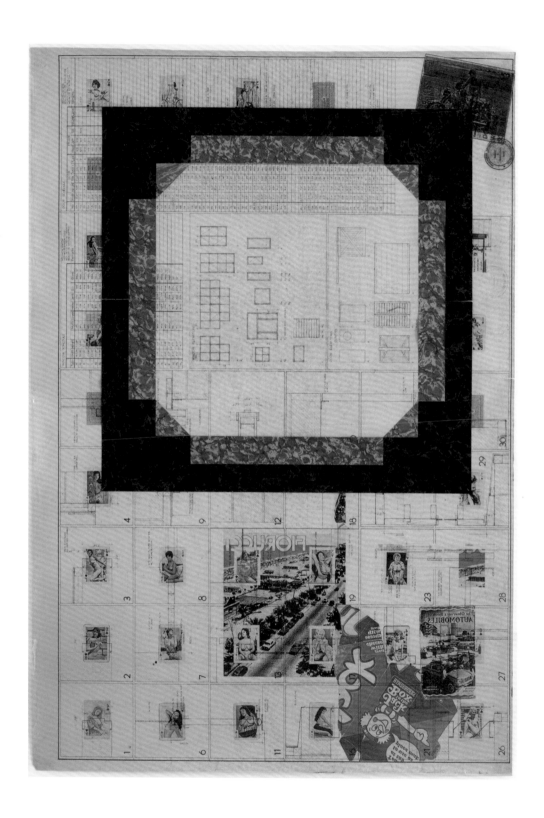

Second Scheme, working drawing collage, 1978
Collage on diazo print. 32″ x 45″

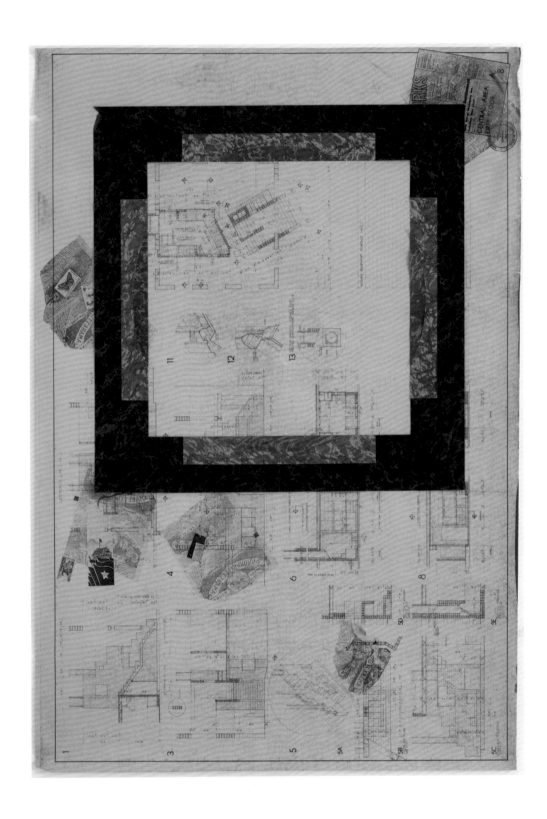

South Side Settlement
Columbus, Ohio, 1975-1980
Studio Works (Craig Hodgetts and Robert Mangurian)
Second Scheme, working drawing collages, 1978
Collage on diazo print. Each 32″ x 45″

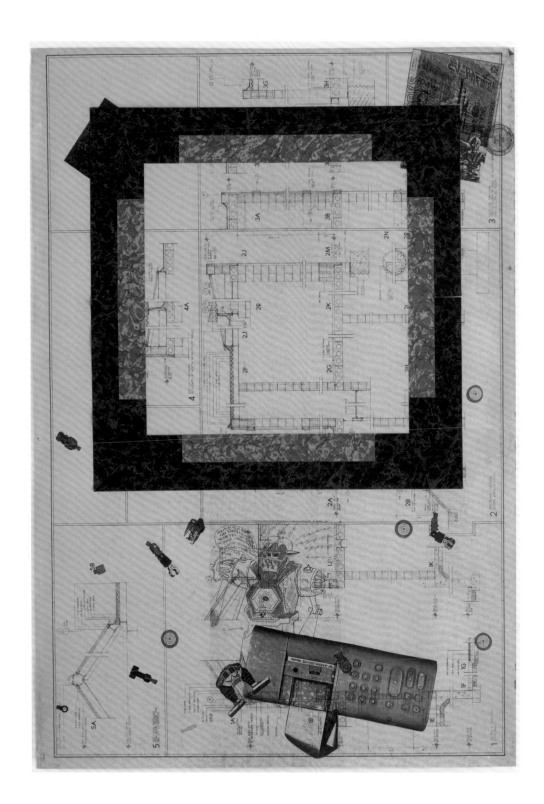

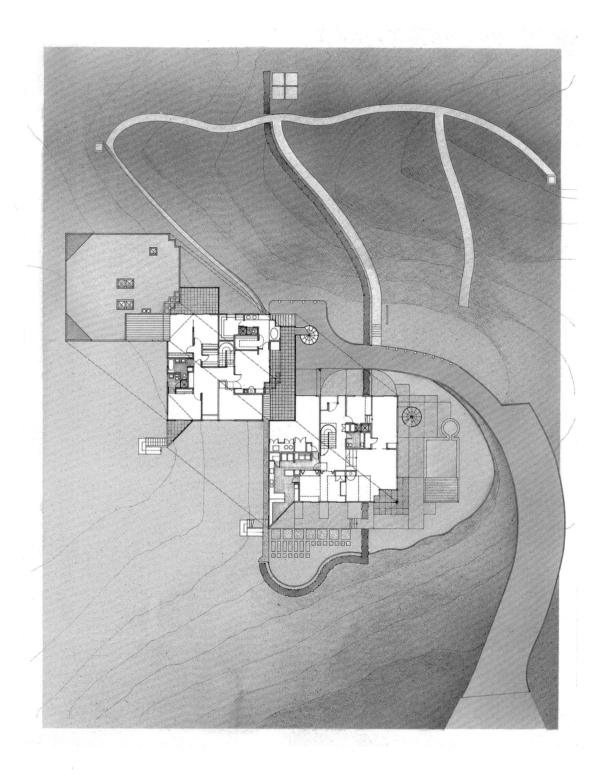

Dimster Residence
Los Angeles, 1983
Frank Dimster
Floor plans
Airbrush on board. 30″ x 36″

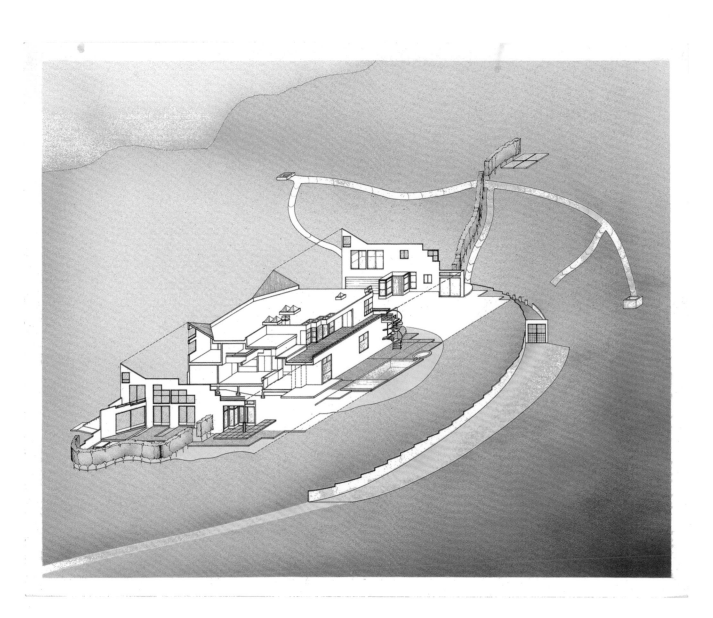

Exploded isometric
Airbrush on board. 36″ x 30″

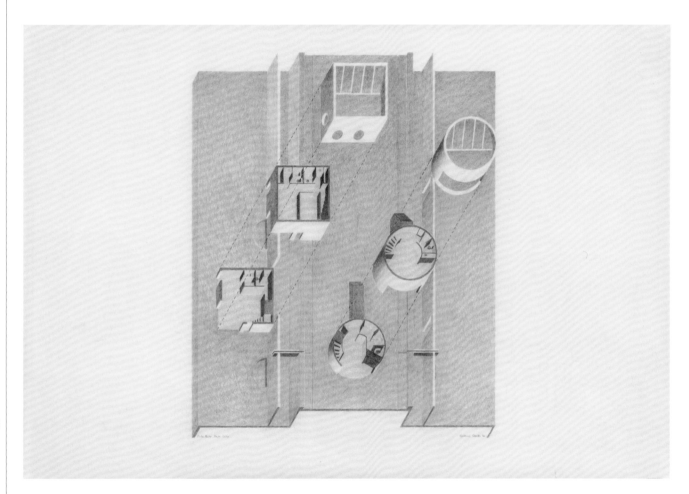

Twelve Houses at Cabo Bello
Baja California, Mexico, 1976
Roland Coate, Jr.
Exploded isometric
Colored pencil on vellum. 36″ x 24″

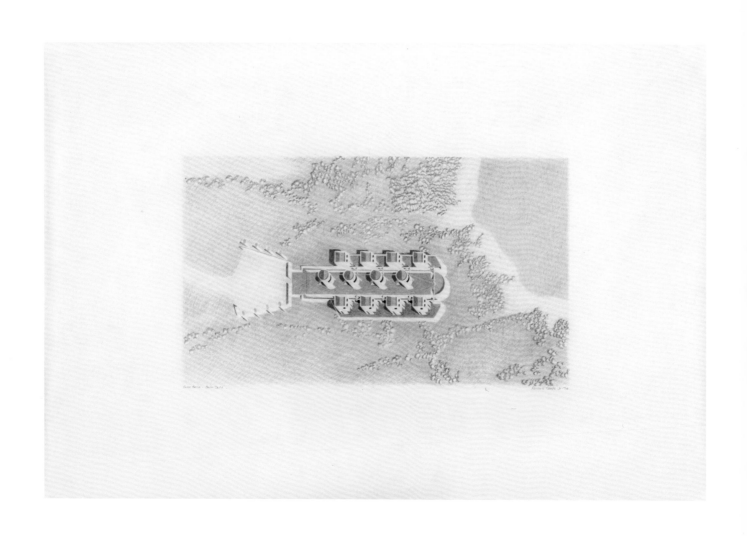

Site plan isometric
Colored pencil on vellum. 36″ x 24″

Observatory
1979
Frederick Fisher
Section
Colored pencil on paper. Two panels, each 28″ x 22″

Solar Crematory
1976
Frederick Fisher
Partial plan, section, and elevation
Colored pencil on vellum. 28″ x 36″

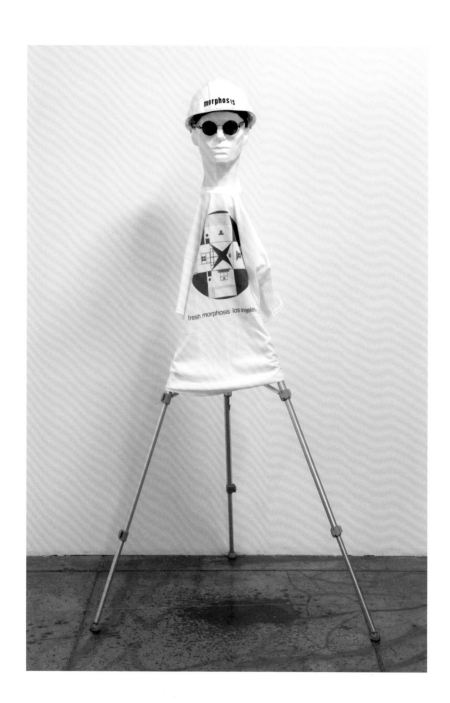

Conscience
1979 (reconstructed, 2013)
Morphosis (Thom Mayne and Michael Rotondi)
Tripod, T-shirt, artist's mannequin head, safety glasses, hardhat

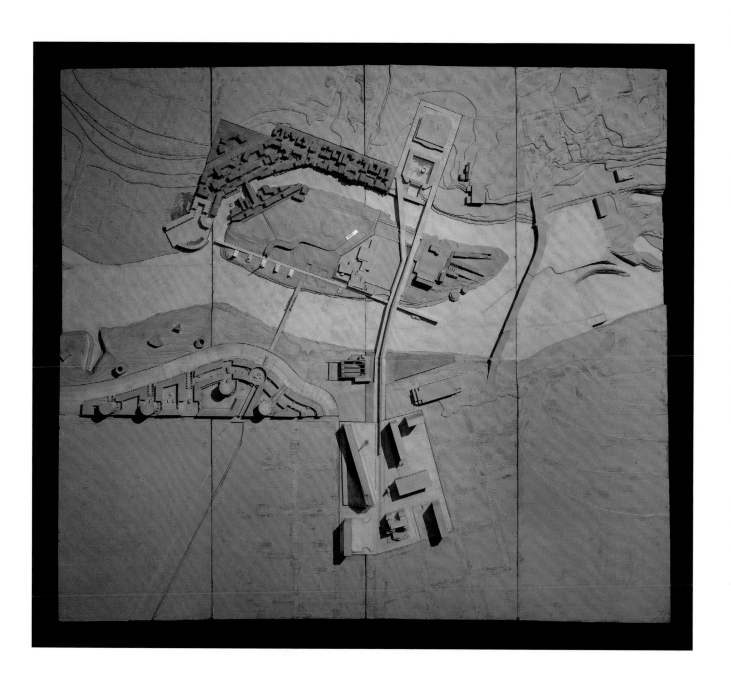

The River and The City
Nicollet Island, Minneapolis, Minnesota, 1976
Studio Works (Craig Hodgetts and Robert Mangurian)
Model
Cardboard, chipboard, and foam. 124″ x 105″ x 4″

132

South Side Settlement
Columbus, Ohio, 1975-1980
Studio Works (Craig Hodgetts and Robert Mangurian)
First scheme, *P/A* Awards submittal book, 1975
Seventeen bound pages. 14″ x 8½″

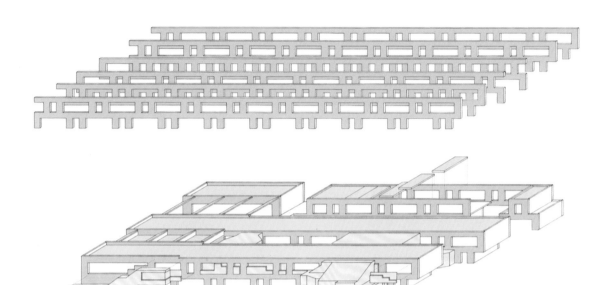

SYSTEMS

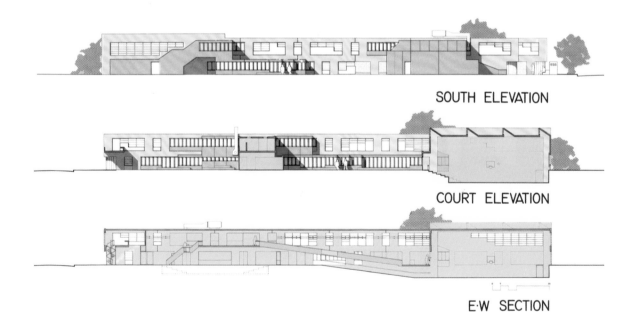

SOUTH ELEVATION

COURT ELEVATION

E·W SECTION

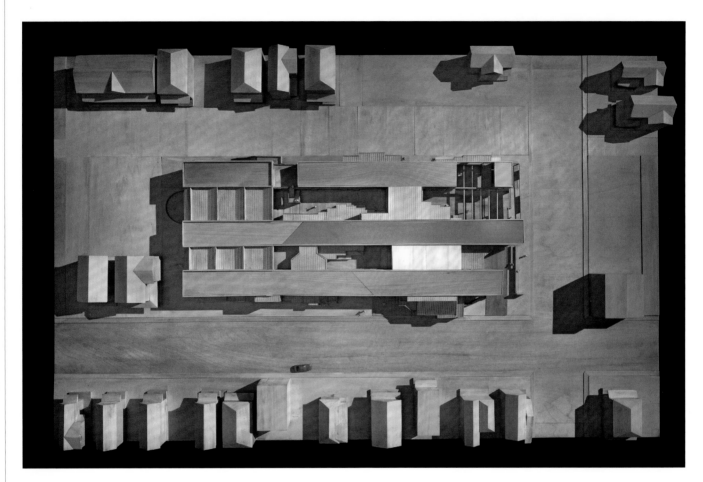

South Side Settlement
Columbus, Ohio, 1975-1980
Studio Works (Craig Hodgetts and Robert Mangurian)
Model, first scheme
Chipboard and wood. 64½″ x 39½″ x 5″

Isometric
Ink, pantone, and collage on paper. 11″ x 17″
Marianne Burkhalter, delineator

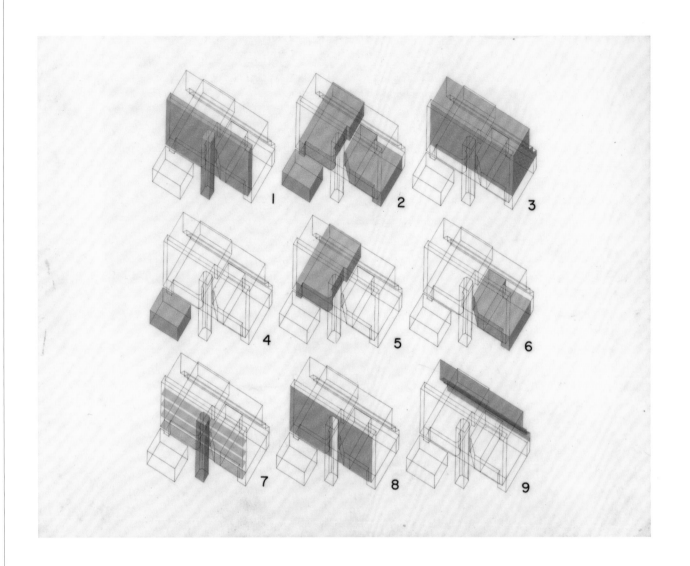

Reidel Medical Building
Tijuana, Mexico, 1976
Morphosis (Thom Mayne and Michael Rotondi)
Diagrams
Pantone and laminated plastic on print. 14″ x 12″

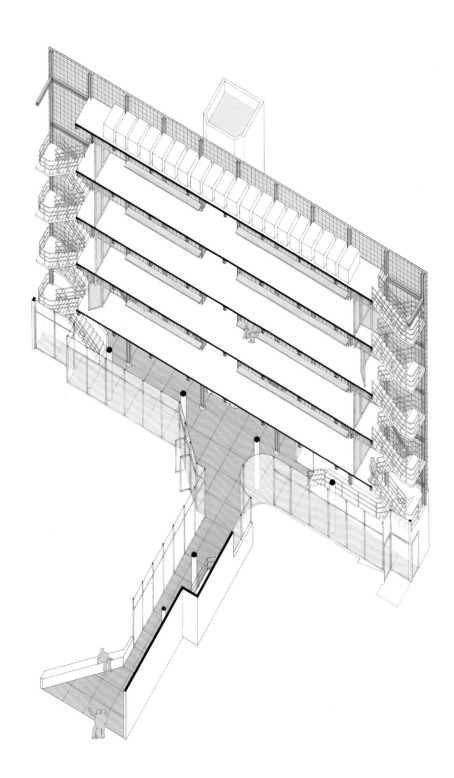

Circulation isometric
Pantone and laminated plastic on print. 14″ x 21½″

138

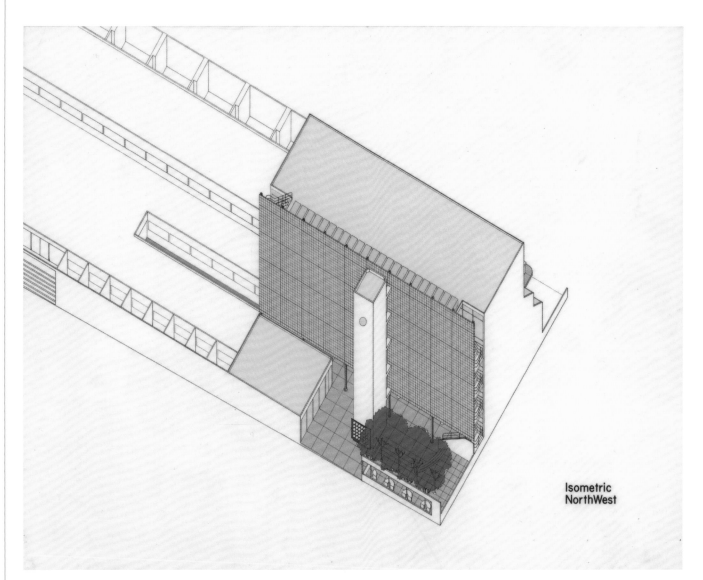

Isometric
NorthWest

Reidel Medical Building
Tijuana, Mexico, 1976
Morphosis (Thom Mayne and Michael Rotondi)
Isometric northwest
Pantone and laminated plastic on print. 14″ x 12″

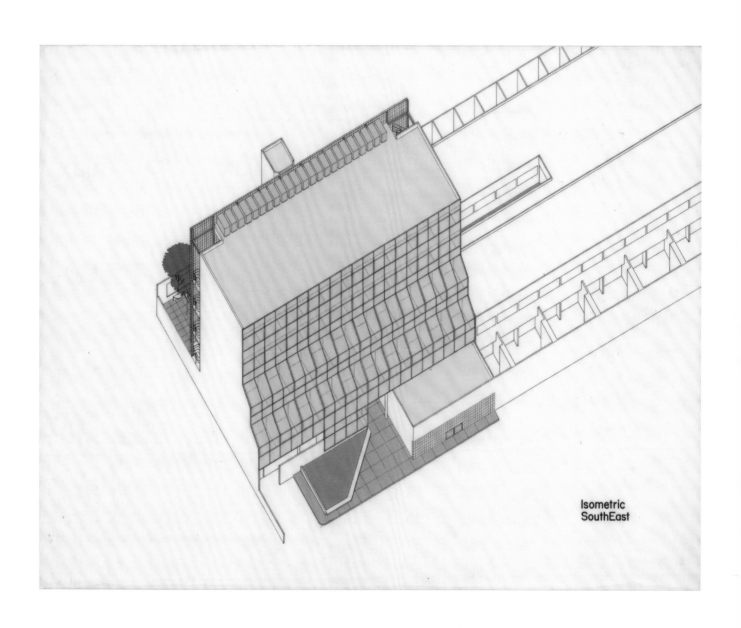

Isometric
SouthEast

Isometric southeast
Pantone and laminated plastic on print. 14″ x 12″

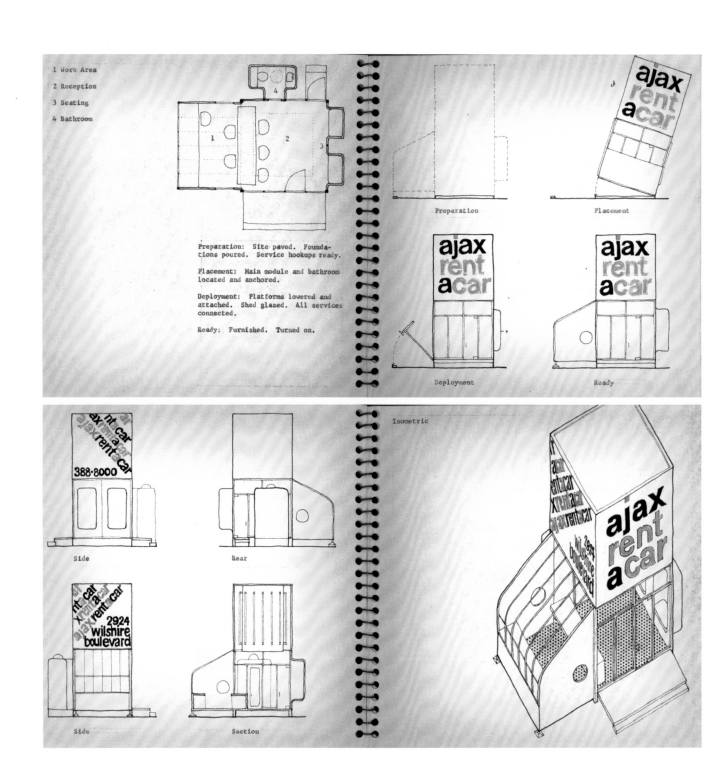

1 Work Area
2 Reception
3 Seating
4 Bathroom

Preparation: Site paved. Founda-
tions poured. Service hookups ready.

Placement: Main module and bathroom
located and anchored.

Deployment: Platforms lowered and
attached. Shed glazed. All services
connected.

Ready: Furnished. Turned on.

Preparation

Placement

Deployment

Ready

Side

Rear

Side

Section

Isometric

Ajax Car Rental
Los Angeles, 1973
Peter de Bretteville, Keith Godard, and Michael Rotondi
Brochure
Twenty four bound pages. 7″ x 7″

Scheme II

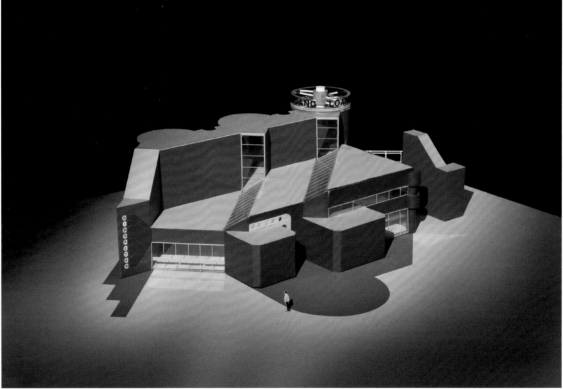

Gibraltar Savings and Loan
Los Angeles, 1979
Eric Owen Moss
Model
Chipboard and colored paper. 23½″ x 24½″ x 5½″

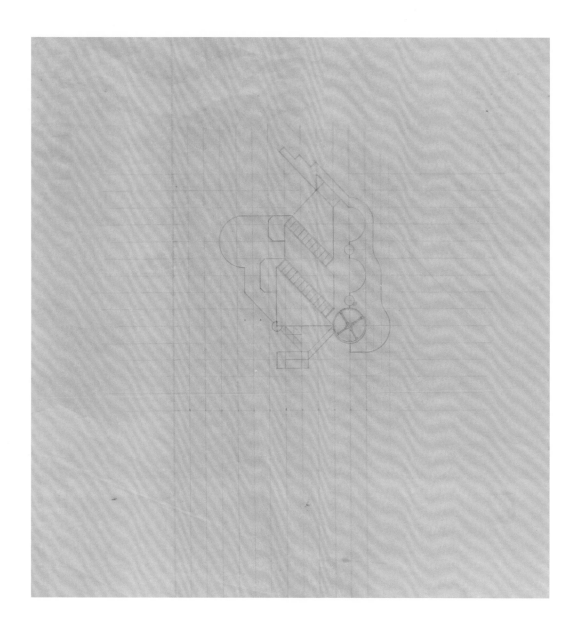

Plan study
Pencil on tracing paper. 9½″ x 8½″

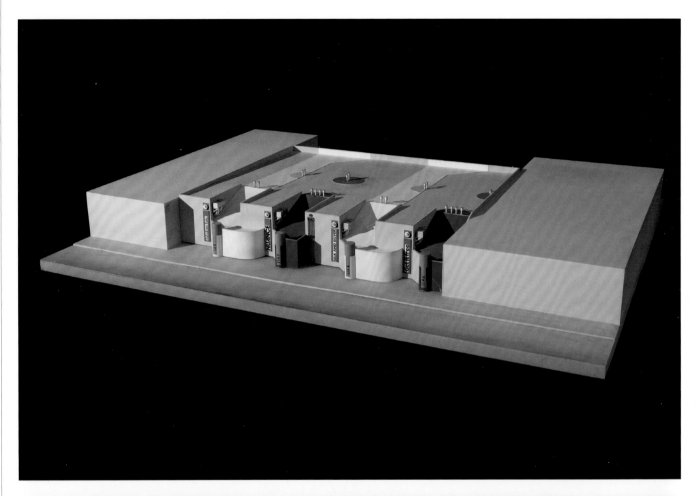

Morganstern Warehouse
Los Angeles, 1977-79
Eric Owen Moss
Model
Chipboard and colored paper. 28″ x 24″ x 3″

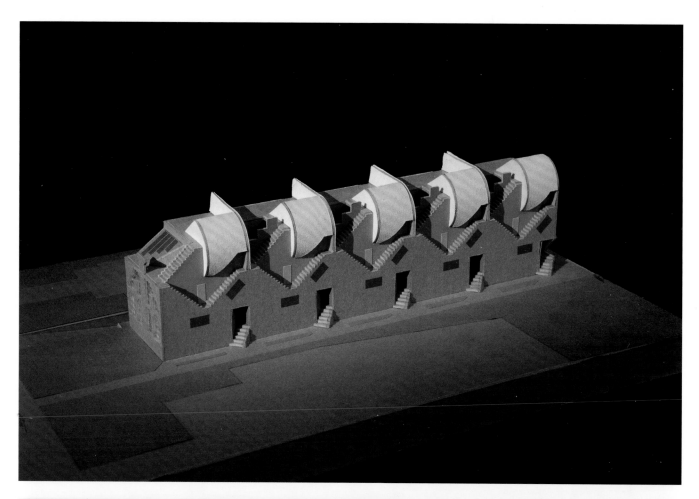

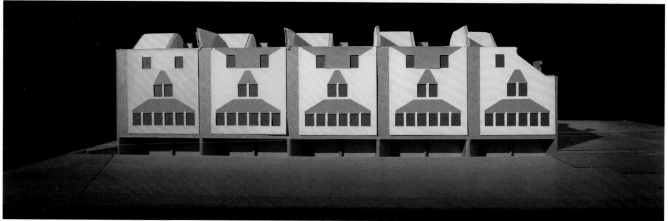

Five Condominiums
Pasadena, 1979-81
Eric Owen Moss
Model, first scheme
Chipboard and colored paper. 14½″ x 9½″ x 3″

Caplin House
Venice, 1978
Frederick Fisher
Model of street façade
Mixed media. 38″ x 45″ x 8″

Model of interior facades
Mixed media. 13″ x 13″ x 2½″

Daniel Studio
Los Angeles, 1980
Coy Howard
Ceiling Drawl
Wood, cardboard, graphite, paint, bronzing. 78″ x 48″

Palmer Eckard Condominium
Venice, 1979
Coy Howard
Drawl
Cardboard, wood, resin, paint. 48″ x 75″

Daniel Studio
Los Angeles, 1980
Coy Howard
Drawl
Wood, cardboard, paper, graphite, bronzing. 31″ x 52″

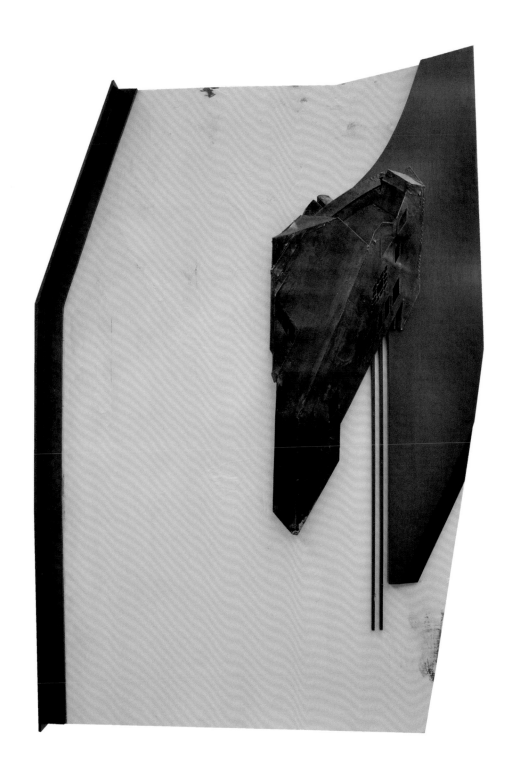

Gross Residence
Hollywood, 1978
Coy Howard
Drawl
Wood, cardboard, paint, graphite, bronzing. 35″ x 55″

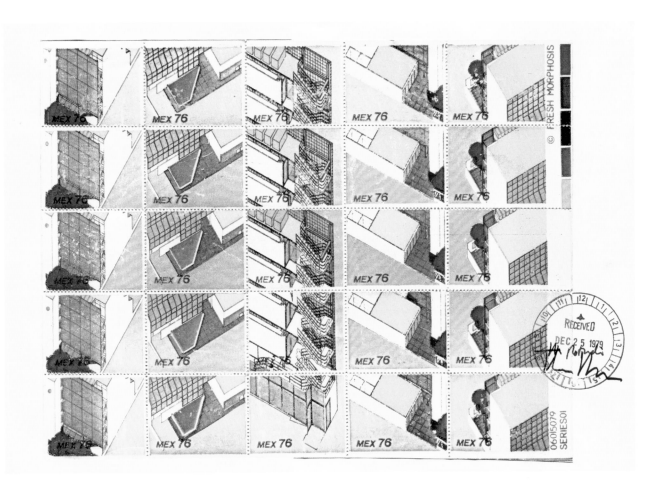

Stamps
1979
Morphosis (Thom Mayne and Michael Rotondi)
Partial isometric views of the Reidel Medical Building
Perforated color copy mounted on board with stamp and signatures.
10¾″ x 14″

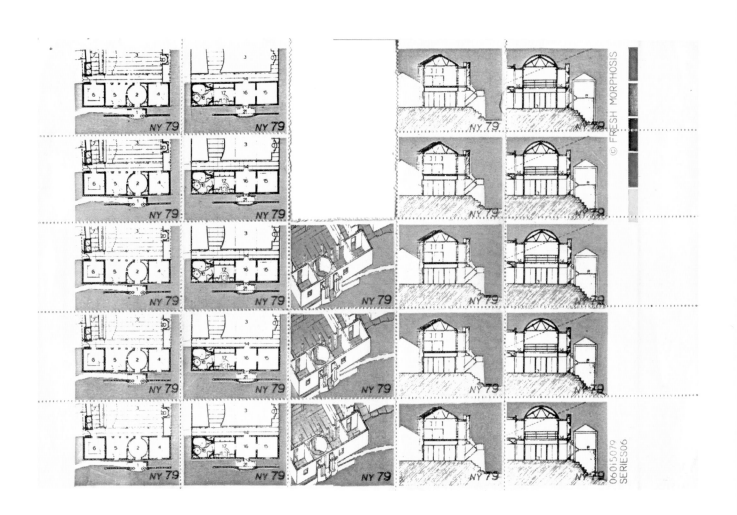

Partial plan, isometric, and section views of the Flores Residence.
Perforated color copy, 10 3/4″ x 14″

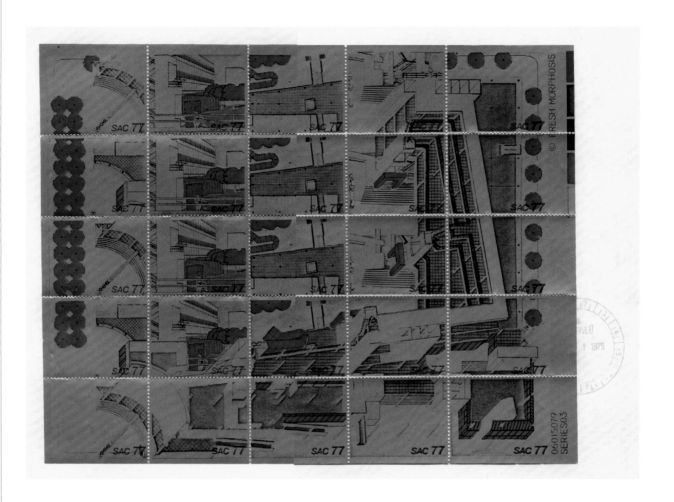

Stamps
1979
Morphosis (Thom Mayne and Michael Rotondi)
Partial isometric views of the Sacramento State Office Building
Perforated color copy mounted on board with stamp.
10¾″ x 14″

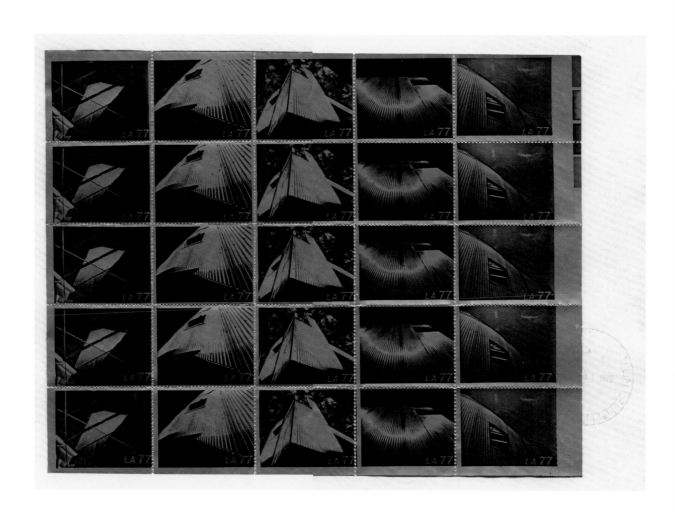

Partial views of the Delmer Residence
Perforated color copy mounted on board with stamp. 10 ¾″ x 14″

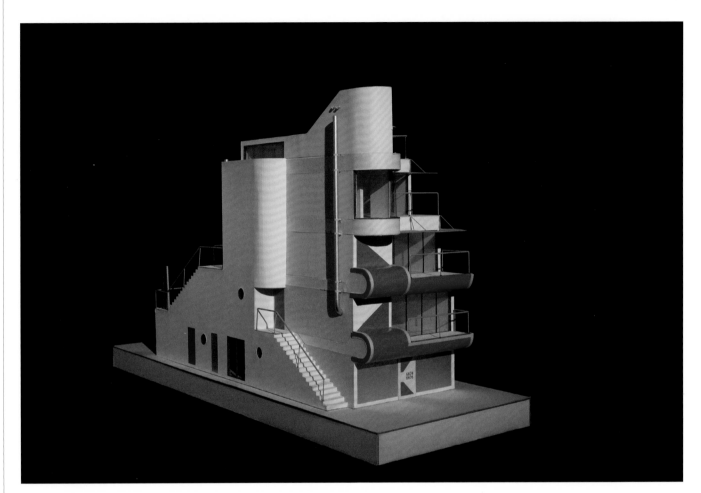

156

Playa Triplex
Los Angeles, 1976
Eric Owen Moss
Model
Chipboard, wood, and colored paper. 33½″ x 11¾″ x 18″

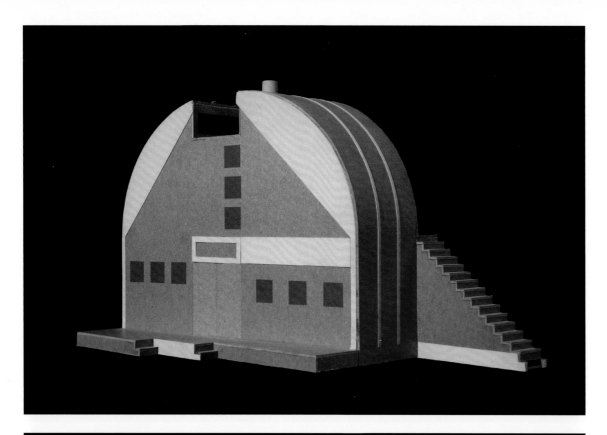

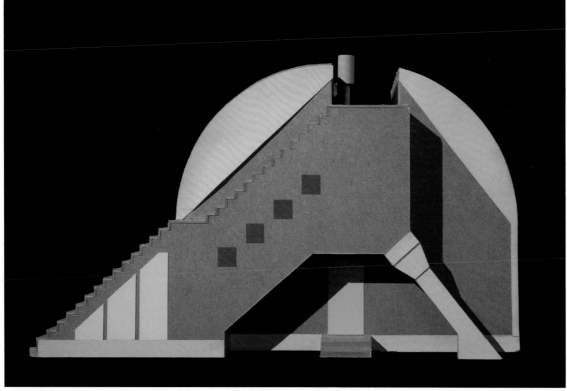

La Faille Residence
Pasadena, 1978-79
Eric Owen Moss
Model
Chipboard and colored paper. 10″ x 5″ x 6″

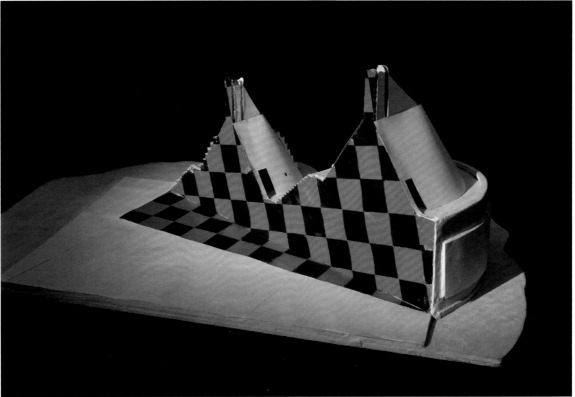

Fun House
Hidden Valley, 1980
Eric Owen Moss
Model
Chipboard, wood, and colored paper. 30″ x 18″ x 10½″

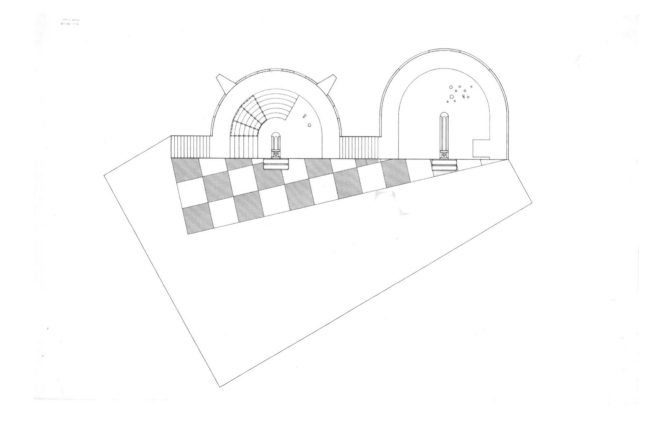

Top: Elevation; Bottom: Roof plan
Ink and pantone on mylar. Each 35½″ x 22″

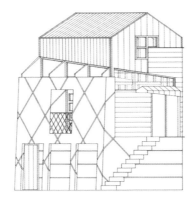

Sedlak House
Venice, 1979-80
Morphosis (Thom Mayne and Michael Rotondi)
Elevation
Ink on mylar. 25¼″ x 18¼″

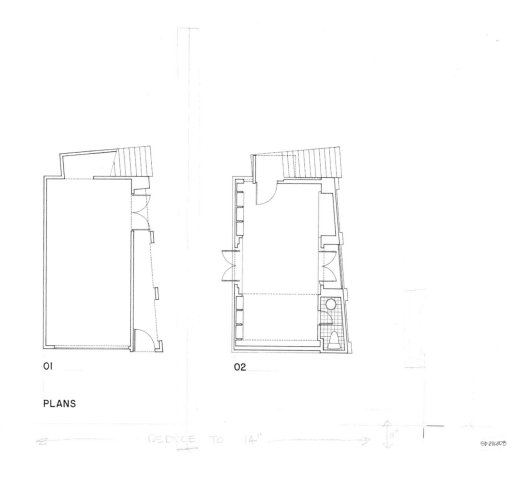

01   02

PLANS

REDUCE TO 14"

Floor plans
Ink on mylar. 24¾" x 14½"

162

Gehry Residence
Santa Monica, 1977-78
Frank O. Gehry
Photographs by Grant Mudford
Gelatin silver prints. 16″ x 20″

164

Gehry Residence
Santa Monica, 1977-78
Frank O. Gehry
Photographs by Grant Mudford
Gelatin silver prints. 16″ x 20″

Gehry Residence
Santa Monica, 1977-78
Frank O. Gehry
Photographs by Grant Mudford
Gelatin silver prints. 20″ x 16″

Gehry Residence
Santa Monica, 1977-78
Frank O. Gehry
Photographs by Grant Mudford
Gelatin silver prints. 20″ x 16″

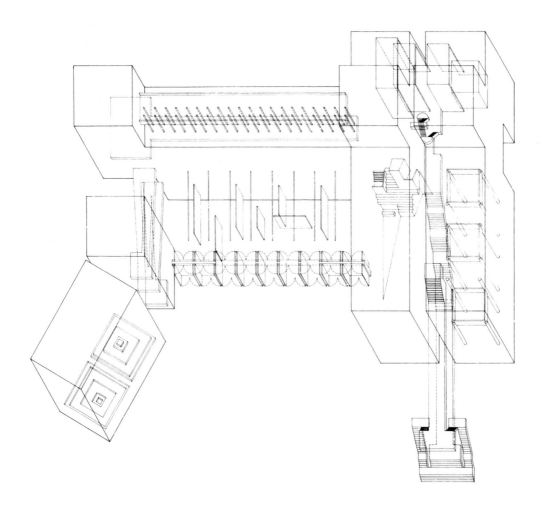

Gunma Museum of Fine Arts
Takasaki, Japan, 1971-74
Arata Isozaki
Analytical axonometric
Ink on vellum. 32¾″ x 22¼″

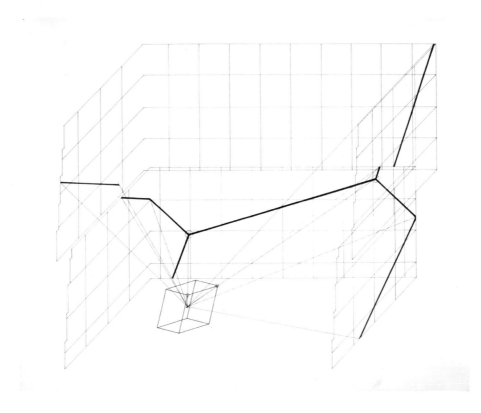

Auditorium: shadow of slanted frame
Ink on vellum. 22¾" x 17"

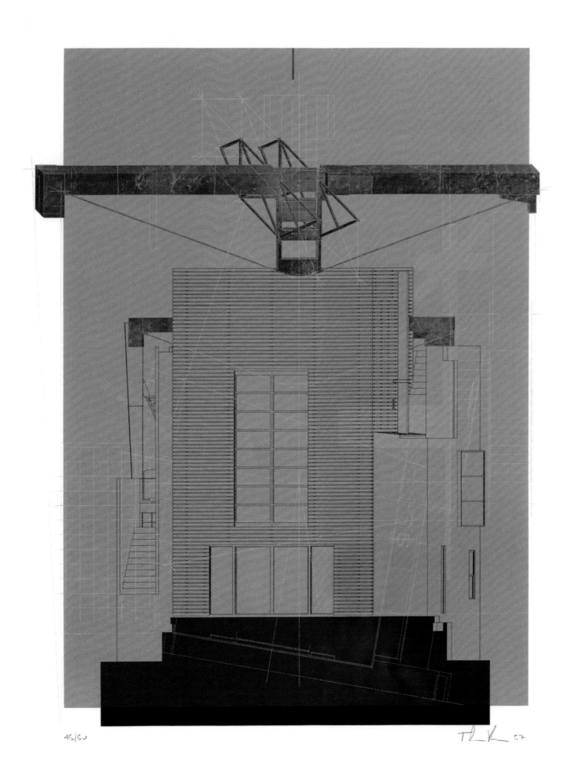

45/50

Sixth Street Residence
Venice, 1987-92
Morphosis (Thom Mayne and Michael Rotondi)
Section
Serigraph with metal foil on paper. 30″ x 40″

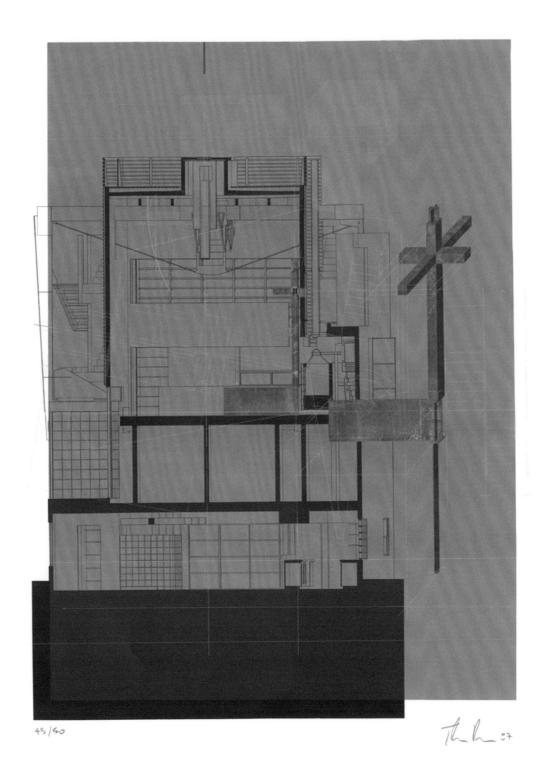

43/50

Elevation
Serigraph with metal foil on paper. 30″ x 40″

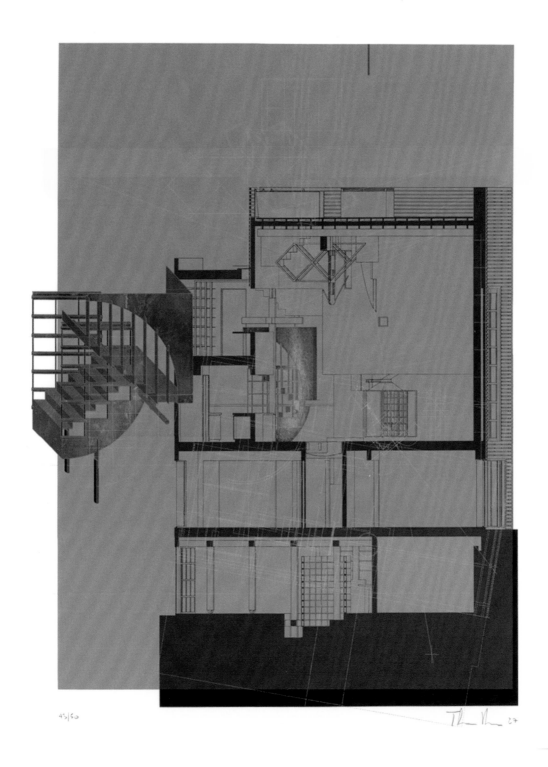

43/60

Sixth Street Residence
Venice, 1987-92
Morphosis (Thom Mayne and Michael Rotondi)
Section
Serigraph with metal foil on paper. 30″ x 40″

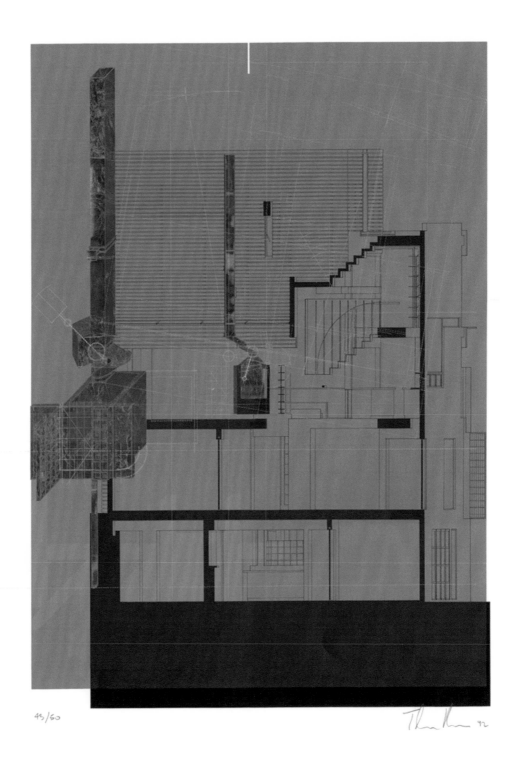

43/50

Section
Serigraph with metal foil on paper. 30″ x 40″

PART THREE

CURRENT
VIEWPOINTS

HOWARD HUGHES'S COLUMN

EWAN BRANDA

The battle lines drawn thirty years ago between "po-mo" and "decon" now seem at best quaint and at worst grossly inadequate. As with the taste wars between metal and punk that raged during the late 1970s, the doctrines that promoted such clear distinctions ignored the fact that the most interesting work from the period did not fall into any clearly defined categories. Regardless of party affiliation (White, Gray, Silver, or otherwise) most of what falls under the label of architectural postmodernism was fueled by shared dissatisfactions with orthodoxy and was underwritten by overlapping philosophical alibis. The work shown at the Architecture Gallery in 1979 demonstrates the inadequacy of such hard-line distinctions. While these Los Angeles architects were actively engaged in the broader contemporary debates of postmodernism they were also isolated from its ideological battles, partly by choice and partly by the fact that Los Angeles was at that time still a remote and somewhat provincial cultural outpost. This isolation, along with the technological and cultural resources nearby, offered a context in which a particularly unique postmodern idiom could develop, one which allowed certain late-modernist tendencies to flourish while also marking a distinct shift in the nature of architectural activity.

The work's significance today stems directly from this ambivalent relationship to late-modernism. To explain how, one might turn to several striking historical parallels between the mid-1970s and the present in which pressure was applied on the discipline from its fringes: the rise of competence and technical excellence as academic values in architecture schools, a broad suspicion of the discipline itself at a moment of environmental and economic crisis, a questioning of a role of architectural design in the face of grassroots social empowerment, and the promise of impending technological revolution brought about by computation. One might also look to the various responses to these conditions by the architects of the Architecture Gallery: a recommitment to the architectural discipline, a validation of the building as a field of cultural and intellectual experimentation, an investment in the superfluous, in risk-taking, improvisation, and the application of architectural will.[1] While most of these responses were characteristic of architectural postmodernism in general, one in particular characterized the architecture that emerged from Los Angeles at that time and differentiated it from the experiments of East Coast postmodernists: the continued interest in technology as a central concern of the architectural discipline. These architects turned to the immediate history of architectural technology, to the techniques and attitudes of hot rod and hacker culture, and to techniques of representation that were coming online, as it were. The result was a renewed discourse on technology in architecture in which technology was no longer a strategy of dissolving disciplinary authority, as it had been in the 1960s, but rather a means by which one could interrogate such traditional concerns of the discipline as the role of history or the nature of authorship.

A number of the attitudes to technology evident at the Architecture Gallery in 1979 built on ideas in play since the 1950s. When Michael Rotondi of Morphosis opened his lecture in 1979 by listing technology among the firm's main interests, he was primarily referring to construction materials and assemblies of interrelated hardware subsystems.[2] This approach built directly upon the systems and industrialized building paradigms that originated in the late 1950s and 1960s and was still in full swing during the 1970s. Rotondi was a committed student of industrialized building and an enthusiastic reader of the obscure and technical European architectural journal, *Industrialization Forum*, which honed his understanding of architecture as fundamentally a problem of part-to-whole relationships within the componentized assembly, an approach which he also likened to visualizing and understanding the parts of a car.[3] Morphosis's projects for the Reidel Medical Building [pp. 136–139] and the Sequoyah Educational Research Center (1977) demonstrate this commitment to the project of industrialized building, but relegate the component and assembly to secondary roles in a more general exploration of the building as an indeterminate container for a complex program. In the case of Reidel, the result was a building that on first glance resembled those from James Stirling's Cambridge and Leicester phase but whose simple, extruded shape suggested something altogether more indeterminate and generic.[4] Ten years earlier, Alan Colquhoun had protested that the tenets of industrialized building and its preoccupation with component assemblies and indeterminate space amounted to an abdication of an architect's primary vocation of making symbolic form. "[A]ny element which is being designed," Colquhoun declared, "must be thought of in the context of the whole of which it is to be a part. A simple system of components based on an additive module, which are interchangeable to suit any situation, does not give this essential condition." Therefore, he went on, "serious thought will have to be given to the question of component design in relation to a particular architectural intention if architecture is not to lose all possibility of symbolic expression."[5] Where Reidel and Sequoyah may have been legitimate targets of that critique, the 2-4-6-8 House clearly brought a preoccupation with systems and assemblies together with an exploration of the semantics of the house, making components out of architectural language itself by assigning architecturally symbolic elements (window frames, lintels, etc.) the same status as fasteners, hinges, and other often overlooked hardware. To blur in this way the distinction between a building's functional-material parts and its symbolic parts and to absorb them into a single organizational matrix points to one possible response to the perceived impoverishment of earlier systems building: rather than draw a distinction be-

tween component and form or assign to the component a metonymic role, as Colquhoun would have it, both material component and semantic component are absorbed into the assembly logic of the whole.

Mayne and Rotondi's drawings of their early houses, and the working drawings in particular, convey a material intensity that the completed buildings do not. This primacy of material was one of the defining attributes of Los Angeles architecture at the time and would offer the world outside Southern California some of its most vivid and enduring imagery. In his 1979 lecture, Gehry encouraged students to develop an interest in building and "getting to know materials" by working in the field, and described his cardboard chairs as fundamentally an experiment in material. A few years earlier, Reyner Banham had located a potential material basis for Los Angeles architecture in the surfboard and the specific relationship between form, material, color, and technological tools required for its production.[6] But the material effects for which Gehry, Morphosis, Moss, and Studio Works would become known—effects based to varying degrees on the use of abrupt materials and improvisational assemblies—were entirely unlike the colorful, precise shapes of the surfboard. These architects nonetheless shared with the surfboard maker (as well as with several Los Angeles artists at the time) a concern for synthesizing coherent aesthetic statements from the opportunistic use of available techniques and materials, whose technologies may or may not have been particularly advanced.[7] As Gehry pointed out, the chain link used for sculptural ends in the Concord pavilion (1975), the Shoreline Aquatic Park in Long Beach (1976), and the Cabrillo Aquarium (1979) were indigenous to each project's immediate environment, while Moss described his use of fiberglass-clad panels in his Playa Del Rey condominiums [p. 156] as merely the sensible use of a material conveniently available at the nearby marina.

Impertinent expediency in the use of materials and building technologies close at hand distinguishes the work of the these architects from the work of the British "High Tech" movement, which in comparison to the work coming out of Southern

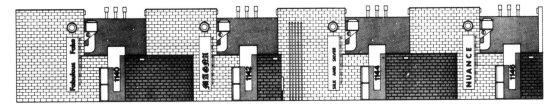

Fig. 1: Eric Owen Moss, Morganstern Warehouse, Los Angeles, 1977-79. Elevation, ink on Mylar.

California seemed rarified and sermonizing.[8] As Moss pointed out in his 1979 lecture, the pipes, vents, and other hardware that appeared on the exterior of his project for the Morganstern Warehouse [Fig. 1] were "certainly not used with any kind of religiosity as Foster or Rogers would use them. They are used selectively and in that sense are conceptually quite different from the use of those things as doctrine."[9] A similar attitude propelled De Bretteville's work. While his Willow Glen house [p. 69] appears on first inspection to be a slick glass and steel box, a closer look reveals an ad-hoc assembly of off-the-shelf components and two-by-four wood and steel bar joist trusses—a building "tuned to the moment" as the architect later put it.[10] De Bretteville explored expedient local solutions that were pragmatic and direct, but which did not necessarily signify highly advanced technology beyond a straightforward approach to optimization. It was an attitude closer to the brutalism of Peter and Alison Smithson's Hunstanton School than to the industrialized refinement of the Eames House and Helmut Schultz's 1976 house in Beverly Hills [p. 25].[11]

These Los Angeles architects, however, did share with High Tech the paradox that all of that technological hardware was ultimately in the service of constructing a social environment. For instance in his Cabrillo Aquarium, Gehry created a theatrical, darkened tunnel for exhibits, outside of which he exposed all of the operations and building services to the broad light of day. Despite the building's technical demands, there were few advanced technologies on display; instead, the exposed services offered a spectacle of administration, maintenance, and other everyday functions in spaces shared by visitor and curator alike. Morphosis too saw their work in terms of such building-human assemblies: as Rotondi put it at the time, "we are

concerned about producing a homeostatic state between building and environment."[12] This explicit reference to the science of cybernetics notwithstanding, the connection between the early Morphosis work and the technological discourses of the 1960s was for the most part limited to a view of the building as an assembly of components. In contrast, the early projects of Works (later Studio Works) developed familiar themes of the 1960s in which technological advancement would allow buildings to dissolve into pure servicing or personalized prosthetic enclosures.[13] Hodgetts and Mangurian opened their 1979 lecture by tracking the trajectory of this mythical dissolution of architecture, starting with the telephone, which made public spaces such as waiting rooms and lobbies irrelevant, and ending with the space suit, which made all architecture irrelevant, since "one only needed electronics and technology."[14] Mangurian's Portable Person [Fig. 2], an x-ray of a human figure (the architect himself) encrusted with various electronic prosthetics, represented one possible endgame, one which, as Hodgetts and Mangurian observed, was not entirely desirable—an every-man-for-himself condition that was nomadic, anonymous, and individualistic.[15]

Despite this eschatological trajectory, their South Side Settlement (started 1975) was a building in the most conventional sense. Yet it was precisely its conventional nature that allowed Studio Works to explore aspects of technology beyond the admittedly glamorous but somewhat exhausted tropes of the 1960s.[16] Their first scheme [pp. 68-69] proposed an arrangement of parallel walls defining a series of programmatically indeterminate zones into which, in their words, "activities were slotted without centrality of focus,…a non-hierarchical mixing chamber."[17] Their second scheme, with its historical and

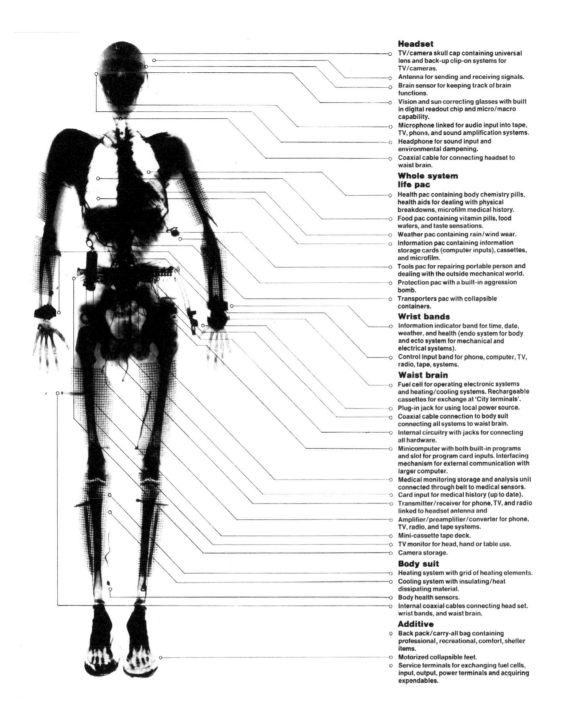

Headset
- TV/camera skull cap containing universal lens and back-up clip-on systems for TV/cameras.
- Antenna for sending and receiving signals.
- Brain sensor for keeping track of brain functions.
- Vision and sun correcting glasses with built in digital readout chip and micro/macro capability.
- Microphone linked for audio input into tape, TV, phone, and sound amplification systems.
- Headphone for sound input and environmental dampening.
- Coaxial cable for connecting headset to waist brain.

Whole system life pac
- Health pac containing body chemistry pills, health aids for dealing with physical breakdowns, microfilm medical history.
- Food pac containing vitamin pills, food wafers, and taste sensations.
- Weather pac containing rain/wind wear.
- Information pac containing information storage cards (computer inputs), cassettes, and microfilm.
- Tools pac for repairing portable person and dealing with the outside mechanical world.
- Protection pac with a built-in aggression bomb.
- Transporters pac with collapsible containers.

Wrist bands
- Information indicator band for time, date, weather, and health (endo system for body and ecto system for mechanical and electrical systems).
- Control input band for phone, computer, TV, radio, tape, systems.

Waist brain
- Fuel cell for operating electronic systems and heating/cooling systems. Rechargeable cassettes for exchange at 'City terminals'.
- Plug-in jack for using local power source.
- Coaxial cable connection to body suit connecting all systems to waist brain.
- Internal circuitry with jacks for connecting all hardware.
- Minicomputer with both built-in programs and slot for program card inputs. Interfacing mechanism for external communication with larger computer.
- Medical monitoring storage and analysis unit connected through belt to medical sensors.
- Card input for medical history (up to date).
- Transmitter/receiver for phone, TV, and radio linked to headset antenna and
- Amplifier/preamplifier/converter for phone, TV, radio, and tape systems.
- Mini-cassette tape deck.
- TV monitor for head, hand or table use.
- Camera storage.

Body suit
- Heating system with grid of heating elements.
- Cooling system with insulating/heat dissipating material.
- Body health sensors.
- Internal coaxial cables connecting head set. wrist bands, and waist brain.

Additive
- Back pack/carry-all bag containing professional, recreational, comfort, shelter items.
- Motorized collapsible feet.
- Service terminals for exchanging fuel cells, input, output, power terminals and acquiring expendables.

Fig. 2: Studio Works (with Jeffrey Hannigan), Portable Person, 1973.

vernacular quotations, marked a more significant break from the ideas about technology on which their earlier projects were based **[pp. 114-115, 118]**. In their lecture, Hodgetts and Mangurian showed a slide of the Vitruvian man, arguing somewhat surprisingly given the trajectory of the work they had shown up to that point that the architect's proper vocation was the making of space "with man at its center." They compared unfavorably Cedric Price's Potteries Thinkbelt to Nolli's 1748 map of Rome and condemned Superstudio's Supersurface, claiming that it "marked a spot" rather than created space.[18] Perhaps more surprising than this sudden humanist impulse, however, was their insistence on its reconciliation with their earlier interests in technology. While Mangurian argued that "one of the villains [in the demise of space] is of course the integrated circuit, the emergence of electronics," he went on to describe the second South Side Settlement scheme—with its courtyards, symmetrical composition, historical forms, and clearly identifiable public spaces—as a microchip or integrated circuit. He explained that the making of a microchip involved the etching away of "layers of material to make a pattern to transmit the information" and that by inference one might think of it as a kind of figure-ground condition produced from a physical operation on a material substrate. In the second scheme of South Side Settlement, he pointed out, the undifferentiated loft spaces containing studios and other non-specific activities were analogous to the seemingly infinite and undifferentiated pathways of the microchip, humanized by the insertion of four legible and programmatically specific buildings on the central axis of each courtyard. While this reading was clearly an oversimplification (chips are of course anything but undifferentiated in their organization) the microchip offered an object through which technology might operate within the traditional domain of the architectural discipline, allowing one to talk in the same breath about architectural history and the technologies of telecommunications.

These new roles for technology in addressing questions of materiality and space making also found their way into modes of representation. One of the enduring paradoxes of the architecture that emerged from Los Angeles is its dual commitment to the autonomy of representation and the actuality of buildings, a commitment in which drawings and models constituted neither a "paper architecture" strictly speaking nor merely a process on the way to a realized building. And so if Rotondi could later claim Jean Prouvé as an important influence on Morphosis, it was with the tacit acknowledgement that Prouvé's relocation of architectural thinking from the architect's studio to the fabrication floor and building site was an oversimplification that their drawings and models sought to correct.[19]

One of the strategies by which representation bridged the gap between paper architecture and actual buildings involved assigning to the drawing or model the aesthetic and ontological properties of

the building. As Rotondi later reflected, "there was an anatomy to the building as there is an anatomy to the body, anatomy to the car, and even to the very complex drawings where we were looking at plan, section, and elevation simultaneously, and then layering in a lot of black ink." At a time when there was little work for young architects, meticulous and obsessive drawing and model making offered a simulation of building in which the organization, materiality, and even the construction sequence could be explored, and with a comparable investment of effort. For Morphosis, "the drawings became the architecture, not just symbolically but in the amount of labor that went into them."[20] These were presentation drawings done by architects, not by professional renderers, in a traditional academic sense for consumption primarily by other architects.[21] Fisher, for instance, made several models of the Caplin House [pp. 146-147] as part of a personal exploration of the project some time after the building was completed and which was not conceived as something to be shown to the client.[22] This completeness of representation—the sense that the drawing or model did not merely describe the building but substituted for it—was crucial to the high degree of visibility of this work in the architectural media, and in particular was useful in convincing the juries of the *Progressive Architecture* Awards program not only of the virtues of the project itself but of the effort, obsession, and commitment that went into its conception.

The axonometric projection played an important role in this search for a synoptic mode of representation, particularly in its atypical and degenerate forms such as the frontal plan oblique, the worm's eye, and the exploded view. The axonometric and the worm's eye view in particular were enjoying renewed attention in the late 1970s. Testimony to the enormous influence of Stirling, the worm's eye offered a representational device through which one might achieve a synthesis of the material, the spatial, and the figural. Like all parallel projection, the worm's eye axonometric was a species of engineering drawing. As it had done for Auguste Choisy, who invented it in the late 19th century, it rejected the floor plane as the primary theoretical and physical surface upon which space was organized and instead proposed that volume and spatial articulation resulted from the organization of services, systems, and structure as much as from walls.[23] For Moss and Studio Works in particular, the distortions of the visual field introduced by the axonometric, and of the worm's eye in particular, allowed for the exploration of a latent figuration [**Figs. 3-5**].[24]

The early axonometrics of Morphosis were drawn on Mylar film, at that time still a relatively recent invention generally restricted to technical drawings.[25] When used with Rapidograph pens, Mylar allowed for precise line work that anticipated later computer-generated drawings. When colored synthetic ("Pantone") films were laid over this needle-sharp line work using the precision of a X-acto knife, the result was imagery that negotiated between the technical ambitions of High Tech and the pastel colors of postmodern classicism. In the work of Morphosis, Mylar made explicit the connection between new experimental practice and the more prosaic world of Los Angeles corporate architecture of the 1970s: during SCI-Arc's first summer, Rotondi was working in the offices of Robert Alexander, in whose print room he found a stack of discarded blank Mylar sheets with pre-printed title blocks from the Bunker Hill Towers.[26] These sheets were trimmed down and the film re-used for several of the early Morphosis drawings. Despite these prosaic origins, the material con-

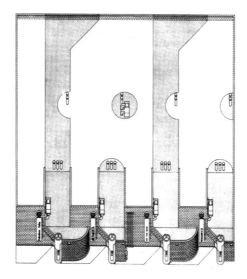

Fig. 4: Eric Owen Moss, Morganstern Warehouse, Los Angeles, 1977-79. Axonometric, ink on Mylar.

Fig. 3: Studio Works, South Side Settlement, second scheme, 1978-80. Worm's eye axonometric, ink on vellum.

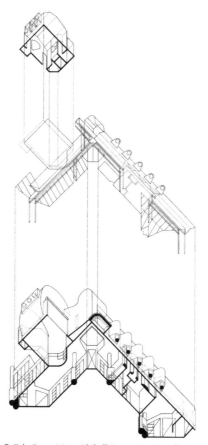

Fig. 5: Eric Owen Moss, Pinball House, Los Angeles, 1979-84. Worm's eye axonometric, ink on Mylar.

tained the potential for experimentation, and Rotondi later recalled the sensuality of layering precisely cut films over 6X0 ink line work on the front and back of those sheets. As the New Romanticism movement in pop culture would do in the early 1980s, this visual language drew out the latent sensuality of a highly technical and precise medium.[27] This sensibility also motivated Morphosis and Mangurian's use of drafting linen, a material as prosaic in its applications as Mylar and which allowed equally precise line work, but which revealed beneath its smooth, plastic surface a dense papyrus-like weave that spoke to its impending obsolescence.

Mylar and linen were not to only drawing media to offer this potent combination of the technical and the sensual. The 1970s saw the introduction of several technologies of reproduction, including what was later known as the fax machine, digital typesetting and color standardization.[28] None was more exciting than the color photocopier. The first electrostatic color copier appeared on the market in 1973, and by the late-1970s this new technology had been absorbed into the visual artist's toolkit.[29] These machines could produce a proliferation of images that were relatively cheap and whose colors were crude and saturated. This fault was of course an aesthetic opportunity, and both Morphosis and Works made extensive use of visual effects afforded by these early machines [Fig. 6].

A more ambivalent attitude to the role of new technology in representation was encapsulated in the use of the airbrush. Invented in the late 19th century for amateur artists and industrial applications, the airbrush signified by the 1970s an ethos of improvisation borrowed from popular illustration and hot rod culture that only hinted at an advanced technology. The smooth, pastel colors of the airbrush drawings of De Bretteville [Fig. 7] and Dimster [pp. 122-123] at first seem closest to the colored pencil renderings of their East Coast counterparts. These airbrush drawings differ from watercolor and colored pencil, however, in the degree of mediation between hand and paper imposed by the tool.[30] Like all airbrush drawing, they aspire to technical perfec-

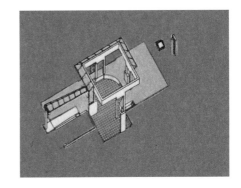

Fig. 6: Morphosis, stamps (detail), 1978-79. Color photocopy.

tion within the realm of the handmade, an ambiguity that Roland Coate exploited in the paintings exhibited at the Architecture Gallery in 1979 in which semi-abstract gradient forms suggested the use of a mechanical drawing instrument yet were neither masked nor airbrushed but meticulously stippled by hand with a brush [pp. 45, 47]. To use the airbrush in architectural drawing was at once nostalgic and futuristic, and directly invoked hot rod aesthetics and science fiction counter-cultures in which it had provided the definitive visual language of a teenage male culture unable to decide between rebellion or reclusiveness.[31]

The airbrush, the color photocopier, and Mylar were all suited to a culture united, as Reyner Banham put it, by "a common admiration for high finish and high style."[32] Mangurian later observed that the interest in the surfboard among designers at the time was in its material and finish, not in its shape. Several of the Works models employed the metallic sparkle paint used for cars, echoing the paintings of Los Angeles artist Mary Corse from 1968 onward in which she created subtle optical effects using an emulsion of glass microspheres normally used for reflective road striping and highway

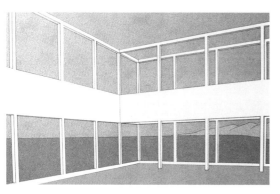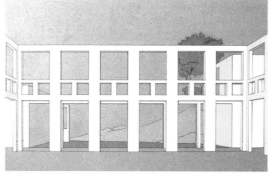

Fig. 7: Peter de Bretteville, Villa Cambiamento, Malibu, 1979-80. Perspectives.

signage. In the world of Los Angeles architecture, however, the smooth and the glossy raised uncomfortable associations with a recent past that had produced, as Charles Jencks later put it, "high tech, hard gloss silvery buildings... a swank, glamorous, brain-dead formalism, but done with great style."[33] The emerging generation of Los Angeles architects did not reject their corporate past wholesale but absorbed it with only partial suspicion. In 1979 Gehry could therefore quip that he included in his Cabrillo Aquarium a "little Cesar Pelli building" (referring to the mirrored glass box housing the administrative offices), but also acknowledged that it was "damn hard to follow his act."[34] Indeed, while the abruptness of chain link fence and corrugated metal in Gehry's work and the explicitly handmade troweled effects of the Morphosis models seemed to reject the hard gloss technological aesthetic of both the surfboard and the corporate architecture of 1970s Los Angeles, it shared with them a concern for the synthesis of a uniform, photogenic coherence.

The attack on the prevailing architectural culture of Los Angeles in the 1970s mounted by this emerging group of architects was therefore less a critique of the earlier generation's "swank, glamorous, brain-dead formalism" or its complicity in the shaping of the city by corporate interests than of its complacency.[35] Their response was an attitude that was as intense and committed as the work of their corporate colleagues was detached, and it was enacted through a new kind of architectural subject: the inventor-in-the-garage. When Banham visited the Venice studio of the sculptor Vasa and suggested to him that the artist's sleek, colored glass monoliths

were made possible because of the technologies available in Los Angeles, the artist agreed but added another reason: the culture of artistic freedom that was a side effect of the isolation in which such artisans worked.[36] This condition, which Mayne described as "connected isolation," was largely due to the urban morphology of Los Angeles, where one could experiment fully immersed in urban conditions and close to resources yet in the safety of the anonymous alleyway garage. As Mayne later put it, "we all had very isolated offices. You couldn't find them."[37]

As in Silicon Valley, a web of strong social and academic ties connected these isolated workshops. For several of these architects, the culture of the hot rod formed the basis of this connective tissue and suggested a shared working method. As Hodgetts put it in his 1979 lecture, the hot rod approach involved taking a standard car and "hopping things up, putting double carburetors on them, putting dual exhaust headers, shocks and high-ratio rear axles. We approached buildings that way."[38] He described their first commission as a "completely customized and accessorized box." "In disadvantaged countries," he went on, "ancient buildings are simply tuned up, hopped up." You provided ancient buildings with services, keeping their spaces intact. The Minneapolis project was "an accessorized hopped up riverfront," and even the more historicist second scheme for South Side Settlement could be seen as an accessorizing of generic gallery spaces through unique elements. Car culture involved iterative experimentation and brash risk taking. As Rotondi later reflected:

You drag a 227 to get it up to a 309. Or you'd drop a 409 into a Hillman, and then the car would blow up because it was just way too big. And you'd say, 'Oh, okay. We shouldn't put one in that big or we need another transmission.' In retrospect, probably just wanting to know how everything works and why does everything have to be like that? Why can't it be another way?"[39]

Tinkering with race-cars, hot rods, and go-karts was part of Southern California middle class culture, and it proposed a mode of operation in which simply staying in your garage and doing what you are good at was a viable mode of cultural resistance.

The improvisational strategies of "hopping up" practiced by the inventor in the garage formed one of the more powerful operative myths of innovation in Silicon Valley.[40] This ethos was encapsulated by the cult of the hacker, which emerged during the mid-1970s at the MIT Artificial Intelligence Lab and other centers of academic computer culture. Prior to its later misappropriation to mean a "security breaker," the term hacker originally referred, in the words of Richard Stallman, "to someone who loves to program, someone who enjoys playful cleverness, or the combination of the two."[41] Therefore, "hacking means exploring the limits of what is possible, in a spirit of playful cleverness."[42] Despite connotations of radical dissent, the hacker belonged to nothing as dramatic as "street culture" or an "underground" but rather to mainstream academia; indeed, as Mayne later observed, UCLA and SCI-Arc were the connective medium for these architects in the undifferentiated and dispersed topography of Los Angeles. But the myth of the hacker points to another paradoxical aspect of 1970s counter culture, particularly as sponsored by technology. Much as Stewart Brand's *Whole Earth Catalog* movement modeled its technological self-help ethos on think tanks like the Rand Corporation, the hack exploited a situation in which the line between counterculture critique and the techniques of institutions of power were increasingly indistinct. It is only in this context that Jencks could refer to the conversions of warehouses into corporate office space as "convivial bazaars... particularly suited to the small, fast-

changing and networked companies that occupy them for brief moments."[43]

Fifteen years after their lecture at SCI-Arc, Hodgetts left Studio Works and the firm moved its offices to the original Hughes aircraft factory in Playa Vista. Outside the building—leading to what they assumed was Howard Hughes' original office—was an unremarkable outdoor stair and column. On closer inspection, the column could be seen to be made of redwood painted with the same green aluminum primer used for aircraft cowlings and other exposed parts. The only means by which one might identify the wood was the scratches and other wear. When Studio Works moved again, the column went with them, and it was repaired using plywood splints and inserts **[Fig. 8]**. While this single object was a totem of the military industrial complex, its low-fidelity technology was also reminiscent of Carlo Scarpa's improvisational details. As Filarete's Column was for Aldo Rossi in the late 1970s, the Hughes column is a synthesis of personal historical anecdote and architectural memory.[44] To locate the architectural metonym in a column rather than, say, in the cyborg of the Portable Person is a reminder of the various commitments to the architectural discipline reflected by this work: an investment in problems of representation, the identification of other architects as principle interlocutors, a commitment to the building as a vehicle for intellectual speculation, the desire to reconcile extra-disciplinary technologies and environmental concerns with the willful shaping and organizing of space.[45] In this architectural postmodernism, double-coding went beyond the simultaneous accommodation of popular taste and elite erudition to something far more inclusive in which intensely personal and occasionally solipsistic investigations of aesthetics, form, and representation might co-exist alongside concerns for a building's responsiveness to its context.

Fig. 8: Column from Hughes aircraft factory, Studio Works offices, 2013.

ENDNOTES

1. As Fisher pointed out in his introduction to the 1979 lecture by Morphosis, "they have a commitment to architecture" and to "the development of the field." Thom Mayne and Michael Rotondi. November 28, 1979, "Thom Mayne and Michael Rotondi of Morphosis" (lecture). In SCI-Arc Media Archive. Southern California Institute of Architecture. <http://sma.sciarc.edu/video/0629_morphosis_b_w/>.

2. Ibid.

3. Michael Rotondi, interview with the author and Todd Gannon. Los Angeles, 13 June 2012.

4. Jonathan Hughes, "The Indeterminate Building," in Non-plan: Essays on Freedom Participation and Change in Modern Architecture and Urbanism, ed. Jonathan Hughes and Simon Sadler (Oxford: Architectural Press, 2000). Reyner Banham, "A Clip-On Architecture," Design Quarterly, no. 63 (1965): 2–30.

5. Alan Colquhoun, "Symbolic and Literal Aspects of Technology," Architectural Design (November 1962): 508–9. He applied his argument to a critical review of the Centre Pompidou. Alan Colquhoun, "Critique," Architectural Design 77, no. 2 (1977).

6. Reyner Banham, Los Angeles The Architecture Of Four Ecologies (New York: Harper & Row, 1971); "Reyner Banham Loves Los Angeles," One Pair of Eyes (BBC, 1972).

7. See, for example, the work of Ron Davis and Mary Corse (cited later in this essay).

8. Piano and Rogers' Centre Pompidou, the first monument of High Tech, opened in 1977. For more on the relationship of Los Angeles to High Tech, see Todd Gannon's introduction to this volume.

9. Eric Owen Moss. December 5, 1979. "Eric Owen Moss: Armageddon or Polynesian Contextualism" (lecture). In SCI-Arc Media Archive. Southern California Institute of Architecture. <http://sma.sciarc.edu/video/1883_moss_eric_owen_1-00-00-00/>.

10. Peter De Bretteville, interview with Todd Gannon. New Haven, 26 April 2012.

11. The term High Tech was coined to describe an attitude to the readymade and the found object and was only later applied to refined systems of industrially manufactured building components. See Emilio Ambasz's introduction to Joan Kron, High-Tech: The Industrial Style and Source Book for the Home (New York: C. N. Potter, 1978).

12. Rotondi, interview, op. cit.

13. The former is encapsulated in Banham's famous essay, "A Home is Not a House," and the latter by Archigram's "Suitaloon" project (among others). See Reyner Banham and François Dallegret, "A Home Is Not a House," Art in America (April 1965).

14. Studio Works. November 21, 1979. "Studio Works" (lecture). In SCI-Arc Media Archive. Southern California Institute of Architecture. <http://sma.sciarc.edu/video/studio-works-part-one/>.

15. Another endgame might be represented by the Mobile Theater project (1972), designed by Hodgetts, De Bretteville, and Kupper.

16. Among the most troublesome of these theoretical cul-de-sacs were put forth by Superstudio in their films "Supersurface: An alternative model for life on earth" (1972) and "Cerimonia" (1973). In 1970, Martin Pawley wrote a scathing essay on the decline of these ideas. See Martin Pawley, "Caroline: Go to Canvas City Immediately—Your Friend Linda Has Been Busted," Architectural Design (November 1970): 558–65.

17. Hodgetts and Mangurian, "Studio Works (lecture)." Price's project was from 1965 and Superstudio's from 1971.

18. This argument was not as conservative as it might at first seem. Nolli's map was still a novelty and had only the previous year made its first widespread appearance in the Roma Interrotta exhibition and Rowe and Koetter's Collage City.

19. Rotondi, interview, op. cit.

20. Ibid.

21. The late 1970s saw a surge in the interest in architectural drawing. At the Museum of Modern Art in New York, Drexler curated the controversial The Architecture of the Ecole des Beaux-arts in 1975, while Robert Stern and Richard Oliver curated Drawing Towards a More Modern Architecture at the Drawing Center and the Cooper-Hewitt respectively in 1977. In Los Angeles, Coy Howard organized Architectural Views: Physical Fact, Psychic Effect, an exhibition of drawing at the Los Angeles Institute of Contemporary Art (LAICA) in 1978. For a discussion, see Gannon in this volume.

22. Frederick Fisher, interview with the author. Los Angeles, 10 May 2012.

23. Hilary Bryon, "The Worm's Eye as a Measure of Man: Choisy's Development of Axonometry in Architectural Representation," in Scale: Imagination, Perception and Practice in Architecture, ed. Gerald Adler, Timothy Brittain-Catlin, and Gordana Fontana-Giusti (London and New York: Routledge, 2012).

24. In their 1979 lecture, Hodgetts and Mangurian showed a slide of a car carburetor as an inspiration for the form of the Gagosian Gallery, which allowed the building to be understood as a "large casting." (Hodgetts and Mangurian, "Studio Works (lecture)," op. cit.) John Hejduk had already explored the figural potential of the axonometric. The Swiss graphic designer Jean Widmer had also experimented with the figural qualities of parallel projection, particularly in searching for a language to describe the new forms of industrial design in the late 1960s.

25. PET polyester film was launched under the trade name Mylar by Dupont in late-1950s.

26. Rotondi, interview, op. cit.

27. This sensibility would play out in Los Angeles in the graphic hedonism of Wet Magazine and the China Club. For a discussion, see Paulette Singley's essay in this volume.

28. Hodgetts and Mangurian recount participating in a conference in New York using the "telecommunicator" (an early fax by which you could transmit images). Hodgetts and Mangurian, "Studio Works (lecture)," op. cit.

29. The first book on the subject seems to be Patrick Firpo, Lester Alexander, and Claudia Katayanagi, Copyart: The First Complete Guide to the Copy Machine (New York: R. Marek, 1978). By the mid-1970s, the gallery Copie Art was already well established in Montréal and in 1979 the International Museum of Photography in Rochester, New York put together Electroworks, an exhibition of photocopier artwork.

30. De Bretteville had taken an airbrush drawing class with the Los Angeles airbrush illustrator Ed Scarisbrick. De Bretteville, interview, op. cit.

31. Ridley Scott's Alien, whose antagonist was designed by airbrush master H.R. Giger, was released in 1979 and pointed out the connection between the aesthetic of gradient tones and the junkyard imperfection of science fiction's technology on the decline and on the shift from machine to biomorph. For a discussion of this film in the context of the work of Morphosis, see Sylvia Lavin, "Morphosis: From Machine to Machinic," in Morphosis: Complete Works (Madrid: Ministerio de Fomento, 1999).

32. "Reyner Banham Loves Los Angeles," op. cit.

33. Charles Jencks, interview with Todd Gannon, 30 May 2012.

34. Frank O. Gehry. November 7, 1979. "Frank O. Gehry" (lecture). In SCI-Arc Media Archive. Southern California Institute of Architecture. <http://sma.sciarc.edu/video/frank-gehry-part-one/>.

35. On the response of the Architecture Gallery architects to established Los Angeles architectural practice in the 1970s see Gannon in this volume.

36. He added that it was also due to the presence of people crazy enough to buy the stuff. "Reyner Banham Loves Los Angeles," op. cit.

37. Even the location of the Morphosis office was concealed by the decoy label, "The Stray Dog Cafe." Thom Mayne, personal interview, July 14, 2012. Mayne would later publish a book of the same title. See Thom Mayne, Morphosis: Connected Isolation (London: Academy Editions, 1993).

38. Hodgetts and Mangurian, "Studio Works (lecture)," op. cit.

39. Rotondi, interview, op. cit.

40. The story of the development of the first Apple computer in Steve Jobs' garage in 1976 is one of the enduring myths of Silicon Valley.

41. Richard Stallman, "The GNU Project," 1999, <http://www.gnu.org/gnu/thegnuproject.html.> Stallman was an activist in the early free software movement.

42. Richard Stallman, "On Hacking," 2013, <http://stallman.org/articles/on-hacking.html.>

43. Charles Jencks, Heteropolis: Los Angeles, the Riots and the Strange Beauty of Hetero-architecture (London: Academy Editions, 1993):8. The relationship between Stewart Brand and corporate/military think tanks and cyberculture is discussed at length in Fred Turner, From Counterculture to Cyberculture: Stewart Brand, the Whole Earth Network, and the Rise of Digital Utopianism (Chicago: University of Chicago Press, 2006).

44. Aldo Rossi, A Scientific Autobiography (Cambridge, Mass.: The MIT Press, 1981).

45. Citing Rowe's introduction to Five Architects, Mayne argued in his 1979 lecture that architectural action involves finding a position between the willful and the responsive. See also Mayne's architect's statement in this volume.

A TALE OF TWO VENICES

PATRICIA A. MORTON

This tale of two Venices takes place in the years 1979 and 1980. In Venice, Italy, the Architectural Biennale spun a tale of postmodernism that would reinstate history and meaning to architecture, dubbed "The Presence of the Past." In Venice, California, the Architecture Gallery promulgated no such overarching storyline, instead displaying a marked skepticism toward any totalizing narrative. While two characters, Frank Gehry and Eugene Kupper, feature in both, the exhibits in the two Venices told divergent tales. A radical pluralism and surface eclecticism linked the two exhibitions, but they shared little else. The suspicion of grand narratives, so evident at the Architecture Gallery, was a symptom of a wider malaise that permeated postwar architecture as modernism's hegemony dissolved and a chaotic pluralism ensued. And, according to a leading philosopher of the moment, even telling tales was itself a dubious enterprise in the postmodern era.

In 1979, philosopher Jean-François Lyotard published a brief, polemical assessment of the state of knowledge, *The Postmodern Condition: A Report on Knowledge*, which became one of the foundational texts of postmodern culture and aesthetics. Presuming a radical break with modern systems of thinking, Lyotard posited a new postmodern attitude founded on incredulity toward the "metanarratives" that had legitimized knowledge in the modern era. In place of Enlightenment narratives of truth, reason, and the universal, he diagnosed the postmodern condition as a propensity to accept difference and fragmentation in place of totality. Abandoning Jurgen Habermas' search for legitimization of knowledge through consensus and discussion, Lyotard celebrated the dissolution of metaphysical philosophy into "clouds of narrative language elements" and language games.

When the English translation of *The Postmodern Condition* was published in 1984, it included another essay that expanded Lyotard's analysis of postmodern knowledge into a direct application to postmodernism generally.[1] This essay, "Answering the Question: What is Postmodernism?," elaborated on Lyotard's thesis that postmodernism jettisoned narratives of certainty and wholeness in favor of instability, fragmentation and difference. Lyotard characterized the postmodern moment as a "period of slackening" in which the heritage of the avant-garde was being liquidated," and described postmodern culture in terms of a lack of attachment to stable value or taste: "Eclecticism is the degree zero of contemporary general culture: one listens to reggae, watches a western, eats McDonald's food for lunch and local cuisine for dinner, wears Paris perfume in Tokyo and 'retro' clothes in Hong Kong; knowledge is a matter for TV games."[2] Denying itself the "solace of good forms, the consensus of taste," Lyotard's postmodern rejected nostalgia or a collective sense of aesthetic criteria in favor of an "anything goes" realism that recognized the dominance of profit as the generator of value.

This conviction that the postmodern condition allowed no consolation in the past or the narratives of the avant-garde might have been the project statement for the Architecture Gallery, exemplified by the exhibition poster [p. 113], which posed "ten viewpoints" rather than a unified vision of recent work in L.A., and by the title of Coy Howard's introductory review, "Erosion, Discontinuity, Incompleteness, Transformation." The terms set by Howard's lecture refused narrative totality resolutely. Elsewhere, however, the search for metanarratives persisted. Architecture culture still needed a narrative after the death of Modernism, and a multitude of tales burgeoned to fill the void. Exhibitions were a favored device for launching new movements—as with the New York Five who were canonized in MoMA's 1969 exhibit—or for telling revised stories about the past or initiating new theories. In the IAUS exhibition *Idea as Model*, for example, Peter Eisenman, displayed the model as a conceptual rather than a narrative tool, making it independent from the project represented. In the 1970s, MoMA produced exhibitions that posed historicist alternatives to the dominant modernist history it had spent decades promoting, such as *The Architecture of the Ecole des Beaux-Arts* (1975-76), and even mounted a revisionist account of modernism, *Transformations in Modern Architecture* (1979). The exhibit of *Roma Interrota* (1978), a set of twelve interventions into Nolli's famous 18th-century plan of Rome, was a key event in the development of postmodernism and Italian rationalism.

In 1977, Charles Jencks attempted to canonize postmodernism *avant la lettre*, publishing the first edition of *The Language of Post-Modern Architecture*, which codified the emerging postmodern style in architecture. He dated the end of modernism and the beginning of postmodernism to 1972 when the Pruitt-Igoe housing project was demolished, marking the demise of modernism's

grand social experiments and its claims to legitimacy. He defined postmodernism initially as a radical eclecticism that used multivalent populist and elite taste codes to communicate with various audiences; later, he espoused postmodern classicism over more a pluralistic eclecticism. When Jencks produced his first manifesto for postmodern architecture, few truly postmodern buildings existed, but a flurry of iconic postmodern buildings appeared shortly after, including Philip Johnson's AT&T Building 1978, Venturi Scott Brown's Basco Showroom 1979, Michael Graves' Portland Building 1980, and Duany Plater-Zyberk's Seaside 1980.

The 1980 Venice Architectural Biennale was the apogee of this particular narrative of postmodernism. Its main exhibit, the Strada Novissima, held in the historic Corderie dell'Arsenale, a half-kilometer-long, disused rope works, consisted of twenty eclectic facades designed by international architects, including Frank Gehry, Venturi/Scott Brown, Stanley Tigerman, Hans Hollein, Robert A.M. Stern, Leon Krier, Rem Koolhaas, Allan Greenberg, Massimo Scolari, Michael Graves, and

Fig. 1: Strada Novissima, Venice Biennale, 1980. General view.

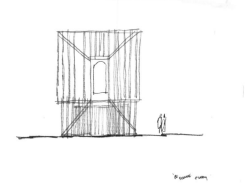

Fig. 2: Frank Gehry, contribution to the Strada Novissima, Venice Biennale, 1980. Sketch.

Arata Isozaki, among others [**Fig. 1**].[3] The Strada Novissima simulated a street in which visitors could come into literal contact with the architecture. Curated by Paolo Portoghesi with critical assistance from Vincent Scully, Charles Jencks, and Christian Norberg-Schultz, the Biennale took the theme of "The Presence of the Past," which emphasized the return of history and a revived role for narrative in architecture. Its partisans were euphoric over what they saw as the end of Modernism's prohibitions and the start of architecture's liberation; Paolo Portoghesi declared: "the postmodern is a refusal,

a rupture, a renouncement, much more than a simple change of direction."[4]

Architecture Gallery participants Frank Gehry and Eugene Kupper exhibited at the 1980 Biennale, Gehry in a prominent place on the Strada Novissima, Kupper on the mezzanine where younger architects' work was displayed. For his designated space, Gehry "drew" a perspective in wood-frame diagonal bracing that framed the window at the back of the exhibition space [**Fig. 2**]. Gehry's façade contrasted with the mannered exaggeration of Michael Graves' classicism on one side or the ironic ghost column of Oswald Matthias Ungers' façade on the other. The stud wall of Gehry's literalized perspective recalled his Santa Monica house, but it also referred to the standardized frame construction of ordinary American buildings, the dominant mode of construction in California. In his statement for the Biennale, Gehry staked out his position: "It is a compelling idea for me to work in the area of making an architectural statement, creating a spirited space, some thing beautiful, maybe using the simplest of available building techniques..."[5] He was impelled by the tectonics of structure and material

Fig. 3: Eugene Kupper, Presentation boards for the 1980 Venice Biennale installed at the architect's studio in Los Angeles.

rather than surface and scenographic effect, by a past of everyday building rather than by historicism. By contrast with Gehry's polemically-simple frame facade, Eugene Kupper presented his UCLA Extension Building, Nilsson House, and Washburn House in a long wall replete with axonometrics, sectional models, photographs, cut-away views, and a range of more conventional drawings [Fig. 3]. The dizzying array of representational forms used to render the Nilsson and Washburn houses freighted them with significance equal to its architect's ambitions: "To make the smallest action within the realm of architecture is to uncover the vital relationships between Place, Culture, and Architectural Work."[6] Kupper's boards exemplified the exuberance and delight in form-making that characterized much of the work in the Architecture Gallery, providing one of the few moments where the two events intersect.

The lack of an overarching metanarrative for post-modern architecture was registered clearly by Suzanne Stephens' retrospective article in the December 1979 issue of *Progressive Architecture*. Searching for a pattern in the myriad emergent trends of the 1970s, she concluded that the attempts to go beyond Modernism had left only incoherence and fragmentation. In a period of such disparate projects as Peter Eisenman's House VI (1977), Rem Koolhaas' *Delirious New York* (1978), Daniel Libeskind's Micromegas (1979), and the Gehry House (1978), Stephens failed to construct an adequate taxonomy that could overcome an inherent distrust of labels. "The decade has been known for its various *isms*, all brought together in the handy catch phrase "pluralism." Pluralism, as a label, *controls* this surface discontinuity. It suggests there is some order in the disorder, in the proliferation of different architectural approaches."[7] As she sifted through the ruins of Modern Architecture, as she put it, she identified theatricality, a return to history, the persistence of modernism, contextualism, kitsch, concern for language, but could only discover promise in an architecture of "bits and pieces," of splendid fragments without unity. According to Stephens, the 1970s were marked by a search for a way of making architecture that would reflect a

consensus between architects and the persons experiencing it, an architecture that would embody the demands and desires of both, in other words a fiction that both sides could believe in. Yet, this quest was doomed by an excess of competing narratives and, as Lyotard noted, by the fundamental lack of consensus during the postmodern period.

In an interview, Frank Gehry rejected the narrative impulse of his Postmodern contemporaries: "Venturi is into kind of a story, a verbal polemic... I'm really interested in this hands-on thing and not in telling stories..."[8] Here is the plot line for this tale of two Venices: the compulsion to tell stories based on history versus the desire to express construction and process. The Strada Novissima was a retrograde attempt to fabricate a metanarrative about Postmodernism as a revived interest in the past, while the Architecture Gallery supported Lyotard's assertion that postmodernism is an "incredulity toward metanarratives." In retrospect, the heretics of the Architecture Gallery left a more lasting legacy, recognizing the death of modern totality and embracing post-modern pluralism without the solace of nostalgia or coherence.

ENDNOTES

1.   Jean-François Lyotard, *The Postmodern Condition: A Report on Knowledge*, trans. Geoff Bennington and Brian Massumi (Minneapolis: University of Minnesota Press, 1984).

2.   Ibid., 76.

3.   In addition to the Strada Novissima, the Architectural Biennale featured an entrance gate and the Teatro del Mondo by Aldo Rossi, homage displays devoted to Ignazio Gardella, Mario Ridolfi, and Philip Johnson, and an exhibition of the work of younger architects on the mezzanine floor above the Strada. A total of seventy-six architects' work was exhibited at the 1980 Biennale. See *Architecture 1980: The Presence of the Past. Venice Biennale* (New York: Rizzoli, 1980).

4.   Paolo Portoghesi, *Postmodern: The Architecture of the Postindustrial Society* (New York: Rizzoli, 1983): 7.

5.   *Architecture 1980*, 154.

6.   Ibid., 222.

7.   Suzanne Stephens, "Playing with a Full Decade," *Progressive Architecture* (December 1979): 49.

8.   Quoted in Heinrich Klotz, *The History of Postmodern Architecture*, trans. Radka Donnell (Cambridge, Mass.: MIT Press, 1984), 395-398.

GUERRILLAS, ARCHITECTS, & CABLE TV: *SCI-Arc's Videos in Context*

KEVIN MCMAHON

Fig. 1: Roland Coate at the Architecture Gallery, 1979.

Each of the original Architecture Gallery exhibitions included a monitor connected to a reel-to-reel deck [**Fig. 1**]. Displayed on the monitor was a black-and-white video of a lecture by the featured architect, presented a few days earlier.[1] While this might have been a novelty elsewhere in 1979, in Southern California it can be seen as one of many applications of independent video in the service of education, art and activism.

Architects first engaged television in the mid-1940s as a physical apparatus requiring accommodation, i.e. designing homes to accommodate television sets,[2] and designing broadcast television production and transmission facilities.[3] The first television sets were substantial objects, and architects viewed them as an unwelcome new gravitational force, distorting traditional interior arrangements,[4] as when *Architectural Forum* exclaimed, "Television: its hypnotic screen will change our approach to designing living rooms and making love."[5]

As television went on to become the dominant cultural force in the U.S., its architectural aspect consisted primarily of the fictional spaces

it broadcast.[6] In subsequent decades there were isolated attempts to use television to present architecture. When BBC1 broadcast the "Reyner Banham Loves Los Angeles" episode of *One Pair of Eyes* in 1972,[7] it was the culmination of a decade of British experimentation, including *The Art of Architecture* (Reyner Banham, 1960),[8] *Great Temples of the World* (Kenneth Clark, 1964), *Master Builders* (John Donat, 1966), and *Civilization* (Kenneth Clark, 1969). In the U.S., the Museum of Modern Art's industrial design curator Edgar Kaufmann Jr. was a regular guest circa 1954 on the *Morning Show*,[9] and between 1963 and 1966, Aline Saarinen presented feature stories on architecture on NBC's *Sunday* show.[10] After the Public Broadcasting Service (PBS) network launched in 1970, there appeared *An Architectural Odyssey with G. E. Kidder Smith* (1978),[11] *The Shock of the New* (1980),[12] *Pride of Place* (1986),[13] and *America by Design* (1987).[14]

An entirely different architectural application of television—as a tool for rendering designs—began to be investigated in the late 1960s. A collaboration between the School of Architecture and the campus television facility at the University of Nebraska in 1967 explored "simulating the scanning of space and the motion through a sequence of spaces," and emphasized video images over digital.[15] At the same time, Peter Kamintzer was working at UCLA on adapting NASA's moon landing simulator into a tool for creating renderings of an imaginary city.[16]

The essential technology behind independent video was the development in the 1960s of a portable, affordable camera and recording apparatus. For the majority of early video enthusiasts, the real beginning of independent video production can be dated to 1967, when Sony introduced its DV-2400 PortaPak. Battery-powered and easily carried by one person, this was the first truly portable video recording system. Scientific institutions were probably the earliest adopters: the National Center for Atmospheric Research, for example, started videotaping lectures in 1967. Police departments also experimented: in 1968 video was introduced for the first time as evidence in a trial, in Costa Mesa.[17]

Those who couldn't afford the equipment individually were quick to organize cooperatives and community video production centers. In San Francisco there was KQED's Experimental Television Workshop (1967-1976), Ant Farm (1968-1978), and Land Truth Circus (1968-1978). Electric Eye (1968-1970) formed in Santa Clara. Later groups were more explicitly engaged in political activism, such as the Media Access Center (1970-1972) in Menlo Park, part of the Portola Institute, Top Value Television (1972-1977), and Optic Nerve (1972-1979).[18] Books like Michael Shamberg's *Guerrilla Television* (1971), J. B. Moriarty, *The Third Eye; a PortaPak Handbook for Teachers* (1972), and the Videofreex Collective's *Spaghetti City Video Manual* (1973) propagandized for socially-relevant grass-roots video documentaries.

In 1975 the Long Beach Museum of Art organized the first major institutional exhibit of video art, and also established a production center.[19] Groundbreaking Los Angeles-based video art includes John Knight, *Site Displacement* (1969); Chris Burden, *TV Hijack* (1972); John Baldassari, *Teaching a Plant the Alphabet* (1972); Susan Mogul, *Dressing Up* (1973); Martha Rosler, *Vital Statistics of a Citizen, Simply Obtained* (1973); Bill Viola, *Olfaction* (1976).[20] The Telethon group, based in Santa Monica, produced in 1973 the exhibit *The TV Environment*, surveying not only the spaces presented on television, but the spaces of television reception.[21]

Reacting to pressure from independent video advocates in the early 1970s, the U.S. government momentarily acted to mitigate the power of broadcast television with a small but consequential infrastructure reform. In 1972, the FCC permitted the further expansion of community antenna television (CATV) or cable TV, with conditions, including "All systems in the top 100 markets...must provide three channels for public access, education, and lo-

cal government."[22] This requirement gave rise to the public access television, which thrived until the Supreme Court declared it unconstitutional in 1979.[23]

The cable franchise in Santa Monica and the Westside was awarded to Theta Cable in 1967.[24] Around the time Theta began broadcasting in 1972, the Episcopal Diocese of Los Angeles, provided a start-up grant for a community video facility, the Los Angeles Public Access Project. The mission of PAP was broadly, "to train anyone interested in the use of video and provide equipment for them to produce their own shows for broadcasting to the public,"[25] but more specifically to provide public access content for Theta. Theta Cable's offices were at the northwest corner of Berkeley and Nebraska streets in Santa Monica. SCI-Arc's building was at the southwest corner, and the school's director, Ray Kappe, invited Public Access to use the unused second floor for their office and studio.

Public Access Project's first public event at SCI-Arc, March 2-4, 1973, was billed as "the first Southern California Video Festival," featuring "workshop, demonstrations and discussions of the use of video and cable television as tools for community self-awareness." Workshops covered "video hardware and teaching video," "community cable franchising and public access to cable," and "video as a tool for community organizing and video as a conceptual art form."[26] A week later Public Access Project was offering at SCI-Arc a free, public screening. The program was characteristic of the times: a videotape of the most recent Venice Town Council meeting.[27]

Having a community video facility on the second floor sparked interest in video inside the SCI-Arc community. Morton Neikrug, who transferred to SCI-Arc in 1973 as an undergraduate student, recalled:

> I had always been interested in electronics. I just started helping them out. They helped me do some video documentation of Venice with their PortaPak. My background was photography and I wanted it to look beautiful, like Kenneth Clark's *Civilization*.

It didn't; it looked like the surface of the moon. ...But working with Public Access, I realized that that wasn't the most important thing. Video was about empowerment. The power that had been confined to studios and media corporations was suddenly accessible to ordinary people, to tell their own version of events. In those days the phrase everyone kept using was "We finally have access to The Box!"[28]

Neikrug and other students encouraged by Shelly Kappe also experimentally videotaped events at SCI-Arc: seminar discussions, studio presentations, deliberative "All-School" meetings, and public lectures. The range of school events taped is a reminder that the videos weren't intended primarily as time capsules for the distant future, but as conveniences for the immediate community—permitting people who couldn't attend an event to keep current.

By 1974, out of frustration with the unreliability of Public Access Project's resources, SCI-Arc invested in its own video equipment. Videotaping the Wednesday night public lectures started that fall. Working within the freedoms and the limitations of the situation, Neikrug and other students developed a pragmatic production strategy. After graduating from SCI-Arc, Neikrug stayed on until 1980 as Media Manager.

At SCI-Arc, public lectures took place in the double height atrium in the middle of the scaffolding structure in which students lived and worked. Since the Main Space hosted not only the lectures, but every group event that happened at SCI-Arc, equipment couldn't be permanently installed. Chairs, projectors, lights, cameras, and microphones were set up before each event and put away afterwards. Moreover, the audio/visual set up had to balance the needs of the taping with the live event needs of the speakers and the audience, to see and hear comfortably.[29]

The crew used two cameras: one on the speaker, the other providing a wide view of the slides. Later that year, students built an editing console, SCI-Arc's first media facility. The equipment consisted of two open-reel ½-inch playback decks for "crash" editing. Later they acquired a more sophisticated Sony deck. Still later they acquired a mixer to permit live switching during taping.

SCI-Arc alumna and Media Manager in the 1980s, Julee Herdt, remembers the original venue with affection:

The Berkeley Street building lecture space was relatively small, which gave immediacy between audience and lecturer. There was a casual feel to the scene. The lecturer walked from the parking lot, through the big metal doors and to the podium; which was just a step or two up from the floor. If the lecture was at night, the windows and doors to the large, un-insulated steel warehouse were usually open and the cool Santa Monica air drifted in. Folding chairs were placed in rows on the concrete floor. Video cameras on tripods taped the lectures. If you got there early you could climb up the modular scaffolding system that surrounded three sides of the lecture space and find a seat. Students jammed onto the scaffolding, which offered a great view. The lecturer's slides or films were projected from the administrative/computer room floor above onto a screen next to the podium. A pretty simple set up but it worked. The space had great atmosphere and hopefully this will read through in the old recordings.[30]

Public Access Project's last public event at SCI-Arc was a May 19, 1977 presentation of Douglas Davis's performance *Two Cities, a Text, Flesh, and the Devil*, which was broadcast live on Theta Cable.[31]

Video in Southern California in 1979 was not a novelty: it was a featured player in a diverse array of contexts—entertainment, educational, artistic, activist and technological. As such, it was almost inevitably part of The Architecture Gallery.

ENDNOTES

1. A full list of Architecture Gallery lectures available on the SCI-Arc Media Archive (http://sma.sciarc.edu) may be found in the bibliography.

2. M. J. Alexander, "The Architect and Television," *Pencil Points* 26 (August 1945): 93-95.

3. "Television Transmitter Station," *Architectural Forum* 83 (November 1945).

4. "House Planned to Check Off Television War," *Los Angeles Times* (August 7, 1949): E7.

5. *Architectural Forum* 89 (September 1948): 118-120.

6. See Mark Bennett's witty series of plans of television spaces, "As Seen On TV," accessed December 6, 2012 via <http://www.artnet.com/artists/mark-bennett-2/>

7. Julian Cooper (dir), Malcolm Brown (prod.) "Reyner Banham Loves Los Angeles" 1972. *One Pair of Eyes* (BBC Television series 1967-84) Cooper and Banham went on to make *The World About Us: Roads To El Dorado A Journey With Reyner Banham* in 1979.

8. *The Art Of Architecture* (series) by ATV with Reyner Banham: *The Good Old Rules* (March 21, 1960); *The Age of the Spaceman* (April 4, 1960); *The Architecture We Deserve* (April 18, 1960). See BFI's *Film & TV Database,* accessed December 10, 2012 *via* <http://old.bfi.org.uk/filmtvinfo/ftvdb/>

9. Beatriz Colomina, "The Media House," *Assemblage* 27 (1995): 64.

10. See the finding aids for the *Aline and Eero Saarinen papers 1906-1977* at the Archives of American Art, accessed December 5, 2012 via <http://www.aaa.si.edu/collections/aline-and-eero-saarinen-papers-5589/more>

11. Wolf von Eckhardt characterized the show as "a maddening bore." See "TV's Monumental Miss; Buildings and TV: A Failure of Vision; The Networks' Blind Spot on Architecture." *The Washington Post* (August 2, 1978): Wednesday, Final Edition, Style; Preview; p. D1.

12. John O'Connor, "A Provocative New Series on Modern Art," *New York Times* (January 11, 1981): Sunday, Late City Final Edition, Section 2; p. 25.

13. Paul Goldberger, "Architecture View; A Grand Tour of Spaces and Places Just Misses the Mark," *New York Times* (March 30, 1986): Sunday, Late City Final Edition, Section 2; p. 25.

14. Paul Goldberger, "American Architecture and How It Grew," *New York Times* (September 27, 1987): Sunday, Late City Final Edition, Section 2; p. 34.

15. Stuart Rose and M. Scheffel Pierce, "Television as a Design Tool," *Journal of Architectural Education*, Vol. 21, No. 3 (March 1967): 5.

16. Peter Kamnitzer, "Computer Aid to Design," *Architectural Design* (September 1969): 509-514.

17. "Prosecution to Use Video Tape at Mrs. Tucker's Murder Trial: Introduction of Recording of Death Scene at Opening of Proceedings Today Will Set Precedent, DA Aide Says." *Los Angeles Times* (October 3, 1968): C1.

18. Barbara London, "Video: A Selected Chronology, 1963-1983." *Art Journal,* Vol. 45, No. 3, Video: *The Reflexive Medium* (Autumn, 1985): 249-262.

19. Long Beach Museum of Art, *Southland Video Anthology* [exhibition], June 8-September 7, 1975. (Long Beach: The Museum, 1975).

20. Glenn Phillips, *California Video: Artists and Histories* (Los Angeles: Getty Research Institute, 2008). Two of these pioneers taught at SCI-Arc: John Knight, from 1977 to the mid-1980s, and Susan Mogul, 2003-2004. Two of SCI-Arc's Media Managers—Keith Downey, 1994-9; and Reza Monahan, 2009-present—have also worked in video.

21. "Since its beginnings in the 1930s, television has become a vital force in determining our culture, our values, and our fantasies. ... Television has changed our conception of information, and has transformed the way we spend our time. ...With the continuing growth of television it will become more and more difficult to separate what is inside and what is outside The TV Environment." Billy Adler, John Margolies, Van Schley, Ilene Segalove, *The TV Environment* (New York: Gordon and Breach, 1973).

22. "Cable TV Gets Signal from FCC to Move into Big City Markets," *Los Angeles Times* (April 1, 1972): B9.

23. Mann, Jim, "Court Rules Cable TV Needn't Offer Public Channels," *Los Angeles Times* (April 3, 1979): 1-1.

24. "Santa Monica OKs Cable TV Franchise," *Los Angeles Times* (September 17, 1967): WS5.

25. Skip Ferderber and Doug Smith, "Public-Access TV: Revolution May Come in a Tube," *Los Angeles Times* (April 22, 1973): WS1.

26. "L.A. Access Project to Hold Festival" *Los Angeles Times* (March 2, 1973): 121.

27. "Town Meeting Tape," *Los Angeles Times* (March 15, 1973): WS6.

28. Morton Neikrug, Telephone interview with the author, April 1, 2012.

29. "I took pains to light the lectures appropriately. This was always a problem—the Main Space was not very friendly. I found Fresnel spotlights at Olesen Lighting that ran on house current. There was also a Lekolite that we otherwise used for model photography. But sometimes the space worked to our benefit: daytime events usually had daylight coming through the skylights. ...I insisted on shooting in black and white long after color became accessible. I argued that we didn't have any way to throw enough light, and actually we would get a worse image with color. I was told I was obstructing progress, but I still think I was right." Ibid.

30. Personal email, February 20, 2012.

31. "Video Performance Artwork," *Los Angeles Times* (May 19, 1977): G1.

PORTRAITS OF THE ARTIST, AMONGST MEN

JOE DAY

Though hardly a lost decade, the 1970s are elusive years in Los Angeles architecture. For L.A.'s boutique practices in particular, it was a slow stretch. Though some of the Case Study Houses were still being completed in the '70s, the momentum of that program peaked earlier with the publication of Esther McCoy's *Modern California Homes* in 1962 and had run its course by the last issue of John Entenza's *Arts+Architecture* in 1967. Reyner Banham's *Los Angeles: Architecture of the Four Ecologies*, though released in 1971, was largely a product of the previous decade. On the other hand, the major postmodern compendia of Moore, Gebhard, and Jencks arrived at its end, or early in the '80s, but featured little recent work. The 1970s were, however, a decade of consolidation for larger firms, and a catalytic ten years in the L.A. art world. The downtown skyline hardened into its familiar, mirrored, taut-skin silhouette, thanks to the corporate ascendency of late modern and "Silver" partnerships such as DMJM and Ellerbe Beckett. As the city crystalized at the mega-scale, a new generation of Light and Space artists, led by Robert Irwin and James Turrell, recalibrated its minute interiors. Though dismissed by many contemporary critics,[1] these ambient investigations would eventually eclipse the Minimalist and Pop "Cool Schools" of both L.A. and New York.

It was also, and not coincidently, the decade in which Frank Gehry reached a first plateau of maturity and recognition. For Gehry, born in 1929, it was the make-or-break decade of his forties. Against formidable odds—little support from local modernists, waves of East Coast condescension, and the economic malaise of the Carter years—he took ownership of an intractable decade and entered the 1980s worlds removed from his American contemporaries in disciplinary terms, and on a very different trajectory from his peers and protégés in California.

Not many published photographs of Gehry date from the 1970s, and those that do often show him in a state of anxious "repose." These were the years before he shifted, as Warhol had, to Brooks Brothers button-down convention to counter the presumed outlandishness of his work. (I've searched in vain for an image of him I remember—though now I'm willing to admit, perhaps only in my mind's eye—sporting an Adidas tracksuit and Gucci loafers, circa 1976.) However singular he was to become in subsequent years, Gehry was avidly social in the 1970s, and landed in a number of group photos that reveal his startling gift for moving between disparate, if not antagonistic milieus. Whether in the company of artists or of architects at very different stages of their careers, Frank Gehry appears, Waldo-like, everywhere and all at once.

The first of these group portraits finds Gehry among like-minded pranksters at a LACMA Art Day in 1968, the caboose of a conga-line of luminaries from the Ferus Gallery including Larry Bell, Billy Al Bengston, elder statesman John Altoon, and his wife Babs [**Fig. 1**]. It is worth noting that while these artists shared a gallery, their work overlapped little in terms of media or sensibility. The artists span from AbEx to Finish Fetish—from Altoon's gestural canvases to Bell's glass boxes, with Bengston's airbrushed insignias somewhere in between—but were united in their taste for revelry. (M.I.A. at LACMA that day from the Ferus stable, but soon to reap its rewards, are the three Eds— Kienholz, Moses, and Ruscha.)

In a second portrait, ten years later, Gehry

Fig. 1: Frank Gehry, Babs Altoon, Billy Al Bengston, Larry Bell, John Altoon, and Tony Berlant at Culture Day at LACMA (L.A. County Museum of Art), 1968.

sits to the left in a formal ensemble to mark Philip Johnson's AIA Gold Medal, awarded in 1978 [**Fig. 2**]. Though the night belonged principally to Johnson, the tableau marks a watershed for all the rest in frame, and the three of the New York Five included—Graves, Gwathmey, and Eisenman in the back row—appear particularly pleased. Gehry, though, looks considerably less festive, with his high-contrast tie, full mustache, and casual eyewear marking him (and Charles Moore, even more so) as westerners at an East Coast banquet. Missing, in terms of bracketing sensibilities, were Robert Venturi and Richard Meier.

The third group, including most of the participants in the Architecture Gallery 1979, has some of the nonchalance of the LACMA shot ten years earlier, but also quite a bit of the focus and strategic contrivance of the line-up for Johnson [**Fig. 3**]. Gehry's role in this context is more ambiguous. Rumor has him conscripted into this rehearsal for the "Santa Monica School" by Thom Mayne.[2] Gehry is foregrounded, and looking not toward the camera—and posterity—but at whoever or whatever has

lifted the camera high enough to clear Mayne's 6′-5″ frame. The oversights on the beach that day were also the players most deeply connected to SCI-Arc: Ray Kappe and Michael Rotondi (though Eric Owen Moss was mistaken for the latter in the caption).

In all three portraits Gehry evades direct, frontal exposure, looking around, to the right or left, but never squarely into the camera lens. Though hardly marginal, he is always to edge of frame. He appears *vested* in each photograph, but differently in each one, and at almost a spatio-temporal remove from all the others represented. These photographs reveal less Gehry's shifting alignments than his catalytic ability to be *present*: in all three ensembles, he is uniquely, informally attentive to the instant being captured. In each, he is caught observing the specific circumstances of the photograph being taken, the scene behind or off-camera, not the potential historical gravity of the gathering—the moment, not the Moment. He learned this from the artists: the only artist acknowledging the camera in the LACMA shot is the one I hadn't heard of, Tony Berlant, to the far right. All the other architects—the

Fig. 2: From left to right: Frank Gehry, Michael Graves, Charles Moore, Cesar Pelli, Philip Johnson, Charles Gwathmey, Stanley Tigerman, Peter Eisenman, and Robert A.M. Stern on the occasion of Johnson's receiving the AIA Gold Medal, 1978.

Santa Monica heretics as much as the New York New and Old Guard—are playing strictly to the camera, convinced they are staring down the future.

This remove is equally apparent when one expands the frame to include not just the visage but the work of the artists and architects in each grouping. While Gehry has consistently claimed his work is best understood in terms of art practice, his projects in the 1970s had little to do with either the lingeringly polychrome, painterly ambitions of Altoon or Bengston, or (yet) with the reflective surfaces of Bell. If there is a local connection, it is the one Grant Mudford found in his early photographs of Gehry's own home, reintroduced in this show, which render its interiors not as a series of violations, but as a sequence of plays between environment and illumination in the tradition of Light & Space [pp. 162-169]. Retrospectives of Gehry's career often begin with the "rupture" announced by his home, completed at the end of the 1970s, but it's more instructive to see that project as a symptom or residue of a variety of conceptual moves away from mainstream architectural production he tested through that decade: cheap studios for artists, furniture, forays into real estate. Few of these projects and ventures outside his home had an audience before the 1980s, and their significance is still under-appreciated in the arc of Gehry's development.

In the 1970s, Gehry's work often transposed approaches from one discipline to the next, and his appearance in all these contexts at either end of the 1970s reflects less his centrality in any of them,

more his active transmigration between them. Gehry's material ingenuity and appetite for abstraction were the keys to his credibility with artists, who hired him to design their studios on the basis of his furniture and lighting design; his play on Ruscha's mega-graphic signage at Santa Monica Place, as much as the declensions of his home, endeared him to a New York architectural scene preoccupied with larger-scale projects. Within the Santa Monica School, Gehry's "strengths" were more controversial, as some, especially Coy Howard and Robert Mangurian, could claim even closer ties to artists, while others, including Craig Hodgetts (as well as the other Architecture Gallery 1979 participants missing from the beach photo—Eugene Kupper, Roland Coate, and Frank Dimster) were as well-versed in harnessing new technologies or subverting corporate practice. In the peculiar hindsight provided by this revisiting of Architecture Gallery 1979, Gehry might seem more indebted to the younger generation than ahead of it. But here, the interpersonal and the historical diverge. Gehry almost certainly drew valuable insights from younger, possibly more "with it" architects.[3] But if Thom Mayne pulled him into frame, the rest needed Gehry there even more.

Though attendant to each context in ways that his colleagues are not, Gehry remains, for posterity, a moving target in these three group portraits. Cavorting artist, ill-at-ease Californian, reluctant paterfamilias: we see him testing each role for its potential, its demands, and its limitations. On at least one level, it's easy to see why Gehry was so much happier with the artists—however simpatico, they weren't his kind, and thus not his rivals. Both Johnson's distant but fatherly embrace and the double-edged respect of new L.A. architects must have raised complicated Oedipal "anxieties of influence" for one as devoted to psychotherapy as Gehry was then. A portrait missing from these years, and one that might explain Gehry's demeanor in the others most succinctly, would capture Gehry in the company of his fellow group therapy participants under the guidance of Milton Wexler. By his own account, Gehry attended for two years, without uttering a word.[4]

Fig. 3: From left to right: Frederick Fisher, Robert Mangurian, Eric Owen Moss, Coy Howard, Craig Hodgetts, Thom Mayne, and Frank Gehry, 1980.

ENDNOTES

1. cf. Rosalind Krauss on James Turrell in "The Cultural Logic of the Late-Capitalist Museum," *October* 54 (Autumn 1990): 13: "It was also a function of the new centrality given to James Turrell, an extremely minor figure for Minimalism in the late 1960s and early 1970s, but one who plays an important role in the reprogrammation [sic] of Minimalism for the late 1980s."

2. The photo was published in *Interiors* (Dec 1980) to accompany Joseph Giovannini's article, "California Design: New West Side Story."

3. Howard and Kupper in particular were emphatic on this point in interviews conducted by the curators for this exhibition.

4. Audrey Nelson, "The Strong Silent Type: The Male Advantage," *Psychology Today*, April 23, 2011. <http://www.psychologytoday.com/blog/he-speaks-she-speaks/201104/the-strong-silent-type-the-male-advantage>.

WICKED ARCHITECTS
PAULETTE SINGLEY

The Gagosian Gallery, by Craig Hodgetts and Robert Mangurian of Studio Works, marks the intersection of two significant cultural sites that emerged from *fin de la decennia* Los Angeles. In Venice, California, *Wet* magazine and Market Street concentrated design debates between contextual or historical approaches and conceptual or technological strategies into a mutually inclusive philosophy wherein it was possible to simultaneously reference architectural history and contemporary art in a single building. Located on the block-long stretch of Market Street between Ocean Front Walk and Pacific Avenue, Larry Gagosian's 1980 gallery forms the nexus of this intersection between architecture and art practices that emerged in the late 1970s.

Despite the presence of a central, circular courtyard, the Gagosian Gallery stands as a pivotal project in which classical and avant-garde approaches to architecture relied upon each other as accomplices in a postmodern discussion concerning fragmentation and rupture. The courtyard is an originary whole that registers disarticulation, a center that evidences destabilization [**Figs. 1-3**]. In this game of *ludus geometrico*, Hodgetts and Mangurian perform as "wicked architects," a designation coined by the historian Manfredo Tafuri in 1980 to describe Piranesi, whose work established a classical language of architectural order only to pervert it. The Gagosian Gallery invites the counter-critique of a neo-avant-garde "systematic criticism of the concept of 'center'" in a world where the measured archaeology of neoclassicism gives way to the compositional bricolage of an inherently ahistorical spatial revolution.[1] The postmodern shift towards classical revival, then, carried within itself the seeds of its own immediate deviation into the romanticism of deconstruction, delineating the model of one paradigm shift embedded within another during a moment of highly accelerated change.

Fig. 1: Studio Works, Gagosian Gallery, Venice, 1980.

Fig. 2: Gagosian Gallery, view of courtyard.

Fig. 3: Gagosian Gallery, street facade.

MARKET STREET

From the 1960s to the 1980s Market Street was the epicenter of a burgeoning art scene in Venice. When Thom Mayne opened the Architecture Gallery in 1979 at his house on 209 San Juan Avenue, his address joined a constellation of significant Venice galleries and studios: Billy Al Bengston at 110 Mildred Street, Eames Office at 901 Washington Boulevard, Robert Graham at 69 Windward Avenue, L.A. Louver gallery at 55 North Venice Boulevard, Ed Moses at 1905 Ocean Front Walk, and Studio Works at the corner of Rose Avenue and Ocean Front Walk. On Market Street alone there was Larry Bell at number 76, Robert Irwin at 72, DeWain Valentine at 69, and the Gagosian Gallery at 51.[2]

In May of 1970, around the time Irwin gave up studio art to explore environmental research, his studio at 72 Market Street hosted NASA's National Symposium on Habitability as part of their research into living conditions on long-term space projects. Dr. Ed Wortz, who ran a research laboratory at Garret Aerospace Corporation, describes Irwin's installation for this event:

> [T]here were these big two-foot-diameter white tubes along the entire length of the other end of the room, standing vertically, floor to ceiling. It was very elegant, very pristine. Larry Bell had created two wonderful plated-glass skylights, and Frank Gehry had helped Bob design the interior, which consisted of various raised acoustic platforms and islands but no chairs.[3]

Continuing these experiments with emerging technologies, Irwin's studio also housed the Market Street Program, a series of group exhibitions lasting from 1971-73 in which artists were partnered with each other based on information derived from questionnaires that computers correlated into compatible affinities. In May of 1980 Irwin returned to 78 Market Street, next to his former studio, where he removed the entire storefront to replace it with scrim, eroding the boundary between gallery and city as well as inviting viewer's to participate in a play of light, shadow, and translucency.

Soon afterward in 1984, Morphosis's Thom Mayne and Michael Rotondi completed 72 Market Street, a restaurant located in Irwin's former studio space that also functioned as an art gallery. By opening the façade to frame the street and placing a room with a bar and seating area adjacent to the public sidewalk, Morphosis played off Irwin's subject-object oscillation between looking in and looking out [**Figs. 4-5**]. This cubic antechamber was the first in a series of their inserting disruptive machines into ideal geometric rooms. A metal column located at the center of the cube supported a square structural frame rotated off axis that performed as an earthquake tension ring. As the architects explain, the rotated and fragmented structural systems addressed "issues of loss of center, destabilization, and the breaking and making of architecture."[4]

Irwin and other artists in the Light and Space movement of the 1970s explored non-object based environments and site specific installations that probed the potential of light, shadow, and retinal spectrums to bend space and erode the distinction between sculpture and architecture, wall and space. In exploring light's transformative potential, Irwin and Turrell worked with Wortz in order to study the perceptual experience of environment. They conducted experiments in UCLA's anechoic chamber, a sensory deprivation room, where they would isolate themselves (as well as volunteer subjects) for extended periods of time without light or sound in order to heighten perception of the world they would observe upon being released from the cell. These experiments led Irwin to develop installations that sought higher levels of phenomenal engagement with their subjects, as well as leading Turrell to the Roden Crater, a sensory enhancement observatory that heightens visitors' perceptions of the sky. With the Roden Crater, Turrell completed a trajectory of inquiry that started in the '70s with his "Skyspaces," enclosed rooms holding roughly fifteen people and open to the sky. Turrell explains that light and space "can be formed without physical material like concrete or steel." He continues: "We can actually stop vision and the penetration of vision with where light is and where it isn't."[5] Similarly, on observing, the firmament Irwin writes: "We know

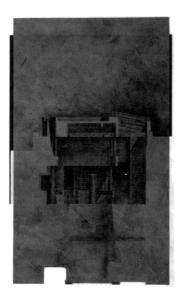

Fig. 4: Morphosis, 72 Market Street, Venice, California, 1983. Perspectival Section.

Fig. 5: Morphosis, 72 Market Street, interior view.

the sky's blueness even before we know it as 'blue,' let alone as 'sky.'"[6] Hodgetts' description of the Gagosian courtyard similarly focuses attention on an infinite vertical axis where "intersecting jet streams fade across a sky criss-crossed by kites and clouds" and where "the ellipse of the sun's shadow crawls around the circumference. Two feet per hour at the solstice."[7]

The Gagosian Gallery's massing emerged as a *sui generis* diagram in response to the client's needs and the city's requirements. For the tight lot at 51 Market Street they designed a building that housed a four-car garage and a 1200 square foot art gallery on the ground floor with 1700 square feet of living space on the upper two floors. Gagosian required that the building be anonymous to the street so that his valuable art collection remained secret. The rotunda, then, solved the problem of day-lighting the residential interior that stepped back from the blank façade and provided necessary outside space for a project that filled every corner of the site at ground level. The circular courtyard—rendered sharply against the sky with a knife-edge detail—performs as a light-space installation, an ob-servation vessel positioned historically and formally

somewhere between an anechoic chamber and the Roden crater.

WET MAGAZINE

In 1976, Leonard Koren, a graduate of UCLA's newly created Master's program in architecture, published the first issue of *Wet* out of his apartment-studio in Venice. Operating at the edge of 1970s culture, *Wet*'s aesthetic trajectory stretched from the fringes of mid-1970s California hedonism to the post-punk context of Melrose Avenue in the 1980s. If the magazine's name alludes to the sensuality of slippery bodies or nocturnal emissions, its subtitle, "The Magazine of Gourmet Bathing," developed pota-bility, ablution, toilets, swimming pools, waterbeds, water gardens, and general liquidity into an alibi for addressing a larger cultural content.[8]

Koren's interest in architecture was evi-dent. Among the buildings and projects published in *Wet* were the Gagosian Gallery, Mark Mack's drawings for conceptual houses, Thom Mayne's addition to Fred Delmer's beach cottage, Frederick Fisher's Caplin house (whose client, Loren-Paul Caplin, suggested the name "wet" to Koren), Frank Gehry's Ron Davis studio, Charles Moore's own house, and Michael Sorkin's essay on "Vegetecture." Setting Los Angeles's cultural milieu to a pop music soundtrack, it published articles by or about Cal Worthington, Timothy Leary, Tom Petty, Talking Heads, Matt Groening, Deborah Harry, Tony Alva, Richard Gere, Mick Jagger, William Burroughs, Robert Smithson, the Dead Kennedys, Helmut Newton, XTC, Elvis Costello, David Lynch, Laurie Anderson, Ed Ruscha, and John Lydon. A crucible of late '70s and early '80s pop culture in Los Angeles, *Wet*'s "graphic sensibilities varied from punk to pre-New Wave to proto-PostMod."[9] April Greiman's and Jayme Odgers's design for the September/October, 1979 issue of *Wet* perfectly distilled Melrose's New Wave ethos, as did her identity and interior design for the China Club [**Figs. 6-7**]. Bold black and red geometries of circles and triangles pierced by pre-cisely rotated lines recall László Moholy-Nagy's Proun spaces and Kasmir Malevich's Suprematist paintings.

In its March/April, 1981 issue *Wet* described the Gagosian Gallery as "a gigantic automobile carburetor, a monolithic warehouse mass, cored by a round, *palazzo italianato* courtyard."[10] *Wet*'s framing of the Gagosian among the pages of this "Melrose aesthetic" introduces a neo-Suprematist, even proto-Deconstructivist, reading of the gallery into this discussion. Seen through Melrose and Malevich, the Gagosian's jigsaw step stair leading up to a small balcony pierces the rotunda's perfect circular geometry as an aberrant, asymmetrically placed compositional device. Likewise, Hodgetts and Mangurian used galvanized tread metal on the gallery façade not only to pervert industrial material into decorative appliqué but also as the *lingua franca* of the artist's loft. As with the courtyard stair, rough details with highly exposed construction techniques rendered the project as willful bricolage.

NEOCINQUECENTISMO

Hodgetts rhetorically questions the project's sources when asking: "Like early Corb? Or was it Palladio?"[11] His and Mangurian's deft connois-seurship layered rarefied historical precedent upon explicit vernacular context. Through a large blank

Fig. 6: Wet Magazine cover by April Greiman and Jayme Odgers, 1979.

Fig. 7: Advertisement for the China Club by April Greiman, 1980.

wall flanked by symmetrically placed windows and doors, the Gagosian façade refers both to Le Corbusier's Villa Schwob and to Larry Bell's gallery storefront just a couple of doors away. Studio Works named this project the Palazzo Gagosian in refer-ence to Venetian palace facades that inspired the front elevation and as a play on words between Ven-ice, California and Venice, Italy.

But it was Lombardia more than the Vene-to that inspired this project. As a fellow of the

American Academy in Rome in 1977, Mangurian visited the Casa del Mantegna in Mantua and photographed its compelling forced perspective [**Figs. 8-9**]. When a visitor stands in the center of this circular courtyard and looks straight up, a shift in the geometry of the upper floors produces a square that aligns tangentially with the circle of the courtyard, a perfect spatial translation of Vitruvius's description of the human body inscribed by both a circle and a square that Leonardo da Vinci translated into the definitive diagram of Renaissance humanism.

Studio Works' turn toward Italy parallels the Museum of Modern Art's 1975 exhibition and catalogue *The Architecture of the École des Beaux-Arts* that disseminated a series of French academic terms, such as *enfilade*, *poché*, and *parti*, into the production of space. The breathtaking watercolor renderings of classical reconstructions reproduced in the exhibition publication returned architecture to its ancient Roman sources of highly sculpted spaces. Symmetrical, thick, layered rooms rendered with excruciating detail inspired experiments with architecture and its representation. While in some cases this would manifest itself as *le rappel a l'ordre* and the conservatism of Hans Sedlmayr or the Krier brothers, in other instances the Italian orientation inspired interpretations by Robert Venturi, Colin Rowe, or Aldo Rossi regarding theories of complexity, collage, and typology. It is Manfredo Tafuri's *explication de texte* of Piranesi's *Campo Marzio dell'Antica Roma*, however, that most closely resembles the avant-garde position Southern California architects developed in response to this region's chaotic suburbs, slipshod construction techniques, and perceived absence of historical urban fabric. Tafuri's description of the *Campo Marzio* serves as an analogue for the architecture and urbanism of Los Angeles: "Piranesi presents organisms that *pretend* to have a centrality but that never achieve one... Piranesi's engravings, however, present to us not merely a set designer's whim, but rather a *systematic criticism of the concept of 'center.'*" [12] Hodgetts similarly writes of the Gagosian:

> The sudden Platonic alignment of the solar plexus with some celestial axis fails to rend

reality. There is no music of the spheres. No Romeo climbs to the tiny porch which interrupts the perfect radius. [13]

Likewise, Hodgetts and Mangurian's rough jigsaw steps disrupting a classical rotunda recalls Piranesi's *Carceri d'invenzione*, in which the stairs and ramps twist normative perspectival space. Indeed, just across the street and three years later, the Robert Graham column and structural system that Morphosis inserted into 72 Market Street—like the Orrery at Kate Mantilini, or the scaffold at the Cedars Sinai Comprehensive Cancer Center—violates space as a bachelor machine or torture device inserted into a buried chamber. At the Gagosian, as Hodgetts claims, "subterranean echoes swirl from a broad, high room. Like a tomb. It is possible to imagine that this place is below the ground. It is time to put away memories of the surface...to the inevitable discotheques and motels." [14] Hodgetts and Mangurian expertly play the game of *ars combinatio, ars contaminatio* at the Gagosian, mixing pure and impure forms into spatial bricolage, a "corrosive" form of "antihistoricism," according to Tafuri, where "everything is now permitted and everything is recoverable...like a labyrinth without exits." [15]

ENDNOTES

1. Manfredo Tafuri, *The Sphere and the Labyrinth: Avant-gardes and Architecture from Piranesi to the 1970s*, (Cambridge, MA: MIT Press, 1987): 27.

2. The *Los Angeles Times* commented on the cultural boom in Venice in the mid-1970s. See Barbara Isenberg, "Is Bohemia Still Affordable?" *Los Angeles Times* (October 30, 1977).

3. Cited in Lawrence Weschler, *Seeing is Forgetting the Name of the Thing One Sees: A Life of Contemporary Artist Robert Irwin* (Berkeley: University of California Press, 1982): 132.

4. "72 Market Street Restaurant," Morphosis Architects, accessed March 1, 2013. <http://morphopedia.com/projects/72-market-street-restaurant>.

5. "Interview with James Turrell," accessed March 1, 2013. <http://www.pbs.org/wnet/egg/215/turrell/interview_content_1.html>.

6. Robert Irwin, *Notes Toward a Conditional Art* (Los Angeles: J. Paul Getty Museum, 2011): 170.

7. Craig Hodgetts, "Building of the Quarter: Palazzo Gagosian, Venice, California," *Archetype* 2, no. 4 (1992): 16.

8. For Koren's account of the history of *Wet*, see Leonard Koren, *Making Wet: The Magazine of Gourmet Bathing* (Point Reyes, CA: Imperfect Publishing, 2012).

9. Michael Dooley, "Bare Bodies, Mud Baths, and Beyond: Wet in Retrospect," *Imprint*, accessed March 1, 2013. <http://imprint.printmag.com/design-thinking/wet-magazine>.

10. "A Palazzo in Venice: Important New Architecture Hides Behind an Anonymous Façade," *Wet: The Magazine of Gourmet Bathing* 30 (March-April 1981): 43.

11. Hodgetts, 16.

12. Tafuri, *The Sphere and the Labyrinth*, 27.

13. Hodgetts, 16.

14. Ibid.

15. Tafuri, 53.

Figs. 8 & 9: Andrea Mantegna, Casa del Mantegna, Mantua, 1476. View of Courtyard.

ARCHITECTURE 1979

THOM MAYNE

The lecture series documented here, which took place in the late '70s, evolved from a serendipitous confluence of events in my life. I had just completed my M. Arch degree at Harvard and had recently returned to L.A. where I was immediately struck by something palpable that was going on in the architecture community. Perhaps it would have been less noticeable had I not been living on the East Coast for the past year, but suffice it to say that the mood was strikingly different, more optimistic, more open, more creative than what I had seen in Cambridge or New York during my tenure at Harvard. After collecting me from LAX but before allowing me to drop my luggage at home, Michael Rotondi insisted that we swing by Frank's house in Santa Monica which was then under construction. It was a powerful blast of something contemporary and new... something that could never have been done anywhere but L.A. That visit was probably the initial seed that fed my sense that something very interesting was going on in L.A. By coincidence it was also my turn at SCI-Arc to organize the annual lecture series. And, as a further bit of good luck, I had just rented a large residential loft space in Venice that had an enormous empty gallery space attached. Things came together quickly.

The available gallery space in my studio provided the opportunity to build a parallel series of exhibitions that would run concurrently with the lecture series. I chose a group of people who were all clearly active and engaged in the vibrant architectural community I had returned to—they were more or less of the same generation and they shared an optimism, inquisitiveness and commitment to pursuing and incorporating their own research and investigations into their work.

The shows ran for five days—they came down on Sundays and the next one went up on Mondays. It was a crazy and intense schedule especially considering that we had no track record and could not predict whether a single person would show up. When the first show opened we had a fair number of visitors including the *Los Angeles Times* architecture critic, John Dreyfuss. He ran a review on the front page of the Arts section in the *Los Angeles Times* that was followed by coverage of each subsequent show. The audience grew rapidly and we were amazed at the hunger for a public architectural conversation. The exhibitions fed into an interest in the lectures—both were made accessible to a much wider audience via John's incisive critical reviews in the *Times*. John sensed, as I had, that this series provided a much needed and appreciated new outlet for exploring what was happening in the Los Angeles architectural community—to an audience much broader than that found in the architecture schools alone. John was instrumental in galvanizing the public interest in the ideas behind the lectures; his enthusiastic reviews provided a platform for developing a much-needed public discourse about the work in L.A. Interestingly the series of pieces John wrote also propelled him in a new direction; his interest in the younger generation of architects in L.A. would continue past the era of the exhibition/lecture series to become a lifelong preoccupation. He would continue, through his career as a critic, to serve as a vital advocate for the unique energy and trajectory of L.A. Architecture.

This exhibition has given me a chance to look back at an event in my history that I haven't thought about for years. The sense I had that L.A. was experiencing a unique phase of creativity has, with time, concretized. The people invited to take part in the lecture/exhibition series in '79 were indeed those whose careers were broadening, their trajectories all led to an expansion of the discourse related to the potentialities of an architecture rooted in experimentation and risk. All in the group were in an early or mid-level place in careers that coincided with being at the peak of an experimental phase that ultimately led to the development of clearly new and more interesting definitions of a more conceptual architectural practice than had been practiced by preceding generations. Outliers all, I see upon looking back that what we all sensed actually did have the legs to carry the momentum forward and beyond the West Coast to contribute to a significant development in the global practice of architecture.

CREDITS

We gratefully acknowledge the following sources for permission to reprint copyrighted material. All reasonable efforts have been made to trace the copyright holders of the visual materials reproduced in this book. Please report any errors or omissions to the publisher for correction in future editions.

TEXTS

All essays by John Dreyfuss copyright © 1979, *Los Angeles Times*. Reprinted by permission.

"The Importance of Being Coy," by Joseph Giovannini is reprinted by permission of the author.

IMAGES

Courtesy of Art Center College of Design/Dlugolecki Photography: p. 21 (top left)

Photo by Larry Bessell: p. 60

Photo by Tom Bonner: pp. 86 top (left and right) and middle (left and right), 92-93 (all), 118, 131, 134, 142 (top and bottom), 144 (top and bottom), 145 (top and bottom), 156-158, 204 (top right)

Courtesy of Peter de Bretteville: pp. 68, 69 (top left), 70-71 (all), 140, 141, 185 (all)

Courtesy of Roland Coate: pp. 45, 46 (all), 47 (all), 124, 125

Courtesy of Frank Dimster: pp. 14 (middle), 19 (left), 57, 58-59 (all), 122, 123

Courtesy of Frederick Fisher: pp. 24, 52-53 (all), 126-129, 146, 147

Photo by Frederick Fisher: p. 24

Photo by Mary Frampton: pp. 34, 36, 42, 48, 54, 66, 74, 82 (top and bottom), 94, 194

Courtesy of Gehry Partners LLC: p. 26 (middle), 64 (top left and right), 65 (all), 192 (top right)

Courtesy of April Greiman: p. 205 (top and bottom)

Courtesy of Gruen Associates: p. 18

Photo by Judd Gunderson: p. 88

Photo by Squire Haskins: p. 200

Courtesy of Craig Hodgetts and Robert Mangurian: pp. 16, 22, 84, 86-87 (all), 114, 115, 118-121, 132-35, 181,

183 (bottom left), 202 (all)

Courtesy of Coy Howard: pp. 98-99 (all), 148-151

Courtesy of Arata Isozaki: pp. 170, 171

Courtesy of Ray Kappe: p. 21 (bottom left)

Courtesy of Eugene Kupper: pp. 20 (top and bottom), 38, 39 (top left, top right, and bottom right); 40 (all), 41 (all), 113

Photo by Eugene Kupper: 191 (left and right), 192 (bottom)

Courtesy of Jerrold Lomax: p. 21 (top right)

Courtesy of the Los Angeles Times Photographic Archive, Department of Special Collections, Charles E. Young Research Library, UCLA: pp. 34, 36, 42, 48, 54, 60, 66, 74, 82 (top and bottom), 88, 94, 194

Courtesy of John Lumsden: p. 19 (right)

Photo by Robert Mangurian: pp. 186, 202 (all), 207 (top and bottom)

Photo by Jacob Melchi/Arnoldi Studio: p. 26 (top)

Courtesy of Morphosis Architects: p. 15 (top and bottom), 26 (bottom), 78-79 (all), 116, 117, 136-39, 152-155, 160, 161, 172-175, 184 (top and bottom right), 204 (top left)

Courtesy of Eric Owen Moss Architects: pp. 25 (middle), 92-93 (all), 142-45, 156-159, 180, 183 (top and bottom right)

Photo by Grant Mudford: pp. 64 (bottom left and right), 162-169

Photo by Morton Neikrug: p. 17

Photo © 1980 Ave Pildas: p. 201

Photo by Marvin Rand: p. 69 (top and bottom right)

Photo by Julius Shulman. © J. Paul Getty Trust. Used with permission. Julius Shulman Photography Archive, Research Library at the Getty Research Institute (2004 R. 10): p. 14 (top), 39 (bottom left and right)

Courtesy of Helmut Schulitz: p. 25 (top)

Photo by and © Julian Wasser. Courtesy of Julian Wasser, Craig Krull Gallery, Santa Monica, and Museum Associates/LACMA: p. 199

Photo by Joshua White: pp. 23 (top and bottom), 45, 47 (all), 50, 53 (top left, top right, bottom left, bottom middle), 5, 57,

210

58 (bottom left and right), 59 (all), 105 (top and bottom),
110 (top and bottom), 111, 119-129, 146, 147

Photo by Jon Yoder: p. 21 (bottom right)

Photo by Daniel Zimbaldi: p. 25 (bottom)

BIBLIOGRAPHY

INTERVIEWS
Branda, Ewan, interview with Frederick Fisher.
	Los Angeles, CA, 10 May 2012
Branda, Ewan, interview with Robert Mangurian.
	Los Angeles, CA, 26 Apr 2012
Gannon, Todd, interview with Peter de Bretteville.
	New Haven, CT, 26 Apr 2012
Gannon, Todd, interview with Craig Hodgetts.
	Los Angeles, CA, 5 Mar 2012
Gannon, Todd, interview with Craig Hodgetts.
	Culver City, CA, 2 Jul 2012
Gannon, Todd, interview with Ray Kappe.
	Los Angeles, CA, 29 Jun 2012
Gannon, Todd, interview with Ray Kappe.
	Los Angeles, CA, 17 Jul 2012
Gannon, Todd, telephone interview with Peter Cook.
	Los Angeles, CA and London, UK.
	26 Jun 2012
Gannon, Todd, telephone interview with Charles
	Jencks. Los Angeles, CA and London, UK.
	30 May 2012
Gannon, Todd, telephone interview with Eugene
	Kupper. Los Angeles, CA and Scottsdale,
	AZ. 23 Mar 2012
Gannon, Todd, telephone interview with Eugene
	Kupper. Los Angeles, CA and Scottsdale,
	AZ. 9 Jun 2012
Gannon, Todd and Ewan Branda, interview with
	Roland Coate. Venice, CA, 21 May 2012
Gannon, Todd and Ewan Branda, interview with
	Frank Dimster. Los Angeles, CA, 11 Jun
	2012
Gannon, Todd and Ewan Branda, interview with Coy
	Howard. Los Angeles, CA, 16 May 2012
Gannon, Todd and Ewan Branda, interview with
	Thom Mayne. Culver City, CA, 5 Mar 2012
Gannon, Todd and Ewan Branda, interview with
	Thom Mayne. Culver City, CA, 14 Jul 2012
Gannon, Todd and Ewan Branda, interview with
	Michael Rotondi. Los Angeles, CA,
	13 Jun 2012
Gannon, Todd, Ewan Branda, and Andrew Zago,
	interview with Eric Owen Moss. Culver
	City, CA, 7 Jun 2012

LECTURES
Note: Unless indicated otherwise, all lectures are available
for viewing at the SCI-Arc Media Archive. http://sma.sciarc.
edu.

De Bretteville, Peter, lecture from Southern
	California Institute of Architecture, Santa
	Monica, CA, 14 Nov 1979

Coate, Roland, lecture from Southern California
	Institute of Architecture, Santa Monica, CA,
	17 Oct 1979 (recording lost)
Dimster, Frank, lecture from Southern California
	Institute of Architecture, Santa Monica, CA,
	31 Oct 1979
Fisher, Frederick, lecture from Southern California
	Institute of Architecture, Santa Monica, CA,
	24 Oct 1979
Gehry, Frank, lecture from Southern California
	Institute of Architecture, Santa Monica, CA,
	7 Nov 1979
Hodgetts, Craig and Robert Mangurian, lecture from
	Southern California Institute of Architecture,
	Santa Monica, CA, 28 Nov 1979
Howard, Coy, "Erosion, Discontinuity, Incompleteness,
	Transformation: A Critical Review of Recent
	Work in Los Angeles, Part 1," lecture from
	Southern California Institute of Architecture,
	Santa Monica, CA, 24 Oct 1979
Howard, Coy, "Erosion, Discontinuity, Incompleteness,
	Transformation: A Critical Review of Recent
	Work in Los Angeles, Part 2," lecture from
	Southern California Institute of Architecture,
	Santa Monica, CA, 12 Dec 1979 (recording lost)
Kupper, Eugene, "Doing Architecture," lecture from
	Southern California Institute of Architecture,
	Santa Monica, CA, 10 Oct 1979
Mayne, Thom and Michael Rotondi, lecture from Southern
	California Institute of Architecture, Santa
	Monica, CA, 21 Nov 1979
Moss, Eric Owen, "Armageddon or Polynesian
	Contextualism," lecture from Southern
	California Institute of Architecture, Santa
	Monica, CA, 5 Dec 1979

ARCHITECTURE GALLERY REVIEWS
Dreyfuss, John, "One-Week Shows by 11 Architects,"
	Los Angeles Times (11 Oct 1979): C25, 28
Dreyfuss, John, "Kupper Employs Dual Process,"
	Los Angeles Times (11 Oct 1979): C25-26, 28
Dreyfuss, John, "Mystery in Roland Coate's Work,"
	Los Angeles Times (17 Oct 1979): F16-17
Dreyfuss, John, "Showing How to Mix Metaphors,"
	Los Angeles Times (24 Oct 1979): F1, 10-11
Dreyfuss, John, "Designs in Social Relationships,"
	Los Angeles Times (31 Oct 1979): E9
Dreyfuss, John, "Courage of His Conceptions: Gehry:
	The Architect as Artist," Los Angeles Times
	(7 Nov 1979): F8-9
Dreyfuss, John, "De Bretteville in Exhibition,"
	Los Angeles Times (17 Nov 1979): G1, 21
Dreyfuss, John, "Architecture Show: A Sampler of a Duo's
	Whimsy," Los Angeles Times (21 Nov 1979):
	E1, 4

Dreyfuss, John, "Their Aim: Social Change," *Los Angeles Times* (28 Nov 1979): C10

Dreyfuss, John, "Nine Entrées: Eric Moss' Architectural Feast," *Los Angeles Times* (5 Dec 1979): G9-10

Dreyfuss, John, "Gallery Stirs Up Architects," *Los Angeles Times* (12 Dec 1979): E26

Giovannini, Joseph, "Design Views: The Importance of Being Coy," *Los Angeles Herald Examiner* (Dec 19, 1979): B1, B4

ADDITIONAL SOURCES

"25 Years of SCI-Arc," *Volume* 5 (Sep 2007)

"Background: SCI-Arc's Organizational Framework 1972-1987," unpublished manuscript. Kappe Library, SCI-Arc

Current Work Faculty/Current Work Students (Los Angeles: SCI-Arc, 1983)

"History of SCI-Arc's Philosophy, 1986," unpublished manuscript. Kappe Library, SCI-Arc

"SCI-Arc and Change," *L.A. Architect* (July 1978): np

"SCI-Arc Chronology, The First Thirty Years," unpublished manuscript. Kappe Library, SCI-Arc

"Trace Historicism: Ten Los Angeles Viewpoints," *Skyline* (Feb 1980)

Betsky, Aaron, *Violated Perfection: Architecture and the Fragmentation of the Modern* (New York: Rizzoli, 1990)

Betsky, Aaron, John Chase, and Leon Whiteson, eds., *Experimental Architecture in Los Angeles* (New York: Rizzoli, 1988)

Boissiere, Olivier, "The Young Architects of California," *Domus* (March 1980)

Cook, Peter, "Los Angeles Comes of Age," *AA Files* 1 (Aug 1981): 16-24

Cook, Peter, *New Spirit in Architecture* (New York: Rizzoli, 1991)

Crosse, John, "Frederick Fisher and the "L.A. School": The Formative Years and "Frederick Fisher: Thinking by Hand" at the Edward Cella Gallery through May 22," *Southern California Architectural History* (20 April 2010): http://socalarchhistory. blogspot.com/ 2010/04/frederick-fisher-and-venice-rat-pack.html.

Dixon, John Morris, "The Santa Monica School: What's its Lasting Contribution?" *Progressive Architecture* (May 1995): 63-71, 112, 114

Filler, Martin, "Harbingers: Ten Architects," *Art in America* 69 (Jul 1981): 114-123

Frampton, Kenneth and Silvia Kolbowski, eds., *California Counterpoint: New West Coast Architecture* (New York: Rizzoli, 1982)

Futagawa, Yukio, ed., *New Waves in American Architecture*, *GA Houses* 9 (Tokyo: A.D.A. Edita, 1981)

Giovannini, Joseph, "California Design: New West Side Story," *Interiors* (Dec 1980): 50-51, 80-82

Giovannini, Joseph, "A New Wave for Venice," *Los Angeles Herald Examiner* (18 July 1979): Home section

Giovannini, Joseph, Real Estate as *Arts: New Architecture in Venice California* (The Sewell Archives, 1984)

Goldstein, Barbara and Peter Cook, eds., *Los Angeles Now* (London: Architectural Association, 1983)

Hawthorne, Christoper, "Their Declarations of Independence," *Los Angeles Times* (12 Aug 2005)

Jencks, Charles, *Heteropolis: Los Angeles, the Riots, and the Strange Beauty of Hetero-architecture* (London: Academy Editions, 1993)

Jencks, Charles, "LA Style/LA School," *AA Files* 5 (1983): 90-93

Kappe, Ray, "Academe: Free Form School," *Architectural Forum* (Mar 1973): 71-72

Kappe, Ray, "SCI-Arc History," unpublished manuscript, 1997.

Kappe, Ray, "Southern California Institute of Architecture," *Architecture California* (Jul-Aug, 1983): 28-30

Lucking, Maura, "SCI-Arc at Forty: The Original "Alternative" Architecture School," *Design & Architecture* (blog). KCRW. 17 Aug 2012. http://blogs.kcrw.com/dna/sci-arc-at-forty-the-original-alternative-architecture-school

Ross, Michael Franklin, "Young, Los Angeles and Possibly-Post-Modern, Architects" *A+U* (April 1978): 83-85

Slert, N. Charles and James Harter, *12 Los Angeles Architects* (Pomona: Cal Poly Pomona, 1978)

Stephens, Suzanne, "Playing with a Full Decade," *Progressive Architecture* (December 1979)

Stern, Robert A.M., ed., *America Now: Drawing Towards a More Modern Architecture, A.D. Profiles 6* (London: Architectural Press, June 1977).

Zellner, Peter and Jeffrey Inaba, *Whatever Happened to LA? Architectural and Urban Experiments, 1970-1990* (Los Angeles: SCI-Arc Press, 2005).

EWAN BRANDA is an Associate Professor of architecture at Woodbury University in Los Angeles. His research considers architecture's place in the information society. Currently, he is working on a history of the Centre Pompidou in Paris. He is also the technical editor of the Electronic Book Review and co-author of the NETLab software toolkit.

JOE DAY is design principal of deegan-day design llc and serves on the faculty for design and cultural studies at SCI-Arc. In 2012, Day was a Louis I. Kahn Visiting Assistant Professor at the Yale School of Architecture. His forthcoming *Corrections and Collections: Architectures for Art and Crime* (Routledge, 2013) examines intersections in museum and prison design since Minimalism.

JOHN DREYFUSS was architecture and design critic for the *Los Angeles Times* from 1976 to 1983. He began his career at the paper in 1966 covering colleges and universities around California, and wrote for the View section from 1983 to 1993. After leaving the *Times*, he started a construction company with his son, worked as a news writer for KTLA Channel 5, and served as director of planning and communications at UCLA's Jonsson Comprehensive Cancer Center. He died in 2004.

TODD GANNON is an architect and writer based in Los Angeles. He is Cultural Studies Coordinator at SCI-Arc, where he has taught since 2008. His publications include *The Light Construction Reader* (2002) and monographs on the work of Morphosis, Zaha Hadid, Peter Eisenman, and others.

KEVIN MCMAHON manages SCI-Arc's Kappe Library, where he most recently co-coordinated the creation of an online Media Archive. Besides library consulting, he also writes on the interaction of words, history, and media in public spaces.

PATRICIA A. MORTON is Chair and Associate Professor of architectural history at the University of California, Riverside. Her current research projects focus on taste and postmodern architecture and on the relation between human geography and French colonial architecture. She is a book reviews editor of the *Journal of the Society of Architectural Historians*.

PAULETTE SINGLEY is a professor and Director of the Rome Center for Architecture and Culture in the School of Architecture at Woodbury University in Los Angeles. She co-edited *Eating Architecture* and *Architecture: In Fashion* and has been published in *Log*, *ANY*, *Assemblage*, and several anthologies.

ANDREW ZAGO, principal of Zago Architecture, is design faculty at SCI-Arc. He is a fellow of the American Academy in Rome and a recipient of both an Academy Award from the American Academy of Arts and Letters and a Fellowship from the United States Artists organization.